The Labour Movement and the Internet

Labour and Society International

Series Editor: Arthur Lipow, Michael Harrington Centre, Birkbeck College, University of London, and Labour and Society International (LSI).

On the eve of the twenty-first century, a new global economy dominated by transnational corporations is coming into existence. The aim of the Labour and Society International series is to examine the nature of this new global economic order and to explore ways in which the democratic labour movement can offer a response to it: a response based on the politics and ethics of international social solidarity, the defence of human rights, including trade union rights, gender and racial equality, and the right to resist economic and political oppression.

The series is a project of Labour and Society International (LSI). Based in London, LSI works with the international trade union movement on these and related issues.

Already published

Socialism: Past and Future
Michael Harrington

Coping with the Miracle: Japan's Unions Explore New Industrial Relations
Hugh Williamson

Breaking Point: A Guide to Preventing Occupational Overuse Syndrome
In association with the International Federation of Chemical, Energy and General Workers' Unions (ICEF)

Economic Fundamentalism
Jane Kelsey

Power and Counterpower: The Union Response to Global Capital
International Federation of Chemical, Energy, Mine and General Workers' Unions (ICEM)

The Labour Movement and the Internet

The New Internationalism

Eric Lee

 Pluto Press

LONDON · CHICAGO, ILLINOIS

First published 1997 by Pluto Press
345 Archway Road, London N6 5AA
and 1436 West Randolph, Chicago, Illinois 60607, USA

British Library Cataloguing in Publication Data
A catalogue record for this book is available from the British Library

Library of Congress Cataloging in Publication Data
Lee, Eric. 1955–
   The labour movement and the internet: the new internationalism/
Eric Lee.
     p.   cm.
   Includes bibliographical references and index.
   ISBN 0–7453–1119–9 (hbk.)
   1. Trade-unions–Computer networks. 2. Trade-unions–Computer
network resources. 3. Internet (Computer network) 4. International
labor activities–Computer networks. 5. International labor
activities–Computer network resources. I. Title.
HD6490.C616L44   1997
331.88'0285'467–dc20   96-28838
                                                                   CIP

ISBN 0 7453 1119 9 hbk

Designed and produced for Pluto Press by
Chase Production Services, Chipping Norton, OX7 5QR
Typeset from the author's disk by Stanford DTP Services
Printed in the EC by J.W. Arrowsmith Ltd, Bristol

Contents

The Web site http://www.geocities.com/CapitolHill/2808/
labour01.html provides updates and corrections to the text in
this book.

For Noemi Lee Stern

Acknowledgements

While I was researching this book, a trade unionist wrote and asked me if I had considered making the writing of this book an international team project. I had to answer him that it doesn't matter what I *want* to do; a book like this is *of necessity* a joint effort of many people in many countries.

At the International Federation of Workers' Education Associations I have learned about the subject and had the opportunity to research it. Their Executive Committee decided to investigate computer communications even before they hired me to work for them, and they have continued their commitment to the new technology ever since. I am indebted to their President, Dan Gallin, and General Secretary, Aaron Barnea.

The people creating the global labournet all over the world took time off from their efforts and provided me with much extraordinary information, their own informed analyses and predictions, advice and – not least – encouragement. More than a dozen of them in eight countries spread out over four continents read parts of this book. Naturally they are not responsible for any inaccuracies, slanders or outrageous opinions; those are my own.

I should emphasise that without the Internet, the writing of this book would have been impossible. With only a handful of exceptions, I conducted all the interviews using email. Probably 99 per cent of my correspondence was done through the networks, though there was a case or two when someone actually stuffed an article into an envelope, glued a stamp to it, and mailed it to me. The archives of important conferences, like the 1992 and 1993 Manchester conferences, are available online. Even internal trade union documents, like COSATU's programme for introducing email to the South African labour movement, reached me through the net. And of course the World Wide Web has been an invaluable source of trade union information. Using the Internet, I was able to ask questions of, and exchange views with, trade unionists in a dozen countries, in nearly real time, at practically no cost.

I am beholden to Peter Waterman for sending me some of his many writings on this subject, reading parts of the manuscript, sharing his wisdom, and encouraging the project through to the end.

I would also like to thank Jagdish Parikh, John Atkins, Dave Spooner, Chris Bailey, Gregory Coyne, Peter Skyte, Marc Belanger,

Larry Kuehn, Florence Ross, Sam Lanfranco, Martin Nicol, Christian Sellars, Celia Mather, Aslak Leesland, Jim Catterson, Richard Flint, Alice Carl, Laura Carver, Vassily Balog, Kirill Buketov, Adrian Bates, Peter Hall-Jones, Steven Hill, Bob Kastigar, Nathan Newman, Gary Graff, Steve Zeltzer, Edward B. Armour, Jim Devor, Arieh Lebowitz, Charley Lewis, Jerry Fray, Mike Lostutter, Janice Kushner, David St John, David Colee, Laura Sager, Len Wilson and Seth Wigderson.

I am grateful to my editor, Arthur Lipow, and publisher, Roger van Zwanenberg of Pluto Press, who received my proposal for this book, conducted negotiations about it, shared views and discussed timetables, all online, using email.

Writing this book has required the support and understanding of Kibbutz Ein Dor's factory, Teldor Wires & Cables, and in particular its General Manager, Avri Maoz, and Information Systems Manager, Hana Gil. They knew that sometimes when I was pretending to do my job, I was really writing this book. Well, maybe if more trade unionists use the Internet as a result, we'll sell more cables.

Constant encouragement has been coming, as always, from Arieh and Regina Yaari. This is our fifth book together – two of theirs, three of mine. Now the world knows what the three of us talk about over lunch here in the kibbutz dining hall.

Finally, authors always thank their spouses, children and family pets. We don't have any pets, just a couple of boys who think that their big contribution to this kind of effort is, as Medad put it, 'to not get in the way'. He and Yonatan didn't. As for Noemi, to whom this book is dedicated – well, it's your turn to use the computer. I'm done – for now.

List of Acronyms

ACTU	Australian Council of Trade Unions
AEEU	Amalgamated Engineering and Electrical Union
AFGE	American Federation of Government Employees
AFL–CIO	American Federation of Labour–Congress of Industrial Organisations
AMRC	Asia Monitor Resource Centre
AOF	Norwegian workers' education association
AOL	America Online
APC	Association for Progressive Communications
APWU	American Postal Workers' Union
ARPANET	Advanced Research Projects Agency Network
ASCII	American standard code for information interchange
AUT	Association of University Teachers
BBS	bulletin board system
BCTF	British Columbia Teachers' Federation
CALM	Canadian Association of Labour Media
CCF	Cooperative Commonwealth Federation
CD-ROM	compact disc-read only memory
CERN	European Particle Physics Institute
CIS	Commonwealth of Independent States
COSATU	Congress of South African Trade Unions
CTU	Clerical-Technical Union
CUE	Coalition of University Employees
CUPE	Canadian Union of Public Employees
CWA	Communications Workers of America
CWIU	Chemical Workers' Industrial Union
EDIN	Economic Democracy Information Network
FES	Friedrich Ebert Stiftung
FIET	International Federation of Commercial, Clerical, Professional and Technical Employees
FTP	file transfer protocol
GCTU	General Confederation of Trade Unions
GFTU	General Federation of Trade Unions
HSE	Health and Safety Executive
HTML	hypertext markup language
HTTP	hypertext transfer protocol
IASS	International Association of Fire Fighters

IBEW	International Brotherhood of Electrical Workers
ICEF	International Federation of Chemical, Energy and General Workers' Unions (now ICEM)
ICEM	International Federation of Chemical, Energy, Mine and General Workers' Unions
ICFTU	International Confederation of Free Trade Unions
IFTU	International Federation of Trade Unions
IFWEA	International Federation of Workers' Education Associations
IGC	Institute for Global Communications
ILCC	international labour communications by computer
ILO	International Labour Organisation
ILRIG	International Labour Resource and Information Group
ILU	International Labour University
IMF	International Metalworkers' Federation
INMARSAT	International Maritime Satellite Organisation
IRC	Internet Relay Chat
ISDN	integrated services digital network
ITF	International Transport Workers' Federation
ITPA	Information Technology Professionals' Association
ITS	international trade secretariat
ITU	International Telecommunications Union
IUE	International Union of Electrical Workers
IUF	International Union of Food, Agricultural, Hotel, Restaurant, Catering, Tobacco and Allied Workers' Associations
IUGW	International Union of Gas Workers
IUOE	International Union of Operating Engineers
KAS-KOR	Labour Information Centre (Russia)
LAN	local area network
LO	Scandinavian trade union federations
LTC	Labour Telematics Centre
MSF	Manufacturing, Science, Finance Union
NABET	National Association of Broadcast Employees and Technicians
NAFTA	North American Free Trade Agreement
NATCA	National Air Traffic Controllers' Association
NCSA	National Centre for Supercomputing Applications
NGO	non-governmental organisation
NIOSH	National Institute for Occupational Safety and Health

NTUC	National Trades Union Congress
NUJ	National Union of Journalists
NUM	National Union of Mineworkers
NUMSA	National Union of Metalworkers of South Africa
NUTP	National Union of the Teaching Profession
PC	personal computer
PGP	Pretty Good Privacy
PSA	Public Service Alliance
RMALC	Red Mexicana de Accion Frente al Libre Comercio
RTECS	Registry of Toxic Effects of Chemical Substances
SANGONeT	South African Non-Governmental Organisations Network
SMTP	simple mail transfer protocol
TCP/IP	transmission control protocol/Internet protocol
TGWU	Transport and General Workers' Union
TUC	Trades Union Congress
UAW	United Auto Workers
UNA	United Nurses of Alberta
USENET	User's Network
WAN	wide area network
WFTU	World Federation of Trade Unions
WWW	World Wide Web

Introduction

When I began writing this book, I already had more than two decades of experience in the labour movement and another decade in the world of computers. I grew up as an activist in the stormy 1960s. My very first job was working for the United Federation of Teachers in New York City (on a project to encourage high school students to vote). At university, I studied industrial and labour relations. I spent my summers working for the Textile Workers Union of America and organisations close to the labour movement. In 1977 I founded a journal of social democratic theory and analysis, the *New International Review,* which put me in contact with trade unionists around the world. Thanks to that journal, I met and was deeply influenced by men like Chip Levinson and Dan Gallin.

In Israel, where I've lived for the last fifteen years, I've been active in the United Workers Party (Mapam), on whose Central Committee I have served. Today I work for the International Federation of Workers' Education Associations as editor of its quarterly journal, *Workers' Education.* I'm a member of a self-governing community of workers and farmers called Kibbutz Ein Dor.

Since 1984, I've worked as a computer programmer. My specialty has been the family of IBM midrange computers, the S/34, S/36 and now the AS/400, where I have been programming in the RPG II and RPG/400 programming languages. But my exposure to computer communications came more as a result of my work for the labour movement than as a function of my career as a computer professional. Now that I was editing *Workers' Education,* I needed to keep in contact with trade unionists around the world. But international phone calls are too expensive and air mail takes too long. I also have to know what's going on in the labour movement in many different countries. But no newspaper tells me that. Sometimes I want to express opinions and influence the course of discussions. But I can't afford to fly off to meetings in different countries.

It wasn't easy, being active in the international labour movement while living on a hilltop in the Galilee. And then, one winter evening in early 1994, I logged onto the Internet for the first time.

CHAPTER 1

The Decline and Fall of the Internationals

Now and then the workers are victorious, but only for a time. The real fruit of their battles lies not in the immediate result, but in the ever expanding union of the workers. This union is helped on by the improved means of communication that are created by modern industry, and that place the workers of different localities in contact with each other.

Karl Marx and Friedrich Engels,
Manifesto of the Communist Party (1848)

We'll begin our discussion of labour and the Internet more than a century before the global computer communications network became a reality. Back then a net was something one used to catch fish, and a web was the product of a spider's energy.

For readers who were expecting that I'd immediately launch into the World Wide Web and the intricacies of email, I can only urge patience. I'll be getting to the Internet in a moment. But I want to make one thing clear from the very beginning. This is one of those rare books about the labour movement, about its history and its future, and not one of the many books about the wonders of the Internet. I have written this book because I believe that computer-mediated communications offer one way (and only one way) to help to solve some problems that the labour movement has faced for decades. We have to begin, therefore, by defining those problems, and putting them in their historical context.

More than a hundred years ago, an international labour movement was thriving. Workers in far-flung corners of the globe would read in their trade union newspapers about strikes half-way around the planet. Sometimes, they would dig deep into their pockets to raise support for their brothers and sisters who were on strike. International trade union structures and their political counterpart, the International of labour and social democratic parties, were increasingly a force to be reckoned with in world affairs. Today, that is no longer the case. Labour internationalism has declined dramatically. So has the power of the trade unions in nearly all countries. The Socialist International exists on paper only.

Ironically, trade union internationalism flourished when multinational capitalism was in its infancy. Today, with transnational corporations dominating the global economy, a vigorous international trade union movement capable of confronting corporate power has yet to arise. This means that the international labour movement cannot now effectively defend workers' basic interests, let alone lead the world forward to a new and more just society.

This does not mean that people aren't trying. There are the beginnings of important multinational trade union projects at the regional level, including cross-border solidarity activities in North America (following the enactment of NAFTA) and the European Works Councils (a direct result of the strengthening of the European Union). Regional trade union organisations are active all over, including in Latin America, Africa, Asia and the Pacific. There is the giant International Confederation of Free Trade Unions, reinvigorated somewhat by the end of the Cold War and the disappearance of its pro-Soviet rival. It unites national trade union centres from nearly every country, with tens of millions of members. And most important, there are the international trade secretariats, which though understaffed and underfunded, conduct vigorous efforts to defend working people around the world. These secretariats, which are headquartered in Europe, unite national trade unions in particular sectors of the economy. Of all the international trade union institutions, these most closely parallel the structure of the emerging global economy.

These institutions are probably not well known by rank-and-file trade unionists, and they deal mostly with national trade unions and national trade union centres. Their publications, for example, reach only very limited circulations (because they are underfunded); sometimes only the staffs of international departments of national trade unions even know about their existence. This is, I think, part of the problem. One way to bring international trade union institutions closer to the rank-and-file memberships is through the new communications technologies, as I'll try to demonstrate throughout this book.

Before briefly reviewing the history of the Internationals, I think it's appropriate to discuss what we mean by an 'International'. There is no single, agreed-upon definition of the term. In fact, to most people, the word 'international' is an adjective, not a noun. Each successive International has defined for itself what the term means. An International could be a confederation of trade unions, engaged in simple mutual aid projects and solidarity actions. An International could also be the army of world revolution, marching forward to its goal under strict military discipline. An International could be an organisation which by its very nature promotes world peace, and this could be its primary reason for existence. Or an International could just be a forum for discussion among left-wing political parties with similar traditions and goals. The historic labour Internationals have been all of these. Internationals have sometimes been federations of trade unions and sometimes of political parties. Only one of the historic Internationals, the first, included every kind of workers' organisation, including both trade unions and political parties.

Today, a new kind of International has arisen, one largely unconnected to the labour movement and its history. I'm talking about what have been called the 'new social movements' – the human rights, peace, feminist and environmental movements in particular. In recent years, they have created their own Internationals, including such mass movements as Greenpeace and Amnesty International. These Internationals have permanent secretariats, hold world congresses, produce publications, and conduct campaigns that would make them the envy of the historic labour Internationals. Their emphasis on information has turned them into what Peter Waterman calls 'communications internationals'.

Now that we've tried – and failed (for the moment) – to define what we mean by an International, let's take a quick look at what has been tried by the labour movement in the last century and a half. The idea of a workers' International goes back more than a century and a half. Certainly everyone is familiar by now with Karl Marx's and Friedrich Engels's 1848 call – in *The Communist Manifesto* – on the workers of all countries to unite. In fact, the dream predates Marx, and there are examples of attempts to create international labour organisations as early as the eighteenth century.

Sixteen years after Marx and Engels made their call to proletarians of all countries, their dream came true – in part – with the formation of the International Workingmen's Association, which has become known as the First International. Formed in 1864, this was a remarkable experiment. It was not, as the Communist (Third) International would later be, a strictly disciplined, centralised structure, the 'general staff' of the world revolution. Nor was it the 'talking society' that the Socialist (Second) International has usually been. It was not a Marxist International. There was room for socialists of all different types, and indeed, for trade unionists who were not socialists, room even for anarchists (for a time). It focused on real-world issues. Its roots were in the existing mass organisations of working people.

The initiative for the formation of this First International came from the English craft trade unions, which were anything but revolutionary. The London Trades Council's motive was a simple economic one: only by cooperating with unions on the European continent could the British working class preserve the limited gains it had made by organising into unions. The importation of foreign strike-breakers into England in the 1850s and 1860s made the International an economic necessity for those workers.

Simple class self-interest more than internationalist ideology prompted trade union leaders and socialists of all stripes to gather in a London hall in 1864 under a banner proclaiming 'All men are brothers!'. This would hardly have bothered Marx. Unlike the utopian socialists who preceded him, Marx was convinced that working people would create a new and more just society not because it was more moral and right, but because it served their own concrete class interests. If it *was* moral and right, that was fine with Marx too.

Hardly a meeting of the International's General Council, on which Marx sat, went by without a specific call for assistance in strike support. Those meetings were held nearly every week. Striking unions needed financial help and needed to guarantee that 'scab' (non-union) workers would not be imported from abroad. These basic kinds of solidarity work would remain the backbone of labour internationalism for decades to come.

- In early January 1869, the General Council learned that French textile manufacturers had formed an alliance to lower wages in order to compete better with the more technologically advanced English manufacturers. The mayor of Sotteville-les-Rouen, himself a leading manufacturer, proposed to reduce his workers' wages. The men refused the offer, and were locked out of their jobs. They appealed to the International for help. Marx proposed that the organisation immediately offer financial aid to the locked-out textile workers. He suggested a transfer of funds to accomplish this, which was approved.
- In February the Council heard from Switzerland that a workers' newspaper, the *Arbeiter*, was in danger of being closed. It voted to send some money to help keep the publication going. But the money arrived too late, and the paper ceased appearing.
- In April of that same year, following the massacre of some striking workers in Belgium, the General Council instructed Marx to prepare an address on the subject. It was discussed at a subsequent meeting of the Council, and then published as a separate pamphlet in English, and as an article in several French and German newspapers.

These kinds of solidarity actions were discussed *every week*, and acted upon with remarkable speed, considering the slowness of communications in the nineteenth century.

The power of the First International was greatly inflated in the eyes of the European ruling classes. (Although the London *Times*

did call the International 'a great idea in a small body'.) The Paris
Commune of 1871, in which some members of the International
took part, was widely seen as an example of the power of the
International to topple governments and wrest political power.
(Marx understood that this was *not* the case in Paris.)

That first International did not last very long. In the early 1870s,
Marx himself arranged for its dissolution in order to prevent its take-
over by anarchists and other elements not to his liking. In those
days, the way to bury an international organisation or render it
irrelevant was to move its headquarters from Europe to the United
States, which is precisely what Marx did. The International was
formally dissolved at a meeting in Philadelphia in July 1876.

The First International did not fail because of the absence of a
sophisticated, high-tech global communications infrastructure.
The workers' movement of the nineteenth century was able to
conduct solidarity campaigns, raise funds, organise and agitate
even with the most primitive tools, mostly letter-writing. The
International was not able to *instantly* react to events in different
countries, but then again, neither were the capitalists. *Both sides* in
the class conflict were constrained by the same technology. (This
is most certainly not the case today.)

Nevertheless, there *is* a connection between this International
and technology. As Marx and Engels themselves noted back in 1848,
'the improved means of communication that are created by modern
industry' are what make possible 'the ever expanding union of the
workers' – that is to say, the International. Without modern mass
production, there would never have been modern trade unions. (If
the invention of steam power may be said to have given birth to
the First International, then the creation of the global computer
communications network – the Internet – may just as easily be the
parent of the new internationalism.)

The First International was not forgotten; in fact, its legend
grew. As powerful social democratic parties and trade unions
emerged in the 1870s and 1880s, particularly in Europe, they
dreamed of re-creating that International. On the hundredth
anniversary of the French Revolution, in 1889, an international
labour congress meeting in Paris re-launched the International. It
also called for the celebration of 1 May as an international labour
holiday beginning the following year, on 1 May 1890. The
organisation it founded, which came to be known as the Second
International, basically exists to this day. It united then, and unites
now, the various social democratic and labour parties in Europe
and around the world.

A year later, in 1890, the very first international trade secretariats
(ITSs) were formed. The ITSs, which represent workers globally
by industry, have been the most enduring international trade union

organisations. By the time of the outbreak of the First World War, there were fourteen of them and that has remained their number, more or less, to this day. (As we shall see, these ITSs have recently played a pioneering role in the use of computer communications in the labour movement.)

Parallel to the ITSs, which are federations of national unions in *specific industries*, there have also been global confederations of national trade union centres. The International Federation of Trade Unions (IFTU) played that role in the inter-war years. The World Federation of Trade Unions (WFTU) briefly played that role after the Second World War until it was displaced by its main rival, the non-Communist International Confederation of Free Trade Unions (ICFTU). The ICFTU, following the collapse of Communism and the rapid decline of the Soviet-dominated WFTU, is today the sole real organisation of national labour centres.

The years preceding 1914 were a 'golden age' for international social democracy and the labour movement. They were marked by many examples of international labour solidarity. In one notable case, during the 1909 Swedish general strike, Danish trade unionists contributed the equivalent of three days' pay per unionised worker to the Swedish strike fund. In fact, the Danish trade unions during their first fifteen years as an organised national centre spent 50 per cent more money on strike support outside Denmark than they spent on negotiations, travel, agitation, salaries and administration put together. Studies of the labour movement during this period, including a noteworthy one on the Danish labour press, reveal a trade union movement deeply concerned on a day-to-day basis with the struggles of fellow workers in other countries.

The quarter-century following the founding of the Second International and the first ITSs was an interesting time for the international labour movement. Never before or since have internationalist sentiments been so strong. One particularly dramatic moment came during the Russo-Japanese war of 1905, when Plekhanov and Katayama, the leaders of the Russian and Japanese social democratic parties, met at the international socialist congress in Amsterdam and publicly shook hands, to the loud applause of delegates. Such an example of simple human solidarity during a time of war was unprecedented.

As the storm clouds of the First World War appeared on Europe's horizon, many hoped that the International had the strength to prevent the fighting from breaking out. The 1907 international socialist congress meeting in Stuttgart resolved that the outbreak of world war would be met by revolutionary strikes. In 1912, when a Balkan war threatened to ignite the whole continent, massive peace demonstrations across Europe organised by the Second International prompted its nomination for the Nobel Peace Prize. Jean Jaures, the leader of the French Socialists, assured a friend in the spring of 1914, 'Don't worry, the Socialists will do their duty ... Four million German Socialists will rise like one man and execute the Kaiser if he wants to start a war.'

But when the war broke out in August 1914, most labour and social democratic leaders supported their own national governments. The International fell apart with the outbreak of fighting. Repeated attempts by well-meaning reformist and revolutionary social democrats alike to revive the International during the war years all faltered.

During the First World War, Lenin and others on the far left of the Second International became convinced that a new, Third International would have to be created to coordinate international labour activity – or as they would have put it, to serve as the general staff of the world revolution. They were convinced that the old social democratic parties and the trade unions linked to them were finished.

At the very first opportunity, the Russian Bolsheviks summoned left-wing labour leaders, syndicalists and revolutionary socialists to Moscow to launch the new International. Though the founding conference in 1919 was not entirely successful, within a year or two the new International, now known as the Third (or Communist) International (and usually called 'Comintern' for short) did unite all kinds of left-wing movements, including mass movements like the Italian Socialist Party, the syndicalist Industrial Workers of the World in the US (the 'Wobblies') and others.

But this did not last long. The Bolsheviks compelled the new International to adopt the infamous '21 Points' which demanded strict organisational discipline, unswerving loyalty to the Soviet party and state, and relentless warfare against the existing social democratic parties which, to Lenin's chagrin, survived the First World War, regrouped, and even prospered.

The Third International had all the trappings of a genuine internationalist labour organisation. It created sub-Internationals for trade unionists, women and youth. It maintained centralised publications in dozens of languages. It employed organisers who travelled the world, often at great personal risk, building up national sections of the world revolutionary party. Decisions made at the highest levels of the International obligated affiliate parties around the world, down to the local level. No doubt many honest trade union militants and socialists saw here everything the First and Second Internationals had been unable to be: a centralised, militant, effective force.

Tragically, the same cancer which overtook the Russian revolution – Stalinism – killed off the Third International with all its hopes and dreams. That International existed officially for 24 years until its dissolution in 1943. It lasted twice as long as Marx's First

International. In reality the Comintern lasted for more than seven decades, finally dissolving only with the disappearance of the Soviet regime in 1991. Its list of crimes is simply too long to repeat here. Subsequent attempts to form revolutionary Internationals, including the unsuccessful Trotskyist attempt to create a 'Fourth International', were always conducted in the shadow of the failure of the Comintern, that most revolutionary and ambitious of all the Internationals.

Meanwhile, the Second International *was* revived after the First World War (and once again after the Second), and *did* serve as a democratic alternative to the Comintern. In most countries, the social democratic parties and the trade unions affiliated to them remained the dominant parties in the working class in the decades to come. This was particularly true in nearly all the English-speaking countries, where the Communist parties nearly always remained on the sidelines of labour politics (South Africa is the exception).

The international trade secretariats remained particularly effective tools of working-class internationalism even after the Second International went into eclipse. As early as 1918, the International Transport Workers' Federation (ITF) managed to successfully halt arms supplies to the counter-revolutionary armies which were drowning the Hungarian revolution in blood. Three years after that, another international trade secretariat, the International Union of Food Workers (IUF), successfully conducted the first international struggle against the Swiss chocolate industry on the issue of union recognition.

But these were isolated victories in a war which was already being lost. By 1923, the International Federation of Trade Unions proved unable to organise a general strike against the French occupation of the Ruhr. Even though certain far-sighted unionists, such as Edo Fimmen, who briefly served as secretary of the IFTU and later as General Secretary of the ITF, foresaw the necessity of global trade union organisations to combat increasingly transnational capital, labour internationalism went into prolonged retreat. Fimmen 'understood and tried to solve most problems seventy years ago that we are still trying to solve today', writes Dan Gallin, the current General Secretary of the IUF. In his prophetic book *Labour's Alternative*, published in 1924, Fimmen wrote that 'just as the development of capitalism has always determined the organisational form of its opponents, has given rise first of all to local and subsequently national trade unions, so capitalism will become, if not the originator, at least the furtherer of the international organisation of the industrial workers'.

Though international trade union structures, including the ITSs, continued to exist, global trade union activities declined. Instead of growing more centralised and organising more coordinated actions, the international trade union movement grew increasingly decentralised, with national labour movements left largely to their own devices. International trade union activity became largely bilateral or multilateral in character, when it took place at all. As far as the rank-and-file trade union membership knew, there was nothing left of the international labour movement.

Dan Gallin wrote in the *New International Review* back in 1980 about the failure of trade union internationalism to live up to its promise in the twentieth century. The most important reason for the decline of international trade unionism, he noted, was the 'terrible toll exacted by fascism'. Another was 'the polarisation caused by the Cold War'. The international activities of many trade unions in the post-Second World War years – in particular those of the American trade union centre – were dominated by Cold War considerations. The totalitarian labour fronts which made up the bulk of the WFTU membership were also instruments of Cold War activity by the Stalinist regimes.

In addition to the decline of trade union internationalism, the political arm of the workers' International – consisting of the social democratic and labour parties – has not exactly thrived. The United States, the world's leading capitalist power for more than half a century, *never* had a mass socialist party. In the Soviet empire, the Stalinist dictatorship made the outlawing of democratic socialism its very first priority. Western European socialist parties were devastated by two world wars. The flagship German party, mortally wounded by the Third Reich, had become by the late 1950s an officially reformist party, committed to Cold War politics and utterly lacking in socialist vision. Social democratic parties in opposition have largely been unable to develop alternatives to the existing right-wing governments in Europe and elsewhere. When they have managed to win political power, they almost invariably disappoint their working-class constituents. With one or two exceptions, democratic socialist parties have not arisen in the developing countries either.

The Socialist International today is a hollow shell of what it was on the eve of the First World War, unable to do much more than sponsor the occasional gathering of social democratic officials for a weekend of speeches and meetings.

More than 130 years after the founding of the First International, little remains of its vision of a world in which 'all men are brothers'. The institutions created by the men and women of that time continue to exist today in the Socialist International, the International Confederation of Free Trade Unions, and the various international trade secretariats. But their dream of a fighting workers' International, spearheading the drive for a new society, for democratic socialism, was basically finished off by 1945.

The labour movement's timing couldn't have been worse. The decline of internationalism in the trade unions coincided with its rise among businessmen. At a time when the international trade union movement was dying, transnational corporations were being born. Just when labour desperately and urgently needed an International, there was no International left.

Already in the nineteenth century, as Marx was quick to notice, a global marketplace existed. World trade was booming, fuelling technological change – in particular, the revolution in transportation and communications. But in recent years, that global *marketplace* has been transformed into a global *system of production*, and this is something profoundly different, with important ramifications for the labour movement everywhere.

As communications became more sophisticated, the idea of the 'virtual corporation' became a reality. A virtual corporation might consist of a small team of managers who contract out work, ranging from design to production to marketing, to others spread out all over the world. The virtual corporation may itself employ almost no one, own no factories, and keep no inventory. In most cases, contracting out means employing low-paid, non-union workers in the world's South. And this is the case not only when manufacturing textiles or computer chips, but writing computer software or designing clothing.

There are now approximately 37,000 transnational corporations which dominate the global economy. They own another 170,000 subsidiaries outside of their countries of origin. Transnational corporations now control one-third of the world's private sector productive assets. Their out-of-country sales ($US 5.5 trillion in 1992) exceed the total value of world exports. 'We all now live in a borderless global economy made possible by new communication and transport technologies', writes Dan Gallin. One of those new communication technologies is the Internet. In this new world order, national governments, national laws, national political parties, national collective bargaining *and national trade unions* have become increasingly irrelevant.

The trade union movement is nearly everywhere in decline. Union membership is falling or stagnating. Trade union political influence in many countries has dropped to zero. Even within social democratic parties, trade unions have weakened and lost influence. Walter Galenson, in his 1994 book, *Trade Union Growth and Decline: An International Study*, discovered an interesting fact. The decline of trade unions has affected almost all industrial nations and many less developed countries as well.

During the 1980s, trade union density (union membership as a percentage of employed wage and salary workers) fell from 23 per cent in the US to only 16.4 per cent. In France, the fall was even more precipitous – from 19 per cent to 12 per cent – and this under a socialist government. Massive declines were also noted in New Zealand, the United Kingdom and Australia. (Labour governments were in power in Australia and New Zealand during many of these years.) Gains were reported in some of the newly industrialising countries, including South Korea and Taiwan – and in the last bastions of social democracy, Sweden and Norway. In the former, trade union density actually rose in the 1980s from 80 per cent to 85.3 per cent.

Galenson's statistics do not reflect developments in the 1990s which include, on the one hand, huge gains for labour in countries like South Africa, and on the other, catastrophic decline throughout the former Soviet bloc and in certain Western countries like New Zealand and Israel.

These figures are only one way – and perhaps not the very best one – to measure the rise and fall of labour movements. But they at least serve to show us that the phenomenon is global, persistent and threatening to the very survival of an independent and democratic labour movement.

Far more ominous are the statistics collected and published every year by the International Confederation of Free Trade Unions on the violation of trade union rights. The most recent ICFTU report documents abuses of trade union rights in a record 98 countries. No fewer than 528 trade unionists were assassinated in a twelve-month period. This number was double that counted the previous year. Some 4,300 trade unionists were arrested or detained because of their union activity. As the news bulletin of the IUF put it, the trade union movement 'has been targeted by a rising tide of violence and repression'.

Meanwhile, as the unions grow weaker, the corporations grow stronger. And they are being helped by the newest communications technologies, including the Internet. Several books have been published exploring how corporations today can use – and are already using – the Internet to increase profits and competitive advantage. Just as the Internet helps corporations to improve their marketing, purchasing, internal and external communications, and research and development, so it gives employers a competitive edge over unions. That competitive edge is expressed not only across the bargaining table but also in the rough-and-tumble world of global class conflict. The Internet has made it easier than ever before for transnational corporations to outwit and outmanoeuvre unions – a point books on business and the Internet usually tastefully neglect to mention.

In the new world order, no one is more disadvantaged than the emerging industrial working class of the global South. Incipient trade unions there, which are fighting for such basic rights as union recognition and collective bargaining, have no communications tools to match the Internet access of powerful transnational corporations. In fact, those unions usually face extraordinarily high costs just to use telephones or faxes, let alone link up to a global computer network.

But ironically, the very technology which has given corporations such a great advantage over unions – advanced communications, especially computer communications – has become cheap enough and accessible enough to allow unions to move toward a new internationalism.

As just one example of the possibilities, let's look at what happened to the plan to launch global 'company councils' sponsored by the ITSs back in the 1970s. These institutions were conceived of as embryonic international trade unions, which would constitute, over time, a 'countervailing power' (as Charles 'Chip' Levinson of the chemical workers' ITS called it) to the transnational corporations. Some observers expected them to enter into contract negotiations with those corporations, to coordinate global strike action, and to begin the process of reviving labour internationalism. That did not happen, and one of the reasons was a practical one. It cost so much money to fly trade unionists from around the world to meetings that the 'company councils' were unable to function. Today, with the adoption of computer-mediated communications by the labour movement, the possibility of creating 'virtual company councils' is now on the agenda, and with it, the solution to the budgetary problems faced by the earlier experiment.

That process of adopting the new information technologies is occurring not only in the central national and international offices of the labour movement, but at the local, grassroots level as well.

The remaining chapters of the book concentrate on how that process is unfolding today. We'll discuss the various new tools now available for the reinvigoration of labour internationalism, including electronic mail, online databases, discussion groups and electronic publishing. We'll review the first two decades of labour's experiments in using computer communications, beginning with Chip Levinson's original proposals back in the early 1970s and the very first online labour network, launched in 1981.

We'll continue with a tour of local and regional labour networks, focusing on independent trade union networks, labour use of existing employers' networks, and local trade union bulletin board systems (BBSs), including a look at one creative use of computer communications at the local level – the online daily strike newspaper. We'll go from there to the various national experiments, ranging from Canada's pioneering Solidarity Network to Russia's GlasNet. Then we'll focus on the emerging global labournet itself, whose core is to be found in the international trade secretariats based in

Europe's capital cities and – at the grassroots level – in numerous bilateral and multilateral solidarity actions taking place online.

Finally, we'll come to some concrete proposals (and some less concrete visions) of the future – including an online international labour university, an electronic labour news service, 'virtual company councils' and others.

CHAPTER 2

New Tools for a New Internationalism

What is the Internet? How can trade unionists use it to reinvigorate the labour movement? In this chapter, we're going to go on a tour of the global online networks which comprise the Internet. That could itself be the subject of a book – in fact, most books about the Internet do precisely this. They are tours of the various things one can do with the Internet.

Here, I'll be doing something much more modest. I'll begin by going over, very briefly, the history of the Internet. (I think that to understand what something is, you should understand where it came from.) Then I'll look over the five things trade unionists (and everyone else) can do with the Internet, those being: email, databases, discussion groups, online chat, and electronic publishing. These are what I call new tools for a new internationalism.

If the terms on that list didn't make any sense, don't worry. Throughout this chapter, I'll try to define each new term used. I'll explain the differences between the various technologies, even if these are sometimes a little blurry (for example, there are discussion groups that are based on email). And this book will always try to focus on how the *labour* movement can use the technologies described. My emphasis will be on practical information for the novice (and not only the novice), answering questions like 'What do I need to use email?' or 'How do I produce a home page for the World Wide Web?'.

My background in computers is as a programmer. For more than a decade, I have written programs, which are collectively known as software. 'How many programmers does it take to change a lightbulb?' runs one of the many awful jokes making the rounds on the Internet. 'None', goes the answer, 'That's a hardware problem.' So I won't be discussing hardware here either, not modems and not computers. All the basic Internet books have the information needed to buy, install and use a modem.

I should mention that the 'hardware problem' is not only the punchline to a joke, but a real issue for those of us who want to use the Internet. When I first logged on, back in early 1994, I was doing it from my vintage 1990 home computer (an IBM-compatible PC with a 286 chip, 1 MB of memory and a 40 MB hard disk) using a slow (2,400 bps) modem. It is still possible today, barely two years later, to use the same computer and modem – but if I did, I wouldn't have graphical access to the World Wide Web. So today I'm using another computer, a couple of generations more advanced, with a faster modem. But a year or two from now, these will not suffice and I'll have to upgrade again. While it's true that computer prices continue to plummet, there is a constant need to upgrade. This may be one of the reasons why trade unionists and working people in general aren't getting online quicker: it requires substantial investments of money (and time) every couple of years in one's computer hardware.

Of course that's not the only reason. I'll discuss other problems with using the Internet throughout this book. But I want to mention right now the general problem of *fear of computers*. Because I live and work in a multi-generational community in which computers have been introduced over a fifteen-year period, I've been able to observe computer-phobia (and its opposite) at close range. I've met 75-year-olds who have become Internet freaks and 20-year-olds afraid to push the 'Enter' key. There are few generalisations that work when describing people's behaviour around computers. But it is a fact that many people are uncomfortable with computers in general, and will go to great lengths if necessary to avoid using them. (When I was a student at university in the early 1970s, I was required to use a computer for a sociology project. I asked for – and received – special permission from my professor not to use the computer, and to do a conventional paper instead. As a result, I didn't touch a computer for another decade.)

This uneasiness with computers in general is multiplied many-fold when confronting the vast Internet. Having been among the very first people in this village to use the network, I encountered head-on the fear and confusion the Internet brings out in people – and its opposite, the great hopes and enthusiasm. Dealing with these fears is a key task facing the labour movement, and I'll try to point out successful stories of how computer networking was introduced into trade unions with the proper training and support.

In this chapter, I'll focus on advantages and disadvantages of each new technology as I see them: for example, explaining why LISTSERV is preferable to USENET. In the chapters to come, there will be lots of examples from out in the field, on the local, national and global levels. In this chapter, as I review technical issues like these, I remind readers that our goal is not to explore these new technologies for their own sakes – even if that would be fun – but 'the ever expanding union of the workers' which this technology makes possible.

A Very Brief History of the Internet

Men and women have been using computers for a half century now. By the late 1960s, computers were a common sight in universities, government and the military, at least in the United States. The Cold War motivated – and technological advances made possible – the US government's decision at the end of that decade to try to create a network of computers in different cities. Four computers were linked together in the western part of the United States. The experiment worked. Thus was the Advanced Research Projects Agency network (ARPANET), the forerunner of today's Internet, born.

One of the reasons the American defence establishment invested in the ARPANET was concern for the reliability of connections between computers. If computers were connected to each other by only a single cable, the connection could be easily lost. The ARPANET provided many different routes between computers. The computers had to be able to send messages to each other by any available route, rather than by just one fixed route.

Another concern was to find ways to allow computers of two entirely different types, using different operating systems, to 'talk' with one another. A common language, or 'protocol', was needed to do this. The American defence establishment was eager to promote cooperative work between research scientists at different sites, using different computers.

Access to the original ARPANET was closely restricted to security-cleared defence contractors and researchers. A second network known as Milnet was established in the early 1980s and it allowed unclassified communications among academics and scientists. The scientific and academic community began establishing its own networks.

Meanwhile, two other kinds of networks were being created outside of the academic and research communities. One kind was the commercial network which allowed exchange of email, online conferencing and access to data. Among these were the US-based CompuServe (owned by H&R Block), Prodigy (owned by IBM and Sears), America Online and GEnie (the 'GE' stands for 'General Electric'). These networks allowed people and organisations with modems and home computers to dial up local phone numbers and connect to each other.

The other kind of network which began to spring up – its origins go back to 1978, in Chicago – was the local electronic bulletin board system, known as a BBS. BBSs spread like wildfire throughout the 1980s and early 1990s, creating a kind of 'poor man's Internet'. Tens of thousands of them exist to this day in North America alone. They allowed exchanges of email and access to data at a local level. In the 1980s, FidoNet was launched, eventually linking thousands of such local BBSs around the world.

All it takes to run a local BBS is a home computer, modem, telephone line and appropriate software. Because the software was often 'freeware' (programs distributed at no cost) and because the prices of home computers and modems were dropping steadily, the result was tens of thousands of such BBSs across North America by the 1990s, and thousands more around the world.

By the mid-1990s, nearly all of these networks, from the giant America Online with its millions of subscribers down to the local BBS with maybe a few dozen, were linked to the Internet. In the beginning, the sending of email from a local BBS or one of the commercial services to the Internet was a feat demanding technical prowess and often a lot of money. Today, that is no longer the case, and even inexpensive local BBSs can offer access to many Internet services at very low prices. In some cities, there are even 'freenets' allowing Internet access at no cost to the public.

The 'protocol' developed by ARPANET allowing computers of different types to talk with each other (known by its initials as TCP/IP) became the Esperanto of the global computer communications network. (Esperanto was an attempt at an international language. At one time, trade unionists and others greeted the idea with enthusiasm, but although several million people learned the language, it never took off.)

The system of sending data in packets, known as a packet-switching network, was embraced by other networks. Today, instead of the original four computers, the Internet links millions of computers, connecting not only defence researchers, academics, and government officials, but tens of millions of ordinary people – including millions of trade unionists.

Trade unions all over the world have been experimenting for more than a decade creating networks, online databases, bulletin boards, and discussion groups. They are doing this using informal local BBSs, or existing commercial networks, or the Internet itself. In some cases, they have even established their own independent networks.

Email

Email is short for 'electronic mail'. Electronic mail is simply the electronic transmission of data from one user on one computer to another user on another computer. By 'data' we almost always mean text, and usually text in Latin letters, without any kind of accents, underlining, italicising or bold facing (this is usually called 'pure ASCII' text). But it is also possible to send other kinds of text, including Cyrillic, Arabic, Hebrew, Chinese, Japanese and other characters. In fact, email can include computer programs, pictures, and sound. Basically, everything you can now store in a computer, you can send to someone else by email.

That means that a labour journalist covering a strike in some far-flung corner of the globe, with the right tools, can today use email to send not only text about developments in the strike, but also photographs (and even videos) of the strikers on their picket lines; graphic displays (using popular spreadsheet and database programs) illustrating the gaps between labour and management; and sound recordings of a press conference held by the workers. Because it is so easy, fast and inexpensive to send email on the Internet, email is a great way to rapidly spread text, pictures and sound about labour struggles from one part of the world to another.

To send email, all you need is the following:

- A computer. And this need not be a very powerful computer. Old Apple computers and IBM-compatible personal computers from the early 1980s are perfectly capable of sending and receiving email.
- A modem. This is an inexpensive device which connects computers to telephone lines.
- A telephone line. This need not be dedicated (reserved exclusively) for the computer; the line is busy only when being used by the computer. In fact, one does not even necessarily need a phone line. Alternatives include low-earth orbiting satellites (this is an option in some African countries), packet radio and line-of-sight microwave connections.
- A link to the Internet (a dial-up account with a service provider, or a direct connection).
- A communications program to connect your computer through its modem to the network. Free communications programs are available.
- An email program (optional if you're dialling up). Free email programs exist too.

You do not have to understand anything technical about email in order to use it. Millions of people use email every day, but there are probably only a few who actually understand how the system works. (Fortunately, some of those are working for the labour movement.) Anyway, how many people understand how a fax machine works? I want to explain a little bit about it, because I think that the more you know, the more intelligently you'll use email.

The way email goes through the Internet can cause delays in receiving mail, and often mail comes in batches. This is quite obviously the case when one is a subscriber to discussion groups, which will be discussed later in this chapter. Email is often, though not always, instantaneous. And email *can* get lost, or erased accidentally – though it's hard to believe that more accidents happen here than with the ordinary postal service, which is sneeringly (and accurately) called 'snail mail' by email users. (Clifford Stoll, the author of *Silicon Snake Oil,* claims that in an experiment he conducted, the Post Office did better than the Internet, losing no letters while the Internet lost several.)

Probably the biggest problem users face is correctly addressing their email messages. Correctly defining an email address is no harder than correctly dialling a telephone number. Anyone who's ever had to dial a long international telephone number quickly learns the value of automatic diallers on telephones.

If you write a letter to US President Bill Clinton today, and spell Clinton with a 'K', your letter will reach the White House. If you don't know the President's address, and just write to him at 'The White House, Washington, DC', your mail will get there. And as millions of children have discovered, you can write to Santa Claus at the North Pole and get an answer. A friend of mine once wrote to the President of a major transnational corporation by addressing his letter to 'The man in charge'. It got there.

But make even a small a mistake in email, and you get a good lesson in the differences between human and artificial intelligence. If instead of writing to president@whitehouse.gov (which is Mr Clinton's actual email address), you wrote to resident@whitehouse.gov, your mail would bounce right back to you. And you can forget about writing to the.man.in.charge@transnational.com.

I don't think there's an email program yet that can do what any postal clerk in the world does every day, which is to handle minor errors in address. But are telephone switchboards any more forgiving? As I mentioned, the best way to use a phone these days is to record phone numbers in one of those neat new telephones that allow you to store frequently called numbers. Not everyone has phones like that. But *every* email program I've seen allows you to store addresses, meaning that once you've successfully sent mail to someone, you'll never have to retype the whole address again.

One standard set of rules used to transmit email on the Internet is called the simple mail transfer protocol (SMTP), which like other Internet protocols allows the transfer of data from different types of computers, ranging from giant mainframes and supercomputers down to the little IBM-compatible personal computer I'm writing on now. And because the Internet is the 'network of networks', you can send mail from CompuServe to GeoNet, from South Africa's SANGONeT to America Online, and from Canada's Solinet to Russia's GlasNet. Using the so-called 'gateways' from one network to another, you can even send mail from your local computer bulletin board, using the FidoNet network of such boards, through the Internet to any other network.

Now that you know what email is, you may wonder why the labour movement would want to use it. What possible advantage is there in email, as opposed to fax machines or ordinary 'snail mail'? I can think of several reasons.

- *Email is very fast.* It's even faster than fax. Let me illustrate this by a true story. Some time ago, I had to send the text of an entire issue of the quarterly magazine *Workers' Education* (which I edit) from Israel to Buenos Aires, by fax. I printed the issue out on 30 single-spaced pages, and then began faxing. I was extremely lucky. I was able to get an international connection. The fax machine at the other end was not busy. It did not run out of paper in the middle. And most amazing of all – we had a continuous telephone link for the full 30 minutes it took for the fax to get there. If we had been able to use email, I could have send the whole text in about ten seconds. This is, however, not always the case. Sometimes, particularly when using FidoNet, email can take hours or even days. Once you actually make the connection, faxes are received immediately. If someone is in their office when you send them a fax, they will hear the phone ring and see the papers drop out of the fax machine. With email, they'll have to check their electronic mailbox from time to time. So even if it only takes a few seconds to send an email message, it may be hours until the recipient checks their mailbox and reads the letter.
- *Email is very cheap.* With email, you're usually not charged by distance. A letter to the other side of the world costs as much as one across town. The cost in most cases is per hour of use. Let's take a look at that fax story again. The cost of sending those 30 pages by fax to Buenos Aires was roughly equivalent to 30 hours on the Internet.
- *Email is more reliable than fax.* There are countries you simply cannot reach by ordinary telephone, at least not regularly. Some of the international trade secretariats report that email is the preferred way to send messages to some countries in the world's South and to the former Soviet bloc. This was borne out by my own recent experience collecting articles for *Workers' Education* from trade unionists all over the world. The subject of our issue was the defence of trade unions, and this prompted labour organisations on every continent to submit articles. The articles which came in from Canada, Norway, New Zealand and the Philippines came in by email and arrived readable and intact. But our friends in the Czech and Bulgarian labour movements didn't have access to email, and faxed in their submissions. Because the typewriter ribbon was light, I couldn't read the name of the author of the Czech article, and half a page of the Bulgarian article was unreadable.

I had to fax back to Prague and Sofia for more information. The Czechs and Bulgarians responded within a few hours – and I still couldn't decipher the Czech author's name, or read the whole text of the Bulgarian article. Modems usually include built-in, sophisticated error-correction programs, which is not always the case with faxes. And because email usually works on a store-and-forward basis, you don't need a live connection through bad international phone lines, as you do with fax.

- *Email is more flexible than fax, phone or mail.* I can send (and I have sent) colour photos – which I created using a simple and inexpensive device called a scanner – using email. I've received them too. I can send audio files, videos, spreadsheets, formatted text files – anything currently stored in my computer. Try to send a colour photo by fax.

- *Email eliminates the need for re-typing.* As an editor of a labour publication which receives faxed submissions from all over the world, I know how annoying it is to have to type back into a computer what was, originally, a word-processed document that someone else typed into another computer. Email not only eliminates the bother of re-typing but also saves the expense.

- *Email is mobile.* Because your email is usually sent to a host computer, from which you pick up your letters from time to time, you can access that computer from your home, office, or on the road (with a portable computer, or using someone else's computer). While attending an international trade union meeting in Belgium, I was able to use a local computer to download mail which had been received at my email account in Israel. In the course of writing this book, I've had to consult a few times with labour movement experts on this subject while they were on the road. I tracked down one in Peru and the other in India. No matter where they travelled – and this was the case even in developing countries where Internet access is not always simple or cheap – I was able to reach them and get answers to my questions. I simply wrote to their permanent email addresses, and they found ways to pick up, read, and reply to their mail. For travelling trade unionists, or for those of us who sometimes need to work at home, this is a huge advantage over fax machines.

- *Email allows the simple creation of mailing lists.* It requires no effort to create computerised lists of individuals or organisations with email addresses. With a simple click of the mouse (a pointing device connected to a computer), one can send the same message to all of them. When I want to send out news to my own list of 20 or so friends and associates, I simply send out one letter to my local Internet access provider, whose computer reads my 'To' list and sends out the letter to everyone on it. When you try to do this with an ordinary fax machine, you have to send the same fax out again and again, tying up your phone lines. The longer the list, the more time the fax (and phone lines) are tied up.

- *Some Internet access providers offer a service combining the best of fax and email.* You send them your text and list of fax numbers, and tie up their fax machine, not yours, sending the letters out. Those faxes, which are not always instantly delivered, are sent out by local host computers in different countries, saving you the cost of international phone calls.

- *Email invites dialogue.* It's so easy to answer an email message, that one is tempted to answer messages *immediately* after reading them, rather than putting them aside in a pile of unanswered mail. In the email program I use, when I read a letter, I can simply point my mouse to an icon (an icon is a little picture on the screen), click on it, and I get a display showing my own name and email address in a 'From' field, my correspondent's name and email address in a 'To' field – even if I don't know that address (because the program has figured out who to write back to) – and in the 'subject' field, the subject of my correspondent's letter with the phrase 'Re:' before it. And the cursor waits patiently on the first line of a blank page, eager to know how I want to respond. Because it's so ridiculously easy and tempting to answer letters at once, I find that I don't have a pile of unanswered email, as was the case before going online. Nor do I have to begin every letter with 'I'm sorry to have taken so long to get back to you'.

- *Email doesn't distinguish between rich and poor, powerful and powerless.* An email message sent out by an organisation of unemployed workers in a developing country looks just like email sent out by the Chief Executive Officer of IBM. In the past, you could tell by looking at a letter – at the quality of the paper used, for example, or the typing – whether the sender was someone to be taken seriously. The rich and the organisations they sponsor simply produced more impressive letters than the poor. But the Internet has a levelling effect, making all email look equally good – or bad.

I've mentioned some of the advantages of email without going into detail about the problems. Some of these will come up throughout the rest of this book, and others will be discussed only in Chapter 7, where I discuss some of the obstacles to the creation of a global labournet. But it wouldn't be fair not to list here at least a few of the problems with email:

- *It is not always feasible to use email for languages which are not based on the Latin alphabet.* Even though it is *possible* using sophisticated software (like the Windows-based program I use) to attach files in languages like Hebrew, the recipient of such mail must also have the right software – and certain hardware features, like a keyboard with non-Latin characters or a terminal capable of displaying those characters. Over time, this will become more and more common, but for now sending and receiving email in languages other than the Latin-based ones is still a problem. The problem of English-language domination of the networks is one which I will return to, but I should point out now that it's a crucial one for the international labour movement. Not only email, but *everything* on the Internet is designed to work in English. The existing international trade union institutions are trying to solve the problem by hiring translators. In one recent case, an important labour group put up a Web site with colourful flags illustrating the different languages which would be available – and then removed them, leaving instead an apology (in several languages) that budgetary considerations did not allow the site to be multilingual. In the long run, I believe that automatic translation software (computer programs that translate text from one language to another) may offer a solution. Until then, international trade union organisations are going to have to invest money in translating what they put out into cyberspace.
- *The learning curve for email, unlike fax machines, is a steep one.* This was even more true a year or two ago, before user-friendly software began to appear. Strange commands had to be learned to do the simplest email tasks. Meanwhile, fax machines could be used by everyone who knows how to dial a telephone.
- *Email is still an insecure medium* – and this concerns trade unionists as much as it does businesses and government. Email messages may pass through several computers on their way to their final destinations. At any point, they can be intercepted and read. Though this problem is wildly exaggerated by the mass media, it is still a problem. There are many encryption programs available today, including the free PGP (Pretty Good Privacy) program, but these are not especially user-friendly.
- *Though it is extremely rare, email can be a source of viruses in your computer.* This will happen only when you transmit executable programs (software) as attachments to email. There are, of course, ways to protect your computer from this kind of attack. But this is not a danger with telephones, snail mail or fax machines.

Databases

Trade unionists don't have to be persuaded of the advantages of using computerised databases. Many of them use these every day. They maintain their membership lists and keep financial data in computers. And they may even use external databases – for example, corporate or legal information available on compact discs (known as CD-ROMs). Online databases are simply masses of digitised information available through the networks, and they can be powerful tools for the labour movement.

There are five major reasons for trade unionists to use online computerised databases:

- *They're up to date.* Unlike printed materials, it's very easy to maintain current information in digital form. This is the big advantage of online databases when compared to CD-ROMs. A CD-ROM will go out of date just as quickly as a book. But a centrally and continuously maintained database is always current.
- *They're often free.* Books and CD-ROMs are rarely, if ever, given out for free. But online databases often are. Let me give an example. There's an annual publication in the US called the *Thomas Register*, which lists American manufacturers by what they produce, and it includes some information about each company. It could certainly be a useful tool in the hands of a trade union research department. Until recently, the only way to get the information in the current *Thomas Register* was to buy several bound volumes every year. But now the *Register* is available online, free of charge.
- *Computerised databases, unlike printed ones, can be quickly searched by keywords.* For anyone who has ever tried to find a needle in a haystack, nothing compares to the pleasure of typing in a desired word or phrase and having the computer instantly spew out all references to it.
- *Online databases can be integrated with other online tools, like email, for powerful effect.* This was demonstrated as early as a decade ago by the researchers at the chemical workers' international trade secretariat (more on this in the next chapter). They were able to access online databases from the organisation's headquarters in Europe, searching for information requested by affiliate unions around the world. When the digitised information was located, it could be easily incorporated – without re-typing or photocopying – in the emailed response back to the local union.
- *Finally, online databases disperse information widely, thereby empowering those who previously had no access to it.* Information

that was once available only in special libraries, or in expensive newsletters and reports, is now widely available thanks to the Internet.

Just as I mentioned that email also has its drawbacks, I want to say a few words about some of the problems with online databases.

- *Much of the better quality material that we need to find is available only in print, or on CD-ROMs.* This makes sense, because there are still many sources of information (particularly commercial ones) who don't see how they can make a profit by spreading around the Internet information that they usually sell. Some entrepreneurs are looking at ways to charge very small amounts of money to access Internet databases. When this becomes practical, no less an authority than Bill Gates tells us that the sale of information via the Internet will boom. Not only commercial information providers are hesitating to put all their quality information up front on the networks. Governments and non-governmental organisations continue to publish books, pamphlets, newsletters, and the like without a thought to making the same information available on the Internet. An outstanding example is the International Labour Organisation (ILO), which is probably the world's leading provider of quality information which trade unionists can use. Yet until recently very little ILO material was available through the Internet.
- *It's often faster to look things up in print, particularly if one has a slow, dial-up link to the Internet.* I recall seeing an Internet site a couple of years ago offering access to a dictionary. It struck me then that it would be a lot faster for me to reach over to my own inexpensive, paperback dictionary and look up a word than it would be to turn on my computer, connect to the Internet, access this site and run their keyword search program. Certain kinds of information sources, including dictionaries, are probably better left to their current form.
- *Nearly all the databases currently online were not created by the labour movement nor are they under the control of the labour movement.* This means that much of the information trade unions look for, collect, and sometimes publish, is not available. And the information that is available is not necessarily what trade unionists are looking for. This will change as more and more unions put their own information online. But until then, the information we're seeing is collected by and published by sources outside the labour movement, and sometimes hostile to the labour movement.
- *Even the wildest estimates of the size of the Internet in the mid-1990s showed that 99 per cent of the world's population was still*

not online. In the developing countries, the figure is much closer to 100 per cent than 99 per cent. Online data is not going to be very useful to those labour movements in those countries, nor to the great mass of ordinary working people and the poor who still cannot afford to join the network. Only when the Internet becomes universal will online databases be a true replacement for printed ones.

- *Online databases are often not as portable as printed ones.* The science fiction writer Isaac Asimov once wrote an essay trying to define the perfect portable computer. It would have to be lightweight and small enough to be carried in one's pocket or bag. It would have to demand very little energy. Its 'interface' – the way users worked with it – would have to be simple. The clarity of the letters or illustrations would have to be very sharp. And it would have to be extremely inexpensive. Asimov's conclusion was that the ideal portable computer was – a paperback book.

- *Keyword searches, while fast, are not necessarily intelligent.* The way a computer searches a database and the way a human does are quite different. Tell an Internet search program to look up 'labor' and it will return every instance of the word 'laboratory' as well. Machine-created indexes are still inferior to the ones humans create. One can often learn much more from flipping pages in a magazine than from doing keyword searches on computerised databases.

- *Finally, the increasing use of online, computerised databases may create a new stratum of individuals with the knowledge and skills to sift through the mountains of information the Internet makes available.* A decade ago, 'information brokers' were simply those people who had online access. Today, when access is much more widespread, the skills of searching and analysing vast amounts of data are what are needed. Anyone can 'surf' the World Wide Web looking for information, but how many people can do this quickly and intelligently?

That having been said, let's look at some of the online databases trade unionists have been using over the last few years. Two pioneering international trade secretariats, which we'll discuss in greater detail in the next chapter, were also enthusiastic early users of online databases. The chemical workers' secretariat subscribed to a number of such databases, including world-wide company directories, stockbroker reports on companies and industries, abstracts from the financial and trade press, and annual reports from several hundred thousand transnational companies. The transport workers' trade secretariat became the second largest user in the world of Lloyd's Seadata system, which records all the world's ships, their movements, and some ownership information.

Meanwhile, the labour movement was beginning to create its own databases. Very early on, the British Columbia Teachers' Federation built a database of contract clauses. This would then be consulted by union negotiators before meeting their employer counterparts throughout that Canadian province. Elsewhere in Canada, Solinet, the first national labour network anywhere, established a grievance database which proved quite useful to the union.

A large number of databases of interest to trade unionists could be found on GeoNet host computers. Among these were a number of health and safety databases, such as NIOSH (National Institute for Occupational Safety and Health; including workplace environment and toxicology), HSELine (Bibliographic References from the Health and Safety Executive), and RTECS (Registry of Toxic Effects of Chemical Substances). Through GeoNet, it was also possible to access LaborDoc, the ILO's labour-related documents and reports.

Discussion Groups

By the mid-1990s, there were four ways to conduct online discussions involving groups of people using the Internet:

- *LISTSERV mailing lists.* These are email-based discussion groups, open to everyone who uses the Internet.
- *USENET newsgroups.* These are a kind of global bulletin board, with tens of thousands of topics, accessible by *nearly* everyone with Internet access.
- *Conferences on private networks.* These groups are accessible by people who subscribe to private networks, and are closed off to the rest of us.
- *World Wide Web-based discussion groups.* As the Web became the heart of the Internet, more and more Web sites offered their own, internal discussion groups. To join the discussion, you had to be accessing the Web site.

As the Internet evolves, more and more such technologies appear. I'm sure that the labour movement will continue to experiment with new online discussion tools as they evolve. I want to say a few words here about each of the four methods described, and how they are being used today.

LISTSERV Discussion Lists

Perhaps the simplest technology to explain is LISTSERV. LISTSERV is, first of all, the name of a computer program which allows a single user to maintain a mailing list, and to forward messages to everyone on that list. Some basic email programs themselves also allow one to do this, and I actually ran an international discussion list (with about a hundred participants) from a desktop PC using such a program (Internet Chameleon), rather than the more powerful LISTSERV program, which only runs on computers which use the Unix operating system.

LISTSERV is widely used in academia, and many universities offer up several LISTSERV-based discussion lists on a broad range of topics. There are thousands of such groups existing today, with varying numbers of participants, ranging from half a dozen to tens of thousands. The most popular list is the daily mailing of American television star David Letterman's 'Top Ten' comedy routine. Activ-L is one of the more important left-wing lists. Further down the line in popularity are such specifically labour movement related lists as Labor-L (Labour in the Global Economy), H-Labor (Labour History), Union-D (European Labour), Labnews (Labour News), Mundo Sindical (a Peruvian-based Spanish-language trade union list), Publabor (Public sector unionists), Labor-Party (Discussion of a Labour Party in the US), and the like. (For more details about these discussion groups and how to join them, see Appendix 2.)

From the point of view of the user, LISTSERV works pretty simply. To subscribe to a LISTSERV mailing list, you send an ordinary email message to an address, usually listserv@ someuniversity.edu, with the first line of text reading something like 'subscribe labor-l john smith' (without the quotation marks). That's an instruction to the LISTSERV program at the other end to automatically enrol you as a subscriber to the list. (In some lists, you cannot join without the moderator's approval, and you have to send an email message explaining who you are and why you want to participate in the list. This is the case with some scholarly lists.) To get off a list, you send a message like 'Unsubscribe'. You can usually see a list of who else is subscribing, or view archived messages, or a whole bunch of other things, by sending different LISTSERV commands.

To send out a message to the whole list, you usually send the message to *another* address (*not* listserv@someuniversity.edu), which either automatically passes it on to everyone on the list, or gives your message to the list's moderator, who then decides whether to pass it on or not. Messages sent out to subscribers to the list reach them by regular email.

This all seems pretty low-tech. Yet this is actually LISTSERV's great advantage over other kinds of discussions on the Internet. If you're a trade unionist in the Philippines or Peru, you may not have much in the way of Internet access. It's highly unlikely that you can access the graphical World Wide Web, for instance. But if you have a personal computer, modem and telephone line, you can probably get online with a local bulletin board. That BBS might be part of FidoNet, which means that you can exchange email (albeit slowly) with anyone on the Internet. In other words, even people whose only access to the Internet is through a local BBS can often join in LISTSERV discussions with people from around the world.

Does this mean that such LISTSERV mailing lists are actually full of participants from Africa and Asia? No, it does not. Those LISTSERV mailing lists are still largely populated by North Americans. *Potentially*, LISTSERV is a powerful tool that would allow trade unionists in many countries to exchange views. But this is not the case today.

Its simple, low-tech character is not LISTSERV's only advantage. LISTSERV also serves as a bridge between various networks. If you're using the Internet through Poptel or GreenNet in the UK, or if you've joined the AFL–CIO's LaborNET on CompuServe or use instead LaborNet@IGC, you can always participate in LISTSERV mailing lists.

And anyone who has participated in groups like Labor-L and H-Labor, which are two of the older, established LISTSERVs which deal with the labour movement, will find that these are infinitely more interesting and useful than the USENET newsgroups, which I'll come to in a moment. This is true because many of the LISTSERV groups, including the ones I've just mentioned, are moderated. In some cases, as in H-Labor, membership is restricted to qualified participants. This means that instead of having one's electronic mailbox stuffed with every crank's messages about every subject under the sun, the messages are sifted through by someone, usually a volunteer, often an expert. What you get are on-topic messages which are usually brief and frequently fascinating.

A disadvantage of LISTSERV is that it's not always simple to find out about a group's existence. One way to do so is to join the group 'New-List' (itself a LISTSERV mailing list) which sends out a bunch of daily messages to its thousands of subscribers announcing new lists – though admittedly very few of these will be on labour topics. Another way is to check out the growing number of resources on the World Wide Web pointing out which LISTSERVs exist. (One of these may be found at http://www.tile.net/tile/listserv/index.html.) And new LISTSERV mailing lists are usually announced to participants in older ones, so if you subscribe to Labor-L, for example, you'll probably read there about new lists when they appear.

Another disadvantage is the relatively small number of LISTSERV mailing lists, compared to, say, the dozens of labour-related conferences available on the APC or GeoNet networks. There is no LISTSERV mailing list today on the subject of labour and the environment, for example. But there is such a conference, and many others, on LaborNet@IGC.

In my opinion, for anyone who has email, LISTSERV is the discussion medium of choice on the Internet. For trade unionists looking to discuss issues of mutual concern with a broad international audience – including the developing countries – LISTSERV is the way to go.

USENET Newsgroups

When one reads in the mass media about Internet discussion groups – and in particular, the bizarre or pornographic groups – one is usually reading about USENET. USENET was set up in the late 1970s by a couple of students in the US to allow Unix operating system users to exchange technical information. It quickly expanded to include other topics and participants eventually began to include users who were not on the Unix system at all.

Today, there are thousands of USENET newsgroups. They discuss virtually every topic under the sun, and are organised hierarchically. Newsgroups have names like *alt.society.labor-unions*. This means, first of all, that this group belongs to the 'alt' hierarchy, which includes the 'alternative topics'. Other hierarchies include 'comp' (computer-related topics), 'soc' (social and cultural topics), 'rec' (recreational subjects, including music, sport and films) and 'sci' (scientific discussion). There are also newsgroups designed to be accessed in specific countries; for example, newsgroups beginning with the letters 'za' originate in South Africa. Under these hierarchies appear others, and alt.society. Labor-unions appears under the 'society' subsection of the 'alt' hierarchy.

In the past, to read postings to a USENET newsgroup, one had to use a program called a News Reader. Today, software like Netscape, which is the most popular program on the Internet, serves the same goal admirably.

Increasingly, there is overlap between LISTSERV mailing lists and USENET newsgroups, with the latter being 'mirrored' to a LISTSERV list and mailed out to those who don't have USENET access. For example, the USENET newsgroup misc.activism.progressive is mirrored to the LISTSERV mailing list activ-l.

When we compare LISTSERV to USENET as means of conducting discussions within the labour movement, LISTSERV has several clear advantages:

- *USENET doesn't reach everyone.* Unlike LISTSERV, which is accessible to everyone with email, USENET newsgroups are available only to those Internet users whose networks provide them with access to newsgroups. Not every Internet provider does this, and not *every* provider gives out *every* newsgroup. For example, even though the newsgroup alt.society.labor-unions existed for some time, I was unable to access it for many months because my Internet provider did not see fit to retrieve and distribute this newsgroup.

- *USENET newsgroups are more vulnerable to state censorship than LISTSERV mailing lists.* Recently, the commercial network CompuServe made headlines when it blocked access to some 200 'adult' newsgroups, knuckling under to pressure from the German government. CompuServe didn't just block the newsgroups in Germany; it blocked their distribution through CompuServe host computers around the world. While most proponents of civil liberties denounced the move, it was interesting to note that the Chinese government hailed it. This doesn't bode well for the future of an open USENET when it comes to China. That regime, and other repressive ones as well, including Iran and Singapore, have their own lists of newsgroups they want to ban from reaching their shores. It is a technically simple thing to do. (It is possible to circumvent this kind of censorship by instructing one's computer to access a news server elsewhere on the net – but how many of us know how to do this?) But if a country is to be open at all to the Internet, it must be open to email. And LISTSERV mailing list messages come through as regular email, drops in an ocean of electronic messages. To block participation in a USENET newsgroup like misc.activism.progressive, a regime need only order local Internet access suppliers to stop the daily 'news feed' of that group. To block the exact same messages coming through the LISTSERV group activ-l would be nearly impossible. Trade unionists worried about repressive regimes should take note.
- *The quality of postings to USENET is often quite low.* Anyone can read messages from and send messages to nearly any newsgroup. Some of the groups are moderated, but most are not. Therefore, unlike LISTSERV, which is often moderated, and whose membership can even be restricted, there's a lot of garbage floating around USENET. Though USENET newsgroups often reach much larger audiences than LISTSERV mailing lists – sometimes even in the hundreds of thousands – one will sometimes get better feedback from the LISTSERV group. This has been my own experience.
- *USENET requires that you access the group every day.* LISTSERV works on the basis of email. USENET doesn't. If you don't remember one day that you subscribe to a LISTSERV mailing list like Labor-L, don't worry. Your messages will still arrive

and will await you in your mailbox. But with a USENET
newsgroup like alt.society.labor-unions, if you forget to check
for a day or two, you'll miss messages. These messages are
not always archived. (Alt.society.labor-unions apparently
isn't archived anywhere.) Internet providers generally keep
only a day or two's worth of messages online.

• *There's almost nothing dealing with labour to be found on USENET
  today.* With all the popularity of USENET, it is surprising that
  only one newsgroup I've heard of deals with the labour
  movement – alt.society.labor-unions – and I'll be discussing
  it in Chapter 5. Meanwhile, there are a handful of LISTSERV
  mailing lists on labour themes, and dozens within the APC
  and GeoNet networks – which we'll come to in a moment.

Conferences on Private Networks

The Internet is a network of networks. That means that it's made
up of many thousands of smaller networks, and many of these have
their own ways of doing things, including conducting online
conversations.

Until a few years ago, access to the Internet was restricted to
individuals in academia, government, and the US military. But
extensive online networks existed. The largest of these was
CompuServe. If you wanted to discuss stamp collecting or astronomy
with others who shared your interests within an online network,
you could do it through conferences on such commercial online
networks. The very existence of those conferences was a big selling
point for CompuServe and its competitors.

Even with the opening up of the Internet in recent years, allowing
the rest of us to use LISTSERV and USENET, private online
networks and their conferences remain an important part of the
ongoing discussions. One recent report showed that some 30 per
cent of Americans who access the Internet do so through the
America Online network. With the launch of the Microsoft Network
(MSN) and Europe Online, with their hundreds of thousands of
new members, it appears that private networks are far from finished.
They still attract members, and still have much to offer, including
conferences. This is certainly true when it comes to the labour
movement.

The San Francisco-based LaborNet@IGC, which is linked to
the Association for Progressive Communications, will be discussed
in much greater detail in Chapter 5. Suffice it to say here that this
private network claims more than 1,000 paying participants and
has been around in one form or another since the early 1990s.
LaborNet@IGC hosts dozens of 'conferences' on labour issues,
making this probably the most extensive discussion taking place

anywhere online, dwarfing the handful of LISTSERV mailing lists and USENET newsgroups.

These conferences discuss the labour movements of different countries and regions; different sectors of the economy; different issues facing the labour movement; and different things that unions do. They include daily labour news briefings, press releases from labour organisations, and announcements of new online resources for the labour movement. In this last category, there is nothing quite like them. If you want to know who is putting up new Web pages in the trade union movement, or which company can assist unions to do this, or who set up 'alt.society.labor-unions' – the LaborNet@IGC conferences are the place to be.

Anyone who subscribes to LaborNet@IGC can read the messages posted to the groups and post their own messages. All messages posted since the groups went online are still available, some going back five years and more. The conferences work like a bulletin board, with the occasional reminder to the user to check a board they haven't yet looked at. Users can mark items 'read' so that they won't be reminded repeatedly to look at the same items. Users can also designate which lists they want to check regularly, and when signing on to the network, they'll be informed which conferences have new messages since they last looked.

A larger collection of trade unionists, but not nearly as many topics, may be found in the AFL–CIO's LaborNET, which resides on the CompuServe network. I'll be returning to this important example of a labour conferencing system – probably the first one launched by a national trade union centre – in Chapter 5.

Canada's Solinet also runs a number of ongoing conferences, including ones on the environment, women's rights, health and safety, training, pensions, privatisation, workers' compensation, books – and even cooking.

GeoNet conferences are called 'bulletin boards' or 'BBSs' (not to be confused with the dial-up variety we'll discuss in Chapter 4). The GEO2 host computer contained a number of these, including a few with a labour focus. The key labour BBSs there are called 'Labour' and 'ITS-BBS' (maintained by the trade secretariats).

While such conferences within a private network have the advantage of great diversity (more than 40 'labr' conferences on LaborNet@IGC alone), they have several disadvantages:

- *Cost.* They cost money – which is to say, joining the network costs money – above the cost of Internet access and telecommunications charges (what the phone company charges). I can access LaborNet@IGC or the AFL–CIO's LaborNET on CompuServe directly through the Internet (using a function called 'Telnet') but I have to pay extra money to do so.

- *A different interface.* As they do not work within the framework of email or USENET newsgroups, or even the World Wide Web, they require the learning of a new interface, or set of commands. For example, to see an index of messages to the LaborNet@IGC conference 'labr.global', I have to key in the letter 'I'. To see the most recent messages, I have to key in the symbol '>'. These commands are not familiar to users who might very well know how to read their email or 'surf' the World Wide Web, and may constitute an obstacle to their use.
- *System incompatibility.* For several years now, the APC and GeoNet networks have tried to 'mirror' each other's conferences, but without much luck. This means that a British trade unionist who belongs to the Poptel/GeoNet network will not be able to access the 'labr.uk' conference on the APC networks, unless he or she also pays to join those.
- *US dominance.* Despite the best intentions of LaborNet@IGC, and their extensive links to trade unionists around the world through the Association for Progressive Communications, the conferences are dominated not only by US participants but even by a US way of looking at the labour movement. A conference entitled 'labr.party' for example is not about labour parties in general, nor even about existing labour parties in Britain or Canada, but about the *proposal* to launch a labour party in the US. On the other hand, LaborNet@IGC has made a special effort to create some conferences which would interest unionists outside of North America, including the very lively 'labr.asia' group, 'labr.cis' (about the former Soviet Union) and 'labr.uk'. But we cannot expect LaborNet@IGC, which is working hard to get American unions online, to play the role of a global network.

In conclusion, though conferences on private networks have the advantage of quality, and have proven themselves effective over a number of years, as tens of millions of people join the Internet, those conferences have become increasingly isolated from the mainstream.

World Wide Web-based Discussion Groups

With the increasing popularity of the World Wide Web, a number of Web sites began to include discussion groups *within* the home pages themselves. This is a little hard to explain, so let me do it with an example.

One of the bookstores which opened up shop on the Web, Book Stacks Unlimited, tries to offer visitors to its Web site a whole bunch of additional services. Yes, one can buy books there. But one can also read about books. The store also decided to make the site interactive by creating discussion groups within their 'Book Cafe'. These groups have moderators, selected from among customers and bookstore staff. They cover a range of topics, including certain authors, book subjects and even particular titles.

Sometimes the discussion group will exist for only a limited time, serving a specific purpose. Authors will be invited to participate in discussion groups focusing on their books, or the subject of their books. For example, Jill Ellsworth, the co-author of *The Internet Business Book*, moderated a discussion group on the subject of business and the net. Customers would post their messages, and Ellsworth would answer when appropriate.

The interface to these discussion groups, which are accessed through the store's Web site, looks much like USENET's or the conferences in LaborNet@IGC. It requires no arcane set of commands to negotiate. Like everything on the World Wide Web, one is usually just a mouse click away from reading a message or answering one.

Other companies have developed similar discussion groups. The *New York Times* 'Computer News Daily' Web site has built-in conferences. But until recently, no trade unions seem to have integrated this new technology into their own home pages. The first one to do so will apparently be the British Columbia Teachers Federation – and this won't be the first time that the BCTF has gone where no trade union has gone before.

One disadvantage of this method is that you have to visit a particular home page to access a discussion group, rather than simply reading your email. Another disadvantage – for now – is that only a minority of people with access to email can use the Web. On the other hand, the World Wide Web's interface is so simple to negotiate these days, that this may become in the not-very-distant future the technique of choice to develop and run discussion groups for the labour movement on the Internet.

Online Chat

Chat is a real-time discussion system where what you type on the screen appears on the screen of others who are 'tuned in' to the conversation. (All the other methods involve sending some form of message on to somewhere, from where it must be later retrieved.)

I encountered this technique the very first time I used my modem, logging on to a local bulletin board. The system operator happened to be logged on at that time and we were able to exchange a few sentences, painfully and slowly relayed letter by letter over a 2,400 bps modem. For a first-time user, influenced mainly by what the movies had taught me to expect, it seemed neat.

Chat – or in its Internet variant, Internet Relay Chat (IRC), Finland's major contribution to the online world – has been the subject of some recent media hysteria. Online 'chat rooms' in networks like America Online have apparently been places where some pretty risqué talk has gone on. Chat seems to be a world filled with teenagers who have little interest in the labour movement.

Nevertheless, a few unions have experimented with Chat, among them the North American-based International Brotherhood of Electrical Workers (IBEW), which has used Chat on the America Online network. Several AFL–CIO affiliates use CompuServe's LaborNET, which also provides 'chat rooms'.

The way Chat works is this. Someone – a union for example – announces (publicises) the fact that at a certain time, a chat 'channel' will open up. This can be on the Internet as a whole, using IRC, or through some network, like American Online. At the designated time, or thereafter, users log on, and begin to type in their brief messages. One used to need special software to run Chat from a PC, but it's included today in the popular Netscape browser program used by the vast majority of Internet participants.

A disadvantage of Chat is that one has to type quickly to enjoy it. Messages tend to be quite brief. One IBEW member who looked into the union's Chat on American Online told me that while it was sometimes quite lively, on the whole it wasn't worth it. The older technology of LISTSERV was a better way to conduct a discussion, even if one didn't get feedback for a whole day. In most cases, if one wants real-time dialogue, wouldn't a phone conversation or a face-to-face meeting be preferable?

Online Publishing

In the early 1990s, a couple of powerful tools appeared on the Internet scene which allowed access to information on a wide range of subjects. The most sophisticated of these tools – and probably the easiest to use – was called 'Gopher' and it was developed at the University of Minnesota, in the United States. Gopher is a document retrieval system based on menus, and can be used by the simplest personal computer with even a slow modem link to the Internet.

Because of Gopher's simplicity, it remains in use to this day, though its phenomenal growth has largely stopped. Trade union use of Gopher was limited, though there were a number of examples such as the Economic Democracy Information Network gopher in the US, the Labour Studies gopher at the University of Adelaide in Australia, and the H-Labor (labour history) gopher at the University of Maine.

By 1989, Gopher's successor was already being born in Europe – in the mind of Tim Berners-Lee (no relation to this writer), a researcher at the European Particle Physics Institute (CERN) in Geneva, Switzerland. In March of that year he proposed a project which we know today as the World Wide Web (WWW). Work on the project continued for two years. In May 1991, CERN released the World Wide Web for general use. The world yawned. As late as March 1993, at a meeting of Internet 'gurus,' only ten participants showed up for the session on the WWW, while more than a hundred were crowding into a room to talk about what was then 'hot' on the network, Gopher.

The World Wide Web was a European creation, and remains Europe's main contribution to the Internet to this day, but it took an American student, Marc Andreessen, to turn it into what it has become – simultaneously the heart and the cutting edge of the Internet as a whole.

Andreessen developed a program called 'Mosaic' which could be easily installed on computers and would allow simple access to the World Wide Web. Together with Eric Bina of the National Centre for Supercomputing Applications (NCSA), he developed the program and released it to the world early in 1993. In the fall of that year, a Windows version was released, as well as a version for the Macintosh. From that moment, the World Wide Web finally took off.

As recently as June 1993, there were only 130 Web servers (computers that 'hosted' pages on the World Wide Web) on the Internet. That number rose to nearly 12,000 by the end of 1994, and 40,000 by the end of 1995. The number of individual pages available through the Web today is estimated to run in the tens of millions. There has never been anything in the history of human communications quite like this expansion. So what is it all about? And what does it have to do with the labour movement? Putting it simply, the World Wide Web was conceived as a way of organising and presenting information on the Internet using the concept of 'hypertext'. It's a lot easier to use hypertext than to describe it, but let me try.

In a hypertext document on a computer, certain words will appear in a different colour, or underlined, on the screen. These are called links, or hyperlinks. Ordinarily when we read a document, we begin at the beginning and read through from top to bottom until the end. With hypertext, we can pause on such a link and click on it with our mouse to bring up onto our screen another document. And in that second document, we can also highlight certain words and from these, jump to other documents. 'Documents' can mean simple text files, but they can also mean anything else that can be stored in a computer. So using hypertext, we can see pictures, hear sounds, even show videos. This is called 'hypermedia'.

Hypermedia reached its peak with *Internet World*'s announcement in April 1995 that a small company named Idaho Computing had developed an 'olfactory' PC expansion board that read binary scent files and generated smells from them. Most people reading the announcement understood that this was an April Fool's joke, but someone from a division of the US Army wrote a lengthy email message to 'Idaho Computing' about how the Army hoped to use 'ScentMaster' for battlefield simulations. The US Navy had similar hopes.

The World Wide Web consists largely of files written in a language called hypertext markup language (HTML) which is surprisingly simple to use. Ordinary computer text files can be easily converted to the HTML format, allowing them to be seamlessly integrated into the hypermedia world of the Web. I'm saying this from personal experience; I was able to learn basic HTML in about an hour, and I have no experience with personal computers other than word-processing.

With the introduction of the Mosaic program in late 1993, the Web became a spectacular success. Hundreds of new 'home pages' were appearing every day. The Web has quickly become the favourite way of electronic publishing on the Internet, as magazines like *Time* have discovered. Meanwhile, new programs have replaced the original Mosaic – foremost among these is now Netscape – and these allow people with only the most limited knowledge of the Internet to freely explore its resources. These explorations are called 'surfing' in the slang of the network.

Every imaginable kind of information is becoming available on the Web these days. Online newspapers and magazines, government and NGO information sources, art exhibitions, broadcasts of music and talk, and corporate advertising are everywhere. In addition to these, a number of trade unions and social democratic parties have also begun to take advantage of the Web.

The World Wide Web is a powerful tool for the labour movement. I can think of dozens of reasons why this is the case, but I want to focus on only three of them. I'll begin by making my case in the strongest terms, and then we'll see if I can back them up.

- Hypertext – which is at the core of the World Wide Web – *contributes by its very nature* to internationalism and the ideals of global solidarity.
- Hypermedia on the World Wide Web is an incredibly powerful tool for labour educators with limited resources, working in sometimes informal settings, with students who do not always fit well into traditional schools.

- Electronic publishing through the World Wide Web is one solution to the crisis of the labour press around the world.

Visit any of the labour Web pages mentioned in Appendix 1 – with maybe one or two exceptions – and you'll find links to other Web pages. Those Web pages are often in the same region and country as the site of the original page, but very often include links to Web pages somewhere else in the world. Let me give an example.

You're reading the *AFL–CIO News* at the AFL–CIO's LaborWeb site. You see a page of links to other trade union organisations, including several in Britain and other countries. So you connect to them. From there, you see links to other trade unions in other countries, and you follow them. After a while, you've been travelling along a global labour information highway, picking up bits and pieces of information, maybe collecting addresses for future reference. And it's been no more difficult to call up the Web page of the Congress of South African Trade Unions (COSATU) than it has been to call up your local trade union. There are no borders in cyberspace.

There is no other medium in the world that works this way. In the past, an American trade unionist reading his *AFL–CIO News* on paper may have known or may not have known about what was happening to other trade union movements. The leadership of the American labour movement would have seen the internal publications of the AFL–CIO's International Department, and would have seen how it interpreted the world. But if a rank-and-file American trade unionist wanted to read what British or Australian or South African unionists had to say in their own words, he or she would have had to get an address for those organisations and write them a letter. As recently as a few years ago, this was the only way to follow labour developments in different countries. We relied on the various international departments of unions to filter and disseminate information; there was no other source.

This new medium has arisen at a moment in the labour movement's history when there is *already* increased interest in international affairs at the grassroots level. We saw this during the 1980s in widespread trade union involvement in the struggle against apartheid in South Africa, or in the broad-based enthusiasm in the labour movement for Solidarnosc's struggle in Poland. It is becoming increasingly true that violations of trade union rights in one country affect workers in all countries, who thanks to electronic media learn the news and react more swiftly than in the past.

Corporate dominance of the electronic mass media means corporations make the decisions about what news we see, including labour news. The hypertext function of the World Wide Web provides instant and direct access for trade unionists everywhere to events anywhere. The fact that there is no difference between the hyperlink pointing to one's own local trade union or to COSATU's home page in South Africa makes one just as likely to click on one link as on the other.

It means that in *writing* Web pages, whether for the whole world (like the International Transport Workers' Federation page) or for Alberta's unionised nurses, we have to assume that a certain percentage of visitors to our site are going to come from outside our own country. When preparing such pages, we have to keep that in mind. It forces writers of Web pages to begin to think *globally*, just as readers must do. This technology, which does not care about geographic distance, and does not distinguish between Internet addresses, therefore contributes in its own way to the re-internationalisation of the labour movement.

If your trade union or social democratic party wants to have a home page of its own on the World Wide Web, you really need only two things:

- The file (or files) which you want to present.
- A computer which is connected (preferably all the time) to the Internet, and which can 'serve' your page to visitors.

Both of these things can be handled in-house by your organisation, or you can turn to one of the many companies now offering to set up a home page for you. (Some of these are labour-oriented, such as Web Workers in San Francisco.) Whether you choose to do things yourself, or pay someone to do them for you, you should know what's involved. The creation of a file for presentation as a home page on the Web can be extraordinarily simple. A regular text file (often ending with the suffix 'txt') will suffice.

But if you just present a text tile, you won't be taking advantage of the Web to the fullest. You won't be able to create headers, or italic type, or add pictures or colour, or 'links' to other Web pages. To do these things, you'll need to adapt your simple text file and convert it into a HTML file.

This is a lot easier than it sounds. Because all HTML is, is a series of code words embedded in a file which tell programs (called 'Web browsers') like Netscape what to do. Let me give an example. If I want the word 'education' to appear in italic text, I can simply type <I> education </I> in my text file. Programs like Netscape know that you don't want to see the <I> and will hide the codes, meanwhile making the word 'education' appear in italic print.

I'm not going to teach you HTML in this book. I learned the language myself from reading a couple of short manuals which I downloaded from the Web itself. I didn't find any need to buy expensive books or study in classrooms – though some of you may want to follow this route. The point is that HTML at its core is probably about a dozen commands with a simple syntax – and it *is* easy to learn. You don't need any kind of special computer program to write HTML files; any word-processor can do this. There are, however, a number of special editing programs for HTML and these are often available free of charge, though I haven't found a particular need for one myself.

The second thing you'll need for your Web site is, as I have said, a computer. You can create HTML files on your home computer and view them for yourself through your Web browser – in fact, you should do this to test that everything works. But if you want *others* to be able to read your file, you'll need a computer which is connected to the Internet, preferably all the time, and which has the programs necessary to 'serve' up Web pages to incoming callers. There's a hard way and an easy way to do this.

Let's start with the hard way. You can take a computer, install Web server software on it, connect it to the Internet and serve up your files from it. This will demand considerable expertise and lots of money. The easier way is to rent space on someone else's computer – and this is what practically all the labour Internet sites have done. The Labour Telematics Centre in Britain, for example, is using the Web server of Poptel. The International Federation of Workers' Education Associations was given space by the Economic Democracy Information Network at their University of California server.

In some cases, it is possible to have a Web site for free. There are sites run by universities and non-governmental organisations which are eager to post relevant and interesting materials. Because the cost of a few kilobytes of disk space is practically nil, trade unions with very limited budgets should consider this route. In any event, commercial servers are much cheaper than any newsletter or advertisement.

I want to conclude with a few tips for labour Web sites:

- Web pages have to be updated frequently. If you want people to return regularly to your pages, include *current* newsletters, press releases and additional materials.
- The experts say that what brings people back again and again to a Web page are the links to other pages you put in it. If all you're showing is some text about your organisation, people may glance at it once, and maybe not come back. But if your site contains links to many other labour sites, other NGOs, and other useful home pages, it will become a jumping-off point for people 'surfing' the net.
- It's not enough to create a Web page; people have to know about it. First of all, publicise your site through the Internet itself – including postings to USENET newsgroups and

LISTSERV lists, as well as reciprocal linking to other Web sites. Make sure you're listed in the 'NCSA What's New' page, in the popular 'Yahoo' index, and in the comprehensive LaborNet@IGC Web page. Second, publicise your site *off-line* as well – in your publications, in Internet-related publications, and to other labour organisations. It is well-known that mention of a Web site in mass circulation magazines guarantees a huge boost to the number of visitors to such a site.

To sum up – if you want a presence on the World Wide Web, I recommend that you write and design your own home page, include plenty of links in it, update it regularly, find a free or inexpensive Web server, and let the whole world know that you're on the Web.

Conclusion

Is there a place for the labour movement in the new world order? There is – if labour chooses to make a place for itself. Part of that process of choosing to survive and to play a role in the future includes the decision to go online.

Transnational corporations have already adopted the new technology in a big way. They have used email and online databases for years. The World Wide Web was adopted enthusiastically by them. Corporations will continue to explore and adopt the new technology whether labour chooses to do so or not.

There has been much talk, for many years, about the negative effects of technological change on the labour movement. Since the 1950s, the very term 'automation' has had a threatening ring to it, with unemployment seen as the main effect of technological change. Very few writers and thinkers in the labour movement have discussed possible *advantages* for the movement in the adoption of new technologies.

In this chapter, I've discussed several new tools developed through the Internet which offer advantages to the labour movement. Among these are email, online databases, discussion groups, and electronic publishing through Gopher and the World Wide Web. A declining labour movement under attack everywhere cannot afford *not* to adopt these new tools. Only by using the same tools as the employers can unions hope to survive and prosper in the years ahead. This is certainly true in the developed countries, where tools like email have been available to unions for a decade or more. It is also true in developing countries, where the information gap has widened – but also where the costs of the computer communications has declined.

As we shall see in the next chapter, none of this is a passing fad. Trade unionists have talked about computer internetworking for nearly a quarter century. Unions have been online since the beginning of the 1980s.

The 'improved means of communications that are created by modern industry', wrote Marx, contribute to the 'ever expanding union of the workers'. That was true in the nineteenth century and is true in the twentieth as well. That union of the workers (the International) will come to life again in the next century thanks in part to those very same improved means of communication – this time, the Internet.

CHAPTER 3

Rise of the Labournets

The Internet was launched in 1969 and its existence made public in 1972. The first trade union leader of any prominence to discuss how the new technology of computer communications might be of some use to the labour movement wrote about the subject already in 1972. Even though the very existence of the Internet remained hidden from most people until the early 1990s, trade unionists were using computer networks by the early 1980s. By 1990 they were already holding international meetings to discuss their experience.

In other words, this is not something that came up yesterday. The Internet has been around for a more than a quarter century, and trade unions have a decade and a half of experience with it. Frankly, I was surprised that labour involvement in this field went back so far. It wasn't until 1993 that I first heard about trade union use of email and computer networking. But by then, there were already competing global networks, permanent institutions teaching the use of telematics to trade unionists, and several articles and pamphlets on the subject. And all that happened even before the great Internet explosion of the mid-1990s, when the World Wide Web emerged as a global communications medium.

As I reviewed this history, I learned not only how far back labour use of computer communications goes, but also a little bit about how labour adopts new technologies. Some people will tell you that labour simply doesn't adopt new technologies. But that isn't true. There are always some crazy people hanging around the labour movement, sometimes in positions of power, who will push forward an idea whose time has come. In researching this chapter, I got to know some of those people. They fought an uphill battle against overwhelming odds, but they sometimes got what they wanted. Trade unions adopted new and untried technologies sometimes even before corporations and governments did.

This is not going to be a comprehensive history of trade union use of computer-mediated communications. No doubt I've left out all kinds of important experiments. But in the pages that follow, I want to focus on some of the more interesting and, in my view, important efforts that were made to link working people together using the new technology. Among these were:

- The bold experiment begun in British Columbia in 1981, which lead not only to the creation of the first online labour network, but to the very survival of the trade union involved.
- The pioneering years of what Europeans call 'labour telematics' – including the birth of the Popular Telematics Project (Poptel) in the UK, and the adoption of email by the international trade secretariats in the mid-1980s.
- The years of what I call 'spontaneous combustion' when national labournets sprung up in Canada, South Africa, Denmark, the United States and elsewhere.
- Finally, the gradual coming together of activists from all these countries and all these unions in a series of meetings culminating in the April 1992 conference in Manchester, England – the first international gathering of its kind.

But in the beginning, before there was a global labournet, there was a prophet.

The Jules Verne of Labour Telematics

In a 1994 report issued by the Labour Telematics Centre in England it was remarked in passing that some trade unions 'have made substantial use of new [telematics] technologies for ten years or more', thereby dating the beginning of labour's use of computer communications to the early 1980s.

Actually, labour's interest in the new technology goes back even further. In Charles 'Chip' Levinson's 1972 book, *International Trade Unionism*, we can see the first hints of labour's next step – the integration of computers and computer communications in its global activities. Chip Levinson was the Secretary General of one of the most powerful international trade secretariats, that of the chemical workers (then known as the ICF). (International trade secretariats, as I explained in Chapter 1, are global organisations of national trade unions in specific industries.) Levinson was also a visionary thinker almost without parallel in the history of international trade unionism, and authored a number of original, and often provocative books, including *Vodka Cola*, a prophetic analysis written in the late 1970s of the impact of Western corporate capitalism on the Soviet empire.

He was particularly concerned with the growing power of transnational corporations and how the international trade union movement could respond to this. He developed the idea of a 'countervailing power' on the part of the labour movement, which would be spearheaded by 'company councils' which would include representatives from around the world of workers employed by particular transnationals.

In his 1972 book, Levinson was discussing a coordinated bargaining programme drawn up by the AFL–CIO's Industrial Union Department. A programme had been written, he said, 'to make relevant information on the condition of a company *immediately available right across the country*'. Such information was needed because of the growing complexity of these giant corporations, which sometimes owned hundreds of plants. 'Only a computerised information bank', Levinson emphasised, 'could possibly keep bargainers and union strategists tuned into the strengths and weaknesses of the companies and provide them with the current data on financial facts and figures, production, inventories, wages, hours of work, vacations, pensions and all the other factors involved.'

Note these words carefully. Levinson was not merely speaking about collecting data into a computer for trade union use – even though this idea was pretty revolutionary in itself back in 1972 – but in addition was talking about making 'relevant information' about companies '*immediately available right across the country*'. As we'll see in a moment, Levinson wasn't privy to US Defence Department secrets (and remember: the existence of the Internet was a state secret back in 1972). Even though he didn't yet know about the Internet protocol TCP/IP or the idea of packet-switching networks, which are the very basis of the Internet, he was formulating concepts which were the foundation of what trade unionists today call 'labour telematics'.

By the early 1970s, the Geneva-based International Metalworkers' Federation, another international trade secretariat and one for which Levinson had previously worked, had already made great strides in the direction of computerisation. 'Computerised data systems', wrote Levinson, 'have been established for auto plants in Latin America and another is in process for European parent firms.' Further, he wrote, 'the United Automobile Workers of America (UAW) has completed a computerised data bank of pertinent economic and collective bargaining information, for the corporations' operations in North and South America. A similar programme is in process of elaboration for European auto companies and their overseas subsidiaries.'

At the time, Levinson's own international trade secretariat, the ICF, was already making plans to get involved itself in computer communications. 'A medium-term aim', wrote Levinson, 'is to have the most important collective bargaining information programmed for a computerised data bank. A plan has been made for utilising the modern computer equipment of IG Chemie [the German chemical workers' union] for European parent and subsidiary firms and the comparable computer of our International Chemical Workers' Union in Akron, Ohio, for North American parent and subsidiary firms.'

The plan was to have Levinson's international trade secretariat emulate the US example mentioned earlier, and share computerised data between national unions. In an extraordinary passage, Levinson wrote: '*Through a compatible programme these data banks could be linked by telex to ICF headquarters and information rapidly transmitted to affiliates upon request.*'

In case any of you think I'm exaggerating Levinson's prescient vision of a labournet, I refer you to a section of his book on 'training for development', in which Levinson even visualised a computerised training programme over long distance which would not be implemented for more than 20 years. 'Not far off are the truly revolutionary applications of computer-assisted instruction', he wrote. 'At Stanford University, California, a central computer linked by telex to numerous automatic typewriters is giving a programmed course for 5,000 students, opening up vast perspectives for cybernetic pedagogy.' Levinson's interest was not so much in education, but in *labour* education, and he was foreseeing developments decades before their time.

There is something out of Jules Verne in all this. As some science writers have pointed out, Jules Verne was capable of imagining submarines, but the lighting in them was done by gas lamps. Men could reach the moon, but they would get there using a very large cannon. Levinson, too, could imagine a global labour communications system, even one using computers and conducting distance learning, but the technicalities were a little fuzzy. We now know that telex machines and automatic typewriters could not provide the basis of such a network. High-speed fibre-optic cables and powerful yet inexpensive personal computers would do that instead.

Remember that the Internet was not first publicly demonstrated until 1972. By then there were only 50 universities and research facilities connected to it. Chip Levinson's book, which was completed in February 1972, with his vision of globally linked computerised trade union databases serving affiliate unions around the world, actually pre-dates the public appearance of the Internet itself.

For nine years, nothing practical came of this vision of a global labournet. But in 1981, halfway around the world, a teacher in British Columbia, Canada, began to realise part of Levinson's vision.

The First Labournet

In 1981 the Internet was barely twelve years old. The first experimental local electronic bulletin boards were launched only three years earlier. The world we have come to call 'cyberspace' was years away – but the first true labour network was being born on the eastern shore of the Pacific Ocean, in Vancouver, British Columbia.

By coincidence, at about that time a Vancouver author who had no experience with computer networks was writing the book which invented the very word 'cyberspace'. The book was *Neuromancer* (published in 1984) and its author, William Gibson, logged onto a computer network for the first time only in 1995.

But back in 1981, while Gibson was dreaming of a cyber future, in another part of town, a teacher of English named Larry Kuehn was quietly making labour (and Internet) history. Kuehn was then the President of the British Columbia Teachers' Federation (BCTF), a trade union representing some 40,000 teachers in primary and secondary schools across this sprawling province. As an English teacher, Kuehn particularly liked journalism and creative writing. What interested him the most, he says, was always *communications*. He knew nothing then about computers and didn't care much to learn. Kuehn became active as a trade unionist because he cared passionately about two things: public education and the rights of school teachers. In 1981, he was serving one of his three terms as BCTF President.

Arnie Myers was the union's communications officer. Unlike Kuehn, Myers had a background in technology. He had previously worked as a science journalist. And like Kuehn, his main interest was communications.

The two of them, Kuehn and Myers, saw a demonstration of an electronic bulletin board and were duly impressed. They talked about how this brand-new technology, never-before used by anyone, anywhere in the labour movement, might be used by the BCTF.

To understand their enthusiasm – and the project that they launched – one has to have an idea just how big British Columbia actually is. The province, which is Canada's third largest (remember that Canada is the world's second biggest country), is four times the size of Great Britain – nearly 360,000 square miles. The largest school district (geographically) is actually the size of Britain and only 20 teachers are employed there.

The problems faced by a provincial trade union in these circumstances are enormous. How do you involve leaders and rank-and-file members in the decision-making process and in union activities when the cost of an airfare from one end of the province to the other can be hundreds of dollars? How do you share complex information quickly among dozens of locals, especially during periods of collective bargaining?

Larry Kuehn saw electronic networking as a way to strengthen his union, especially during a decade when it was under constant attacks by the provincial government. (The labour-backed New Democratic Party had lost power in the province in 1975, and the rightist Social Credit Party governed until 1991. The Social Credit provincial government 'felt that the BCTF was an enemy', says Kuehn.) The local media called those attacks the 'school wars'. Trade unionists everywhere will recognise them as simple union-busting. The provincial legislature even rewrote the laws on union membership, forcing the BCTF to sign up its thousands of members again, one by one.

In such a situation, one would hardly think that a union president would have the time to fiddle around with a new-fangled, unproved and expensive technology. Yet that is precisely what Larry Kuehn did. Using his position as BCTF President, Kuehn pushed the union to start small – but to start.

They decided to link the eleven members of the union's Executive Committee, who were spread out all over the province, using the telephone company's packet-switching network (known as 'Envoy 100'). The union bought a 'dumb' portable communications terminal for each of the Executive Committee members. (The word portable should probably also be in quotes; these devices were about six times the size of today's notebook personal computers. Kuehn swears you could fit one under an airplane seat – barely.)

The terminals were 'dumb'; they were not PCs. And they had no screens. Messages were printed out on thermal paper. In fact, this proved to be an advantage. Trade unionists using the network – especially back in the early 1980s – wanted to see everything on paper. Texts that were stored only on magnetic disks or that you read off a computer screen didn't seem 'real'.

The terminals were connected to ordinary telephones using 'couplers' placed over both ends of a phone. Using a 300 bps modem, messages could be sent and received. (A 300 bps modem runs at about 1 per cent of the speed of today's 28,800 bps modems.)

Some basic training was given to each member of the BCTF Executive and they then began exchanging electronic messages. They found that this allowed them to remain in touch with one another between meetings of the committee, which took place every month.

The problem faced by the BCTF Executive – solved back in 1981 using 300 bps modems and thermal printing – is still faced today by unions, particularly by the international trade union movement. Some international trade secretariats hold meetings of their Executive only once a year. The International Federation of Workers' Education Associations holds Executive Committee meetings once every six months. The problems of reaching consensus, or reacting to fast-paced events, faced by such Executive Committees, were solved using computer networking technology that today seems Stone Age to us.

The decision to use the new technology and to begin with Executive Committee members raises an interesting point. It has been suggested by some observers that the new communications technologies would contribute to the disappearance of traditional labour movement institutions and replace them, over time, with grassroots networks. Computer networking *did* have its effect on the BCTF and its structure – more on that in a moment – but Larry Kuehn's intention was to *strengthen* the existing union. And Kuehn's gamble paid off: the BCTF survived and grew stronger, in part because of its early adoption of computer networking.

The eleven members of the BCTF Executive used the network for two years, and if we can sum up its most important achievement, it was this: they grew to like it. They liked it so much that they decided to share it with others. Kuehn had succeeded in winning eleven allies for the next stage: linking up all the union locals using the same 'Envoy 100' system and dumb, portable communications terminals.

This was a more innocent age. Today, no one would dare expand a network using the same modems, or the same software, as we used two years ago. Two years in the 1990s represent aeons of time. But back in the Jurassic Age of internetworking, no one thought twice about continuing with a technology that *worked*. The BCTF kept on using the 'Envoy 100' network right up until September 1990 – nine whole years using the same old system. And as Kuehn is quick to point out today, there were certain advantages to the old network that have been lost in subsequent changes – first to the nation-wide Canadian labour network Solinet, and now, to the Internet.

Back in 1983, the BCTF gave out terminals (and training) to every local branch. That year would have been a turning point for the union even if they had never heard of computers. In 1983, for the first time in its history, the BCTF launched a province-wide strike. By this time, the union locals were already online, and they put out messages updating each other on strike news. These messages were then photocopied and handed out to teachers on picket lines.

Larry Kuehn says that these messages gave the striking teachers a sense of solidarity that reached across hundreds of kilometres. But I think they probably had another effect too: they showed the teachers that their union could use what was then cutting edge technology in their interests. An institution like the BCTF seemed unafraid of the future and what it would bring. That's one of the messages a union broadcasts to its members – and others – when it adopts a new technology, like computer networking. It's a way of saying: we're changing because we intend to *survive*.

By the end of 1983 the network had about a hundred users – all 76 local presidents, the original Executive Committee members, and some union staff. As Larry Kuehn flew around the province, he carried his terminal with him. Over the course of one 20-day period, he spoke to 12,000 teachers at 20 different meetings all over British Columbia. And thanks to the network, he was able to approve press releases and deal with other day-to-day issues in the union office while travelling.

All through the 1980s, the union continued to use the network – and it steadily grew. When the 'Envoy'-based network was finally shut down in 1990, the BCTF opened some 300 accounts in the new network, Solinet. The number of uses being made of the network was also growing. Larry Kuehn's list includes (in addition to building solidarity during strikes, which we've already mentioned), the following:

- The union provided teacher unionists with information about legislation and other government actions. The union would provide detailed analysis and suggestions on how to react. Often, the local teacher unionists would be better informed than their employer counterparts, who at that time had no electronic network.
- Problems were solved through the network, using electronic conferencing. At first, this was just email mailing lists. Later, other techniques were used. One example was a request made by one BCTF local for information regarding the rights of teachers infected with the HIV virus. Within hours, several other locals answered with examples and the local was able to develop a policy proposal.
- Strategic discussions could be held involving local and provincial leaders. When formal meetings would be held, consensus had already largely been built. Local union leaders, now better informed than ever before about the union, could act quickly – and in concert.
- A provincial news service was launched, featuring educational and social news of interest to teachers. Not only did such a service provide union news quickly to locals, but it also provided content, already digitised, for local newsletters then just beginning to use word-processing and desktop publishing.
- A database of contract clauses was created as the information flowed from the locals into the provincial office. This growing database would be consulted by union bargainers before meeting their employer counterparts. The unions developed such a clear advantage here that the employers were eventually

compelled to set up their own system of computer-mediated communication in response.
- Finally, the network allowed for the more effective functioning of the BCTF's various advisory committees – these discuss matters ranging from racism to the French language. Those committees, made up of members from all over the province, would previously meet only three times a year. The network allowed members to stay in touch between those meetings.

Computer networking has not destroyed the existing trade union structure, but strengthened it. This does not mean that nothing changed in the BCTF. Larry Kuehn is proud of the fact that his union has always been a participatory democracy, never an authoritarian bureaucracy. Perhaps in a more bureaucratised, top-heavy union, the effects would have been more dramatic. But even in the highly democratic BCTF, networking did change the union.

Previously the union had 'regional coordinators' who served as intermediaries between the far-flung local unions and the central organisation. They were full-time teachers who undertook this job in their free time, and they served as a conduit for information, using regional meetings and telephone conversations. The introduction of the network in 1983 throughout the whole union, with its direct connection between local activists and union staff and officers, made the regional coordinators redundant.

The BCTF experience in the early and mid-1980s demonstrated that a regional trade union can make effective use of computer networks. According to Kuehn, the union's survival during that turbulent decade is a tribute, in part, to the success of that technology. But not only technology. The BCTF's survival, he says, 'also depended on a militant tradition, effective leadership training programs, committee membership and a variety of other things. No technology is better than a variety of human commitments that it can facilitate.'

The BCTF launched its network at the dawn of the age of new information technologies. They have been using networks now for a decade and a half. (In the next chapter, we'll talk about the state of the BCTF network today.) The longevity of the experiment teaches us that this technology is not some passing fad, but is a proven method for communicating within unions, and strengthening them. The BCTF network grew and prospered during a time when the union was under siege. Its experience teaches important lessons to unionists all over the world today whose organisations are under attack by employers who seek a 'union-free' environment backed up by anti-labour governments. Back in 1981, Larry Kuehn and Arnie Myers saw the future, and it worked.

A Global Labournet?

Within a few months of Larry Kuehn's decision to try out the newfangled technology, on the other side of the world a proposal was being considered to create a global labournet. It was so far ahead of its time that it seems almost destined to have failed. It was called the Unite Project, and its sponsor was a Norwegian computer specialist named Kristen Nygaard. Looking back at the project, Peter Waterman – a British-born international labour activist who has written extensively on trade union use of computer communications – called it 'the first attempt to create a systematic international information and communications network for labour'.

Nygaard proposed creating a computerised database, supported collectively by the Western trade unions, taking advantage of the World Centre for Microcomputer Science and Human Resources that the new socialist government was creating in France. It ultimately proved impossible to use the French centre, so Nygaard went to the Norwegian unions for help. 'His efforts seem to have not yet been successful', wrote Waterman. The proposal was, however, written up twice in the publication of the International Confederation of Free Trade Unions, *Free Labour World*.

According to Aslak Leesland, who is in charge of international affairs for the Norwegian workers' education association AOF, Nygaard 'was ahead of his time. In the 60s he developed a computer language that I understand became the basis of Windows. (Unfortunately for him, Bill Gates caught on to the idea).' But, says Leesland, the Norwegian trade union federation (LO) did 'not catch on to his ideas in the 80s. The truth is, we consider LO to be rather slow learners when it comes to this technology. One theory ... is that it has got something to do with their culture and centralised tradition.'

Waterman speculated on why nothing came of the Nygaard proposal, and came up with three probable reasons:

- Ignorance of, or hostility to, the new technology.
- Organisational conservatism.
- A conscious or unconscious strategy of informational deprivation (or limitation) as a membership control device.

Several years after Nygaard's proposal faded away, Waterman still hoped that 'the project will eventually be supported, as an open access system, with the full resources of the Western national and international trade union movements, since it could put them in the forefront of the struggle for the democratisation of international labour communications'. But he was not optimistic. 'One cannot, evidently, depend on them to do this', he wrote.

'This Is Going To Change the Way You Do Things'

While Larry Kuehn was experimenting with packet-switching networks and feeling the effects on daily life in his union, and while Kristen Nygaard was trying to promote his vision of a global labournet, Dave Spooner was working for an English magazine called *International Labour Reports*. He was thinking about how to organise trade union activity across national borders, within the framework of transnational companies. It was a problem that had preoccupied the international trade secretariats and their leaders, including men like Chip Levinson and Dan Gallin, throughout the 1970s and early 1980s.

'Then we were made aware of these remarkable things called modems', he recalls. A friend from the Netherlands turned up in his office with a box one day back in 1983. It looked like a shoe box, Spooner remembers. 'This is going to change the way you do things', his friend said. The box was a home-made, 300 bps modem. Spooner in England and his friend in the Netherlands began typing electronic messages one to the other. 'Hello. Are you there?' Nothing really meaningful, but, says Spooner, 'we realised that this was [full] of tremendous possibilities for trade union activity'.

The trade unionists in Europe were probably unaware of the network in British Columbia which at that very moment was expanding. (The Canadian teachers were equally unaware of the infant 'Poptel', the Popular Telematics Project that Spooner and his associates were launching.) And certainly the two networks could not have communicated with each other even if they had been aware of each others' existence.

At this time, there were no commercial Internet access providers in Europe or anywhere else. The Internet, with its high-speed networks and global reach, was still closed off to all but the academics and defence-related research community it was designed to serve. Trade unionists looking to exchange email with each other were experimenting with different networks.

While the international trade secretariats were experimenting (we'll come to that in a moment), Dave Spooner and the Poptel people were also looking for the right software and network. They began with the European Space Agency. 'They had a system whereby, for free, you could dial in and use their electronic mail system, and we used that for a few months', he recalls. 'The trouble was that the European Space Agency electronic mail system at that time was extraordinarily cumbersome. To send something, you had to sort of go "slash, slash, p, n, x, slash, dot, dot" in order to send the mail. This was impossible.'

Poptel experimented with an American system called 'One to One', a commercial system, and it proved much easier to use than the obtuse commands of the European Space Agency. (One shouldn't have to be a rocket scientist to send email.) The problem with the new system was that it was not designed for trade unionists. It was designed for businessmen with secretaries. And the people at Poptel had no way to influence the way it was developed.

Thanks to contacts in the German Green movement, Spooner and his friends discovered GeoNet, a commercial network based in Germany. (This is just one example of how the various 'new social movements' began using computer communications well in advance of the trade unions.) The Poptel/GeoNet network became, as Spooner called it, the 'de facto communications system for the labour movement' – particularly the international trade secretariats – by the mid-1980s.

The Trade Secretariats Go Online

By 1984, experiments had been conducted in one Canadian province and across the English Channel, but no international trade union organisation had yet begun to use the new technology more than a decade after Chip Levinson had prophecised its uses. Ironically, it was Levinson's own international trade secretariat, the Brussels-based International Federation of Chemical, Energy and General Workers' Unions (ICEF), which pioneered the change.

The role the ICEF Secretariat was to play in creating a global labournet reminds me a little bit of the American legend of 'Johnny Appleseed'. Johnny Appleseed was a man who went around the country planting apple orchards for no particular reason other than the fact that he loved apples. I never really understood this story as a child, except that I guess we apple-lovers were supposed to feel grateful that someone went around planting all those trees. The apple trees planted by the ICEF and other international trade secretariats in the late 1980s and early 1990s were local and national trade unions going online in order to stay in touch with each other and with their international federations. Those trees blossomed and gave fruit by the mid-1990s when the outlines of a true global labournet began to become clear.

'Shortly after the election of new leadership ... in July 1984', wrote Jim Catterson, ICEF Research Officer, 'computerisation of Secretariat activities began with the subscription to a number of commercial databases.' Until then, the only electronic equipment in the office was typewriters.

Whatever became of Chip Levinson's plan to launch a global labournet based on the ICEF? I asked Catterson, who began working for Levinson in 1982, two years before the latter's retirement. Levinson 'was certainly a visionary', says Catterson. When Levinson took over the ICEF in 1964, it had no paid staff. He built it up into one of the most effective trade secretariats. But one of the ways he built the organisation was by what Catterson calls 'great public relations'.

'We were always "on the brink" of all sorts of developments', he recalls. 'Whether it was international strikes, international collective bargaining, or telematics and computer communications.' Catterson read more than once that the ICEF was 'using computers to analyse and track the operations' of transnational corporations. 'We weren't', he admits.

The secretariat's research resources consisted of its library, which held a collection of publications produced by unions and international organisations, as well as a massive amount of trade journals, directories, magazines and newspapers. 'We were able to do a lot with this', he says, pointing to ICEF publications from that period, as well as Levinson's own books.

There were several meetings held in the 1970s to discuss how to implement some of Levinson's bold ideas regarding computer-isation. Terms and conditions of employment and some contract language were stored in computers owned by ICEF affiliates, in particular in Scandinavia, the US and Germany. The unionists talked about ways these databases could be linked together. But 'the technology at that time was just too expensive', says Catterson.

The computerisation of the ICEF was pushed by the newly elected leadership beginning in 1984, which wanted to shift the secretariat's focus from a campaigning one to more of a service organisation. The intention was to strengthen the organisation by making it more valuable to affiliates – which would in turn make its campaigns more effective. The ICEF intensified its cooperation with other ITSs and other organisations at the same time.

The original need for, and use of, computer communications was to obtain necessary information for the global struggles with transnational corporations. 'A major function of any trade secretariat is providing affiliated trade unions with information useful for collective bargaining', said Catterson – and that information was available through commercial databases as early as mid-decade. At the same time, in 1984, the ICEF began to computerise its administration, using personal computers.

Within a few years, the ICEF Secretariat was subscribing to a number of commercial databases, including Data-Star, Dialog, Pergamon Information, Reuters, as well as European Community sources. Included within these was access to more than 1,500 individual databases. What kind of information did ICEF staffers find in these computerised file cabinets? 'World-wide company directories, stockbroker reports on companies and industries, abstracts from the financial and trade press throughout the world, as well as detailed specialist databases dealing with particular industries, subjects and occupational health and safety information', reported Catterson.

The quantity of information available was impressive. 'The range and variety of information available could not be realistically compiled by any other method within the limited resources of a trade secretariats' research facility. At ICEF we routinely gather the annual reports of several hundred multinational companies within our sectors. Through the databases, however, we have direct online access to the annual reports of several hundred thousand multinational companies, with more limited financial information being available on even very small national based corporations.'

But the ICEF discovered several disadvantages to this kind of information:

- Commercial databases turned out to be quite expensive.
- They were almost always only available in English.
- They were not particularly easy to use, and proficiency could be acquired only after taking courses to learn the various interfaces.
- What the ICEF got out of them was often raw data, which still needed to be analysed. Not all the affiliate unions had staff that could do this. If the ICEF research staff had to do it, this became a lengthy process.

Nevertheless, Catterson concluded that within the first few years of its operation, the ICEF's use of commercial databases resulted in 'an information facility that I believe to be far more effective and extensive than that of any other international trade union organisation'.

At the same time the chemical workers' trade secretariat was already 'experimenting with various electronic mail systems. Direct computer to computer connections were made with a number of affiliated trade unions and the MCI Mail System was examined in detail. The final decision was made to use the Poptel GeoNet System.'

By mid-1985 email was being used for routine communications between the ICEF and its Tokyo regional office, as well as a small number of affiliated unions. By 1992, some 30 affiliated unions – a small fraction of the 235 then belonging to the ICEF – were online. 'We have been pressing affiliated trade unions to join the system', noted Catterson. The role of international trade secretariats in promoting the use of computer-mediated communications in the labour movement cannot be over-stated. Dozens and later hundreds of unions went online in order to communicate better with the various trade secretariats in Europe, and with each other.

By the late 1980s and early 1990s, the ICEF established mailboxes for its Seoul and Moscow offices as well, and a special mailbox at GeoNet's GEO4 host, for use by the organisation's General Secretary when travelling in the United States. One key use of email was to send telexes or faxes. (More on how this is done can be found in the previous chapter.) Sometimes this was done merely for convenience, but on other occasions there were clear cost benefits in doing things this way.

A more interesting use of email, and one which may well have contributed to the spread of its use throughout the ICEF's network of affiliates, was in forwarding the results of database searches to unions which requested them. As Catterson pointed out, 'On one level it is ludicrous to obtain information within minutes and then consign that information to the international postal system for delivery. Postage from Brussels may take 2–3 weeks to arrive in some countries.'

With all the advantages of commercial databases, these did not always answer the questions unionists were asking. Labour needed its own databases. Catterson noted that the ICEF began work early on, together with a number of affiliates, to build a database of contract information. In addition, a database on occupational safety and health – a central concern of trade unions working in the chemical industry – was being built.

As early as 1991, over 1,300 requests for information were being handled annually by the ICEF Research Department. Many of those requests were answered within hours. And there were practical results out in the field. 'As a result of mercury poisoning, three workers from Thor Chemicals in South Africa lay in hospital, one in a coma', reported Shirley Miller of the Chemical Workers' Industrial Union of South Africa. 'Rapid and detailed information from abroad was essential in this life-threatening situation. By means of electronic mail, we were able to liaise with the ICEF in Brussels, the World Health Organisation in Geneva, and the Workplace Health Fund and other specialists in [the] USA to help save the lives of those workers.'

Catterson argued that potentially the most important use of email would not be to distribute information requested by affiliates, nor to tighten up communications between the ICEF Secretariat and its various offices, but to conduct solidarity actions. In order to do so, it was important to link up not only those affiliates (and other international trade union organisations) with email addresses, but those who only have fax numbers and no email.

In creating these combined email/fax lists, the ICEF was able by the early 1990s to reach more than 40 per cent of its affiliated trade unions instantly, as well as reaching large numbers of international organisations and journalists. 'Electronic mail', said

Catterson, 'allows this to be achieved far more quickly than any alternative method of communication and, importantly to an organisation such as ours, as cost effectively as possible.'

The ICEF also began distributing information using the GeoNet bulletin boards. A bulletin board called 'ITS-BBS' was established on the GeoNet network and messages were copied to APC network as well, with its own set of labour 'conferences' online. The existing 'Labour' bulletin board on the GeoNet network was also used. The ICEF used this technique to post solidarity requests, to publicise the results of discussions at ICEF conferences, and news of successes by affiliate unions.

But Catterson observed that in the early years of international labour internetworking, even though the existing online labour bulletin boards were wide open to people to read and write messages, and a large variety of organisations appeared to utilise them, it seemed that very few people were actually reading the messages the ICEF and others were taking the trouble to post. (He believes this is still a problem today.)

Richard Flint is the Communications Secretary for the International Transport Workers' Federation (ITF), headquartered in London. By 1993, the ITF represented over five million members in more than 100 countries, organised in some 400 affiliate unions. Those members work as seafarers, dockers, truckers, railway workers, inland navigation workers, civil aviation workers and tourism services staff. Together with the ICEF, the ITF was a pioneer in the mid-1980s in the adoption of email.

Flint reported that by 1993, a 'significant number of ITF affiliates' had adopted the Poptel email system. Nevertheless, the main use of email has been internally, within the ITF itself. In particular, translators working for the ITF – for example, a Swedish translator based in Gothenburg – can send formatted word-processed files using email to the Secretariat in London. Email was found to be particularly effective in communicating with people living quite far from the Secretariat, and was used regularly with unions, labour resource centres, and even one port chaplain in the Philippines.

At a time when many unions were not yet online, an important use of email was to send faxes. Four out of every five ITF affiliates had fax machines, making that (rather than email) the medium of choice for conveying information. Fax bulletins were developed in cases of industrial disputes. During a strike in the early 1990s at Cathay Pacific airlines, the ITF received a fax saying that a number of cabin crew were stranded in various airports all over the world. 'We were able to contact affiliates in those countries and get them to help the stranded crew right away', said Flint.

Like the ICEF, the ITF was an early and heavy user of online computer databases. The trade secretariat has a group user account on Lloyd's Seadata system, which records all the world's ships, movements and some ownership information. It turns out that the ITF is the second largest user of Seadata in the world. Many of the ITF's 50 inspectors have access.

Looking back at the first few years online, Flint reflected on the joint ICEF–ITF decision to use Poptel. It was, he said, 'a decision which would appear to have been correct (though I do remember a time when we could only talk to each other because no one else had a box)'.

Spontaneous Combustion

When one studies the history of the trade union movement or socialist parties, it is remarkable how they simultaneously sprung up all over the world. In the years before the Communist International, there were no such things as international organisers, nor was there any central body coordinating the organisation and growth of unions and parties. But they grew and developed all over the place.

Of course there were the immigrants, cross-pollinating the working classes of different countries with ideas that were germinating in Europe. But on the whole, working people created their own institutions without much outside help or even knowledge of what was happening elsewhere in the world. The process of trial and error did much to slow down the building of working-class institutions, but also did much to give each of them authentic local flavour.

By the mid-1980s, the development of the global labournet began to happen in much the same way: largely spontaneously, based on local people, with lots of trial and error along the way – and lots of authentic local flavour. There were also cases – as in Asia – where local trade unions got a little help from their friends. But on the whole, the process did resemble spontaneous combustion.

The First National Labournet

Back in 1980, Marc Belanger was working as editor of *The Facts*, the monthly research magazine of the Canadian Union of Public Employees (CUPE), the largest union in that country. He knew nothing about computers. There was a computer terminal in the CUPE offices; it was used only to make changes to the magazine's mailing list, which actually resided on a mainframe computer owned by a private company. That company would charge CUPE for rental time on its mainframe computer, and would print out the mailing labels in its offices, which would then be shipped to CUPE.

Wasn't there some way CUPE could print the labels in its own office, Belanger asked. The company representative 'looked me straight in the eye', Belanger remembers, 'and said, "No. And I can't explain it to you because you don't know the difference between synchronous and asynchronous communications". 'Belanger stared at the company representative, who stared back. 'I knew', he recalls, 'he was deliberately using techno-jargon to intimidate me. And he knew that I knew. But there wasn't a damn thing I could do about it. The truth was I *didn't* know the difference between synchronous and asynchronous communications.'

He does now – and he knows a whole lot more. Within a few years, Belanger and his associates at CUPE had set up the first Novell local area network (LAN) connecting personal computers in Canada, and later the first nation-wide, bilingual computer conferencing system in Canada, the Solidarity Network (better known as Solinet). It was also the first national labournet.

But back in 1980, Belanger knew nothing about computer communications. He began to learn, coming into work at five o'clock in the morning, studying computer communications and computers in general. 'I was absolutely determined never to be techno-jargoned again', he says. After a year of doing this, he knew enough to devote a whole issue of *The Facts* to the subject of computers and their effect on work. That issue convinced a few people that Belanger knew what he was talking about when it came to computers. ('The truth', he admits, 'was I had learned just enough to know how much I didn't know.')

In the spring of 1982, he was invited to meet with CUPE's accountants. The union didn't have a computer of its own at that time. They were using something called a 'business machine' which used punched cards, and it was filled to the brim, unable to hold more data. 'If they were to add a new employee', Belanger remembers, 'they would have to take one out.' The accountants, convinced that Belanger was their local computer expert, introduced him to an IBM salesman. Belanger was thrilled; his dream was to get his hands on one of the new IBM personal computers (PCs) which had been introduced a year earlier. His idea was that linking personal computers (also known as microcomputers) together could do the work of one larger computer, which were known as minicomputers and mainframes. IBM didn't know what Belanger was talking about, and eventually he was thrown out of their Ottawa offices for proposing that CUPE buy a whole bunch of microcomputers and create a network of them.

By this point, intrigued with the possibilities of personal computers and communications, but lacking specific technical knowledge, Belanger turned to a couple of better-informed friends, one of whom worked as 'technical wizard' for Canada's social democratic party, the New Democrats. Together with Belanger, they produced a number of briefs for CUPE's top officials arguing the case for microcomputers, and declaring the IBM minicomputers to be 'a dying technology'. CUPE's President at the time 'didn't know what on earth I was talking about', Belanger recalls, 'but knew that the union had to do something bold to confront the growing computerisation of our members' employers'. Belanger was appointed CUPE's Technology Officer and told to begin computerising the union's accounting and administrative functions.

He found a local Ottawa software company which could help. When he asked what they knew about microcomputers, they took the elevator down to the building's basement. There they weaved around big, shiny Digital minicomputers, walked down a small corridor, past the janitor's closet, and there they found a microcomputer the size of a small suitcase. 'It was an AT&T something or other', Belanger says. 'Not plugged in. No monitor. No printer. As an instrument of revolution, it didn't inspire much confidence.'

The software company had a system designer who was something of a visionary, and he was able to put together a computer system which linked microcomputers. At the time Novell was a little company in Utah, not very well known. But in the end, Belanger and CUPE installed the first Novell local area network in Canada. 'We had guessed right', he now says.

In the end, Belanger had set up a real computer department for the union, handling payroll, general ledger, accounts payable and dues collection. But his original goal, of using microcomputers for communications, hadn't advanced far. Early on in the CUPE computerisation project which Belanger spearheaded, he experimented with the use of modems. A friend agreed to call him at a particular time one evening; Belanger's home computer would answer the phone, and they would see what would happen. They had a brief and rather silly 'conversation' – one which scared the hell out of Belanger. It scared him because for a brief moment, he wasn't sure if it was his friend at the other end. That moment taught him something he never forgot about people's fears of using computers.

'I decided', he remembers, 'the labour movement needed a computer communications system to build teams, share information, discuss problems and work on common solutions, nationally.' This was easier said than done. Canada is the world's second largest country, spanning several thousand kilometres and several time zones. CUPE alone has 450,000 members spread out over 2,500 local unions. Its staff consists of some 500 men and women working in 52 different offices. By 1985, Belanger says, 'I began looking for a new way that our members and others in the labour movement could quickly and efficiently communicate amongst each other. I figured a union meant people united.'

He began to take courses – online courses, which he learned about from the *New York Times.* These were conducted by the New School for Social Research in New York City. Students could stay wherever they lived and take courses at the school's centre for media studies. Without leaving Ottawa, Belanger began learning at the New School. In the very first class he took, the teacher was based in New York, but there were students from England, France, Colombia, Japan and the US. 'When we discussed international affairs', he recalls, 'it was a far different experience than sitting in a class at the University of Ottawa.' Belanger learned how to teach courses via computers, and learned the history of computer conferencing.

The Canadian telephone companies were offering a service called Envoy-100, which we discussed earlier with reference to British Columbia. But that offered only email, not conferencing. Conferencing required a shared message base, which could be accessed by other participants. 'Given that trade union work is based almost completely on group work', he says, 'I wanted a real conferencing system that had email as an adjunct.' He didn't know if such a system existed.

One day, Belanger had to go see his doctor. She was working with a group called Canadian Physicians for the Prevention of Nuclear War. And though members of her group rarely met face to face, they were communicating among themselves using a computer program at the University of Guelph. Two weeks later, Belanger was at the university, talking about a computer conferencing system known as CoSy. Some professors were even using the system to teach parts of their courses. It was exactly what Belanger was looking for.

There was one thing missing, and that was the fact that CoSy worked only in English. It was decided to run two copies of the CoSy program, one in English and one in French, sharing the same message files on a Digital Micro Vax computer. By the time they were finished, Belanger says, 'we had developed the first national, bilingual, computer conferencing system in the country. We named it the Solidarity Network – Solinet for short.'

Of course there was no network. There was just a computer with some software in it. The network would consist of people who would use the hardware and software which Belanger and his associates had so painfully put together. Belanger began by buying modems for every CUPE office. Clerical support staff who were already trained in the use of microcomputers were taught how to use Solinet, and they, in turn, would teach their co-workers. In Ottawa, Belanger put together a team who would run Solinet, including people from the union's public relations department, a union negotiator, a graphic designer, and the director of CUPE's employment assistance programme. This committee met in conference using Solinet for two months, as Belanger taught them the basics of computer conferencing – and as they taught each other how to apply the new technology to their work. A highlight of this early period came when one of them – the graphic designer – called Solinet from a hotel room. Little things like that were pretty exciting back in the mid-1980s.

Belanger was already insistent that Solinet could be more than just an internal CUPE network. 'I wanted Solinet to become a public system, accessible by individuals, unions and other organisations', he says. He began marketing the network using leaflets, advertisements, and introductory workshops.

It was important to get as many people online as quickly as possible. 'As anybody who has tried to run a computer conferencing system finds out immediately, the primary organising principle is to get a critical mass of users', he says. People will not return to a system that is rarely used. To succeed, Solinet needed to recruit a large number of people who would use the system at the same time.

Belanger decided to hold Canada's first national conference on technological change – online, using Solinet. He guessed that people interested in that subject might be more likely to have microcomputers – and also because the subject was itself of some interest. He found a sponsor in the Canadian Centre for Policy Alternatives. The conference was scheduled to begin in December 1988 and run for two months. 'That shocked people', he recalls. "Two months? You're planning a *two month* conference?"' But, as Belanger understood, time worked differently in computer conferencing. During those two months, 150 people participated in the discussions. And they were people from all over Canada, who could not possibly have met face to face. 'The ability to allow people to communicate without synchronising meeting times', says Belanger, 'became known as asynchronous communications.'

The conference contributed to Solinet's reputation, and contributed to the decision by Larry Kuehn and the BCTF to move away from the Envoy-100 technology and to link up to Solinet. 'Some of the most creative strategies for using Solinet came from Larry and the people he organised', recalls Belanger. Thanks to the BCTF, Solinet was no longer an in-house CUPE system, but one open to the broader Canadian labour movement.

The BCTF was now using Solinet to coordinate bargaining, produce electronic newsletters and even run committees which 'met' exclusively online. Another early participant in Solinet was the Canadian Association of Labour Media (CALM), an organisation of local trade union newsletter editors. CALM used Solinet to send out a monthly news package to editors, who could use parts of it without re-typing. CALM's staff person was an early 'telecommuter'. Living in a village some 200 kilometres north of Toronto, he participated in CALM Executive meetings, sent out the news package and more without leaving home (and his two children).

Over the next few years, Solinet held dozens of other online conferences. There were special ones which lasted for limited periods of time, as well as permanent online discussions. The special conferences included discussions of free trade, pay equity, employment equity – and international issues like the Russian or American labour movements (more on this in Chapter 6). Permanent Solinet conferences discussed a wide range of issues, as mentioned in the previous chapter. An early attempt at a jokes conference was a complete failure. 'One person's jokes can be another's sexist comment', says Belanger. Some of the conferences were moderated, others were not. There was a general conference area where anything could be discussed called the Lounge. When Belanger tried to break up the topics being discussed in the Lounge, users rebelled – and that's when he realised that Solinet had become a community.

That community – the first national labournet – has been around for more than a decade now. We'll talk about it again in Chapter 5.

From WorkNet to SANGONeT

A decade ago, South African progressives and trade unionists launched one of the first and most important labournets – and it exists to this day. It was called WorkNet. WorkNet's early years, with its successes and failures, are interesting to look at for a number of reasons. First of all, in some ways its experience is typical of what happens in developing countries, though South Africa is certainly not a typical developing country. Second, WorkNet arose in a highly repressive society, under police surveillance. The implications for independent trade unionists and human rights activists in countries like China today are there for all to see. Third, WorkNet had to grapple with the transition to a new, democratic South Africa, to building institutions like trade unions and political parties. There are certainly similarities between the WorkNet experience and the experience of those trying to build a democratic labour movement in Eastern Europe and the former Soviet Union.

Two developments took place which allowed the creation of an online network for South Africa's labour movement in the waning years of the apartheid regime, one of them entirely accidental. In 1986, one of WorkNet's founders came back from a study trip to England – where 'labour telematics' had already begun to coalesce around Poptel – raving about the 'wondrous world of GeoNet', as WorkNet's Taffy Adler called it. By chance, software was discovered which would work on an available machine, and in May of that year the first 'tentative and frustrating links' were made between Johannesburg and the GeoNet host computer known as GEO2, in Britain.

Later that year, a local South African programmer (who was then working as a consultant for the *Weekly Mail*, a newly established left-wing newspaper) wrote the software for both email and an electronic bulletin board which became the basis for WorkNet. The initial users were the *Weekly Mail* staff of reporters, who were the first South Africans to grapple with, and succeed in exploiting, the full potential of the new computer communications technology. (The *Weekly Mail* is still linked, a decade later, to the network. Its archive is available there through the Web site of WorkNet's successor, SANGONeT.)

They were joined over time by the Trade Union Research Project, the International Labour Research and Information Group, research officers at a number of trade unions, the documentation centre at the Centre for Applied Legal Studies, the library/resource centre at the South African Council of Churches, the *South African Labour Bulletin*, and independent newspapers including *Vrye* and the *New Nation*. Ten or more trade unions came online, including the Congress of South African Trade Unions (COSATU). By 1992, WorkNet had amassed some 180 users in the trade union, development, media, human rights, documentation, environmental, academic and peace networks.

As Peter Waterman has written, WorkNet 'provides us with an example of high-level cooperation between the alternative actors in the development of ILCC [International Labour Communication by Computer], with these also being closely articulated with a new, mass, militant, left-nationalist labour movement'.

WorkNet tried to be ecumenical in the world-wide division between the Poptel/GeoNet and Association for Progressive Communications (APC) networks. It linked itself both to the British APC affiliate, GreenNet, and to the GeoNet host in London as well. It made available to its users some 200 conferences from *both* systems. Its priority was, however, south-to-south communication, particularly within the Southern African subcontinent. By the early 1990s, WorkNet was even opening up to the Internet – and this at a time when most networks were closed to the very idea of connecting to what was considered an academic computer network.

Working under the repressive apartheid regime forced the WorkNet pioneers to 'survive police surveillance and interference'. They did this by maintaining a low profile and dealing with the occasional cutting of phone lines and monitoring of their content. This experience will certainly be of interest to independent trade unionists working under repressive regimes which are today slowly opening up to the Internet.

WorkNet had some small successes. It maintained a flow of information to and from local opposition groups and media, most notably the *Weekly Mail*. Trade unions were part of this flow. Wage information from different plants in a transnational corporation would be made available. Health and safety information about a French power station whose design had been copied by South Africa was found. Human rights information, some of it originating at the United Nations, was distributed.

One example of a WorkNet success took place during the Mobil Oil fair disinvestment campaign. 'It was with some air of superiority', wrote Adler, 'that we demonstrated our mastery of the cutting edge of technology by coordinating meetings, information and demonstrations on three continents using email to good advantage. Electronic communication is demonstrably a superior and cheaper form of linking people, campaigns and trade unions.'

A representative of the chemical workers' union (CWIU) in South Africa spoke in 1992 about the uses made of WorkNet's links to international trade secretariats in Europe. Noting that many bitter strikes have taken place in South Africa involving transnational corporations, the local union was able to collect 'up-to-date information on the companies, operations in other countries, and proposed take-overs. Through the ICEF we were able to contact sister unions in the country of origin of the company. Pressure from these unions has assisted in many cases the struggles being fought in South Africa.'

Like most independent South African organisations in the 1980s, WorkNet was funded by anti-apartheid organisations based abroad. Sometimes this funding was conditioned on the purchase and use of certain kinds of computer equipment. This did not always work out, and as a result some state-of-the-art computer hardware attracted dust in trade union offices. As Waterman commented, WorkNet representatives were 'unusually aware (or uncommonly open)' – or both – 'about the ambiguities of its relations with Northern supporters'.

WorkNet also had to deal with the question of how one runs a democratic computer communications network. At first, the WorkNet founders thought that the best way to do this would be to have representatives of the various organisations using the network actually run it. But this did not work out, and eventually it was decided to run the organisation as an independent body. Its board consisted of activists working full-time in the trade unions, church, media, housing and information-processing fields. The question of whether it really represented the interests of its users would be settled by the free market. As Adler put it, 'if more

NGOs were joining the system, then clearly we were servicing the needs of our target community, and would thus be representative of that community'.

Apparently WorkNet was not entirely successful in 'representing' that community. Even though the labour movement was the first group of non-governmental organisations to use email, by the early 1990s, according to Morice Smithers of the *South African Labour Bulletin*, 'the labour movement probably uses less email than most other NGO sectors in the country'. Smithers identified five obstacles to trade union use of computer-mediated communications in South Africa at that time, and these are probably relevant to many other countries as well:

- *Fear of new technology.* 'Many people in South Africa', he wrote, 'are still fearful of computer technology, both the more educated and those who had less access to education.'
- *Unfriendly technology.* 'Hardware or software that is not easy to use, is not going to be used.' By 1993, when WorkNet became SANGONeT, more user-friendly software was finally introduced – and it was finally compatible with the operating system used by COSATU. 'People will only use email as an alternative to fax', concluded Smithers, 'when email is as easy to use as a fax.'
- *Lack of capacity to handle technology.* Only 'a small handful of people in the unions' in South Africa had the skills to use computer communications, and they didn't necessarily have the time, or sense of responsibility, to pass those on to others.
- *Lack of capacity to handle the output.* The new technology was producing information quickly and in enormous quantity. Smithers cited one South African trade unionist: 'People don't even have the time to deal with the pieces of paper that land on their desks. How will they ever be able to cope with the flood of material that becomes available via a modem?'
- *Other priorities take precedence.* Even though many well-intentioned union leaders support the use of computer-mediated communications, 'it is way down on their list of real priorities – as opposed to wished-for possibilities'. The new technology is therefore 'a luxury which they cannot afford in time or money'.

Smithers gave as an example the national trade union centre COSATU, established a year before WorkNet, in 1985. COSATU had the computers, but the staff members who set up the system left the organisation, and the system was hardly ever used. Regional offices of COSATU used to use email to jointly produce *COSATU News*, but that stopped once publication of that periodical was halted. 'Few of COSATU's affiliates use email', he wrote. 'Among those that do, use is generally only between head offices.' Because other non-governmental organisations had already begun to use email, unions used it to communicate with them. Otherwise, the main use was communication between local trade unions in South Africa and international trade secretariats in Europe. This was particularly the case with the metalworkers' union NUMSA and the chemical workers' CWIU. 'WorkNet', concluded Smithers, 'started small and grew quickly, but suffered from being under-resourced ... WorkNet's user base remained small and under-utilised.'

Years have passed, but even today there is a still a bitter taste in the mouth of some South African trade unionists. Email 'was hyped as the future' by WorkNet, says Martin Nicol of the National Union of Mineworkers (NUM). But 'it was very difficult to use, and very unreliable'. All the trade unions bought modems and paid to join the network, he recalls, but they 'could not actually use the technology'.

Meanwhile, South Africa underwent a revolution. Apartheid collapsed, and a new, democratic nation was born. The labour movement became, as it has become all over the world, just another non-governmental organisation. And WorkNet became SANGONeT, in partnership with the Development Resources Centre, taking its place, as Taffy Adler wrote, 'among other NGOs of civil society in working towards the socio-economic development of our fundamentally unequal society'. We'll discuss what happened next in Chapter 5 of this book.

Poptel and the ITSs in Asia

The Asia Monitor Resource Centre (AMRC) in Hong Kong was founded by radical church people from the US. It was one of a number of alternative documentation services and focused on transnational corporate activities in Asia, eventually publishing the *Asia Labour Monitor*. Using the Americans' familiarity with computers and cheap East Asian computers, AMRC became what Waterman called 'a major actor' in the global labournet. 'Its recruitment policy', he wrote, 'has resulted in the training of a number of third world specialists' – including individuals from India, South Africa, the West Indies and elsewhere – 'as well as interaction and exchange between these and others from the First World.'

Derek Hall of AMRC hailed email as the most significant tool for communication since the invention of the telephone, but nevertheless listed a number of problems with it. It was expensive; it required special skills; there are no directories or handbooks; it is not user-friendly. Hall also pointed out the destructive competition between alternative networks. He painted what Waterman called 'a sobering picture of the possibilities for developing and using email not only within the third world but amongst unions and workers more generally'.

Jagdish Parikh was one of the coordinators of AMRC back in 1987–88. At that time, they were working to establish email links for various ICEF affiliates throughout Asia to Poptel in the UK, through the GeoNet host computer known as GEO2. Other trade secretariats, including the ITF and IUF, were also involved. At the time, the Association for Progressive Communications was brand-new, and even six years later had no affiliate networks in Asia.

In the intervening years, Parikh believes that a number of the Asian unions which adopted Poptel have abandoned it, and Poptel's efforts in Asia have faltered. Parikh says today that much was learned about the use of computer communications by the trade union movement in Asia – but emphasises that not many people have any 'real sense of what is feasible in Asia' or of what has been achieved so far.

Poptel founder Dave Spooner also worked for a time in South East Asia. There was already interest in computer communications in the Philippines, he says. His job was 'helping affiliate unions in different countries use modems to connect to electronic mail, to be able to connect to Europe and elsewhere'.

FLOKS, FORKANT and TUDIC

The powerful Danish labour movement began conducting experiments with computer communications as early as 1988. Their first project (called FLOKS) was launched in the county of Middelfart.

Thirty trade unionists, who were also members of the Social Democratic Party, were given terminals that allowed communication using the Portacom system. Some of the participants, who had previously been relatively quiet and inactive, increased their activity and influence. As Gordon McAlpine of the Danish labour federation LO pointed out, 'the social structures around the participants were strengthened, which was an unexpected result'.

A year later, the LO launched a more ambitious project called FORKANT. Using the same computer system, it linked 70 local trade unionists on the island of Fyn. Most of these were users with no computer experience and limited educational backgrounds. Taking that into account, the union bought what seemed to be the friendliest machines around at that time – Apple Macintoshes. Those users who already had some computer experience were provided with PCs. In order to encourage them to use the computers, all the users were given word-processing and spreadsheet software as well. This actually turned out to be one of the great successes of the project. Administrative tasks were handled more effectively –

even though the real point of the project was to test computer communications.

Though email was readily adopted, the conferencing function which proved so successful in Solinet and other networks was under-utilised by participants in the program. McAlpine believed the reason was that users were not sufficiently involved in discussions of how the system should be used.

Another problem which the Danish trade unionists discovered will be of general relevance throughout the labour movement. In order to participate in computer conferences or discussion groups, one has to write. This 'reliance upon written communication', reported McAlpine, 'has been a problem for many users, and has inhibited open and comprehensive debate'. This problem was not reported by other networks, most notably the Canadian ones, and one reason might be that networks based on teachers (BCTF) or office staff (CUPE) might include people with a higher level of education than the Danish group.

In Chapter 6, when we discuss international use of computer networks, we'll talk more about the third stage of the Danish experiments – the TUDIC project. Let us only note here that by the autumn of 1990 the LO started this unique experiment in online labour education in cooperation with two other national trade union centres – the British Trades Union Congress (TUC) and the Swedish LO.

A Turning Point

By 1989–90, one study showed that at least 180 labour organisations were online around the world. A 1990 survey found 70 major trade union organisations using various forms of email. The International Confederation of Free Trade Unions declared that the value of electronic communications was 'clearly established'.

That same year (1990), about 50 people from all over the world took part in a conference in Epe, in the Netherlands. Among those present at the Epe meeting were representatives of the Association of Progressive Communications, which had yet to launch its LaborNet. Representatives of a number of labour-support groups were also present, as well as delegates from some of the new labour movements in South Africa and South Korea. The ICEF also sent a representative – the first appearance within this network of a representative of the traditional trade union internationals.

A labour sector meeting was held, and it called for an international conference of labour email users. 'That decision', wrote Peter Waterman, led directly to the 1992 conference on the labour movement and computer communications held in Manchester, 'at which the traditional unions were present in both number and quality' – something utterly new.

Meanwhile, sometime between the Epe and Manchester meetings, a group of people decided to launch what is today known as LaborNet@IGC. Users of the San Francisco-based Institute for Global Communications (IGC), the US affiliate of the APC, wanted to explore the potential of electronic communications for the labour movement. According to Jagdish Parikh, who had previously worked promoting Poptel in Asia, 'enhancing [the] possibilities of global labour solidarity was one of the key concerns' of this group. Initially, the group contacted existing users of the IGC network – which was largely focused on environmental, peace and women's issues – and found those with an interest in labour, and then surveyed them regarding their needs. The LaborNet initiators brought about an increased presence of labour discussion areas on the IGC network. They worked for more information sharing with the existing Poptel/GeoNet network, which involved the traditional trade union structures. According to Parikh, the flow of information was one-way (from IGC to GeoNet) due to technical difficulties. The LaborNet initiators also provided special support to users who expressed an interest in labour issues. LaborNet@IGC was not constituted as a formal, independent network until 1994.

On 14 April 1992, some 90 trade unionists from two dozen countries representing every continent gathered at a trade union college in Manchester. They came from Africa (South Africa, Ghana, Cameroon), Asia (Philippines, South Korea, India, Singapore), and Latin America (Mexico, Brazil, Uruguay). There were representatives from the US, Canada, Australia and New Zealand. But most of them came from Europe – from the UK, Ireland, Belgium, the Netherlands, Italy, Finland, Denmark and Switzerland. They even came from the newly liberated trade union movements in Russia and Hungary.

The people who came were often themselves pioneers in the field of labour telematics, men and women who for a decade or more had been involved in the field. Among these were Dave Spooner of Poptel, Larry Kuehn of the British Columbia Teachers' Federation, Marc Belanger from Canada's Solinet, Jim Catterson of the ICEF, Richard Flint of the ITF, Taffy Adler from South Africa's WorkNet, and Peter Waterman – theorist of the new internationalist communications. Organising the conference were the very institutions which already in 1992 had accumulated experience of years working with computer communications and the labour movement – among them, Poptel, WorkNet, *International Labour Reports*, and the ICEF.

The conference was organised by email. Its organisers lived in Britain, Hong Kong, Belgium, the US and South Africa. These individuals and others could have continued to communicate using email, but decided to convene a conference where they could meet face to face. That kind of personal encounter is necessary if you want to build something outside of cyberspace.

Taffy Adler and Jim Catterson spoke about using email for international solidarity. Marc Belanger and Larry Kuehn reported on Canadian trade union use of computer networking. Representatives from Britain, Denmark and Korea discussed using computer communications for union education, on the shopfloor, and in community/labour teleconferencing. Several plenary sessions and workshops were devoted to online information sources, including discussions of commercial databases, specifically labour databases, ILO databases and, in particular, health and safety materials online.

Workshops and a plenary on the question of access focused on 'those without the technology', on women's networks, on Eastern Europe and on 'democratic electronic networks' in South Africa and Mexico. Workshops on 'The Future' dealt with labour movement databases, software, European strategies, health and safety information, email for trade union officials and the all-important issue of training. Peter Waterman led a workshop on 'alternative labour communication'.

'So far, information technology has largely been the tool of transnational corporations', said Celia Mather, summing up the conference. 'Trade union organisations must take a determining role in this new international information order. They must take the technology and re-shape it for democracy, justice and social progress, for themselves as organisations and for working people and their communities worldwide. These three days were filled with examples of how *this is already happening around the world*, and with many ideas for the future.'

Other participants were somewhat less enthusiastic. Looking back four years later, one of them told me that 'with a few exceptions, particularly Marc Belanger, Larry Kuehn, and Jim Catterson, it was not very worthwhile'. There was a lot of enthusiasm expressed for email 'with almost no sense of the labour movement and what could be done with it'. And some of the organisers seemed to be supporting a kind of 'techno-anarchism', using email as 'a tool for an intellectual elite to reach the rank and file from the outside'. Another participant told me that a number of people 'responded with great nervousness to even the word "internationalism" at or after the event'. For him, the conference didn't go far enough in recognising the emerging global labournet as not only a *tool* for traditional trade union ends, but as a *community*.

The concrete results of the conference seem small enough: a conference report was published, and was also made available through the GeoNet labour bulletin boards. The Labour Telematics

Centre was established at the same trade union college where the conference was held (more on this in Chapter 5). Personal contacts were made, and ideas exchanged. A follow-up conference was held a year later.

To me, several things stand out about this conference, looking back at it years later. Its style and concerns were entirely *internationalist*, even if a disproportionate number of participants (though not a majority) were British. These trade unionists were talking about the whole world as if there were no borders, as if the working class were something real and tangible that shared common interests no matter where people lived. It focused almost entirely on *practical issues* such as databases, access, email, building trade union solidarity – instead of adopting empty and verbose resolutions on dozens of issues. The participants were not top-ranking officials of the labour bureaucracy or ministers in various social democratic governments, but were activists and pioneers at the national and local levels in the Americas, Africa, Asia and Europe. They were the people who actually work out there in the field, creating the technological and human basis of the global labournet.

And that global labournet, whose creation is a precondition for the rebirth of the International in the years to come, was already becoming visible in 1992.

CHAPTER 4

Local and Regional Trade Union Networks

Until now, I've talked about national and international trade unions and their use of computer networking. I've mentioned Canada's Solinet, Europe's Poptel/GeoNet, WorkNet in South Africa, LaborNet@IGC in the US, and others. In the chapters that follow, I'm going to explore those efforts in greater detail.

For now, however, I'll pause and take a look at the grassroots. This chapter will discuss the five ways local and regional trade unions use computer-mediated communications:

- Online daily strike newspapers.
- Trade union use of existing employers' networks.
- Independent local and regional trade union networks.
- Dial-up local trade union bulletin boards.
- Local trade union World Wide Web sites.

Each of the five methods has its advantages and disadvantages. Each one serves a particular purpose at a particular moment.

Online daily strike newspapers seem to be the most powerful uses made so far of the new communications technology by trade unions. But they have not shown that they can survive the end of the strike, though many readers seem to want them to do so. They are, therefore, wonderful campaigning tools, but have not proven themselves useful for the ongoing work of the labour movement between strikes.

Trade union use of existing employers' networks is not well documented – and for good reason. In some cases, workers are conducting trade union business on employers' email systems quietly, without the bosses ever knowing. Despite its advantages (the networks already exist, it's free of charge, and it works) it is insecure.

Independent local and regional trade union networks were an important development in the 1980s and early 1990s. We talked about the British Columbia Teachers' Federation in the previous chapter. But these networks appear to be disappearing today (or at least changing drastically) with the opening up of the wider Internet. In countries where access to the Internet is still expensive

– and that, unfortunately, is true of most of the world – these independent networks might still be relevant examples.

Dial-up local trade union bulletin boards seem to be another tool whose time has come and gone, judging by the examples we have here. But like the independent networks, that is an illusion. Only in countries where Internet access is almost as cheap as a local telephone call – and that really only describes North America for now – is this the case. Everywhere else in the world, dial-up bulletin boards are still a viable option, and the experience of the pioneers in the US labour movement is worthy of some consideration.

Finally, we'll have a look at some of the local trade union World Wide Web sites. With the rising popularity of the Web, it was inevitable that local trade unions, at least in the advanced industrial countries, would join the national and international trade union centres and use the new medium. Trade union Web sites are being added daily; we'll look at just a few examples here.

Online Strike Newspapers

If the labour movement in general has a difficult time getting its message across, the problem is exacerbated a thousand-fold during a strike. If the strike is widespread, prolonged, affects the daily lives of ordinary citizens, or is punctuated by violence, it is even more likely that the mass media will throw their full weight against the workers and possibly against the labour movement as a whole.

Sometimes, trade unionists have published daily strike newspapers. According to one editor of such a paper, a union launches a daily strike newspaper in order to 'refute the lies of the boss press, give the true facts about its own aims and policies, and expose the antilabour schemes of the bosses and the government'.

A very early example, published from 1883 to 1892, was called *The Boycotter*. It was the organ of New York City's Typographical Union No. 6, which was boycotting the *New York Tribune*. The year *The Boycotter* ceased publication, striking union printers in Toronto launched the *Evening Star*, which continues today, a century later, as the *Toronto Star*, one of the largest circulation newspapers in Canada. There were other strike newspapers that persisted long after the strike ended, including the *Citizen's Voice* in Wilkes-Barre, Pennsylvania.

An early, and important, example of a strike newspaper was the daily *Strike Bulletin* published during the 1919 general strike in Winnipeg, Canada. Historians have been unanimous in their evaluation of that paper as a success. The Winnipeg *Strike Bulletin* maintained order and discipline among the strikers.

The *Strike Bulletin* was such a powerful tool in the hands of the unionists that the Canadian authorities decided to put a stop to it. The paper's editor, William Ivens, was arrested, though he was quickly replaced by J.S. Woodsworth, who was destined to become the leading figure in the Cooperative Commonwealth Federation (CCF), forerunner to today's New Democratic Party. Woodsworth lasted barely a week at his job, and he too was arrested.

After Woodsworth's arrest, the paper's third editor went into hiding and tried to continue the project under new names. But by then the strike was broken.

Even though the strikers had the muscle to shut down rival newspapers, they remained dependent on privately owned presses. When the authorities ordered the Winnipeg Printing and Engraving Company to stop printing the newspaper, the fate of the *Strike Bulletin* was sealed.

Fifteen years later, the first daily strike newspaper published by a trade union in the United States was launched. It was called *The Organizer*, and it was published by Local 574 of the Teamsters in Minneapolis, Minnesota. *The Organizer* was launched on 25 June 1934, at first as a weekly. The editor was officially Farrell Dobbs, whose book *Teamster Rebellion* is an eyewitness account of the strike. But the real editor was American Trotskyist leader Max Shachtman.

On 16 July *The Organizer* became a daily, on the eve of the outbreak of one of the three strikes organised by Local 574 that year. The union leaders realised early on that a weekly was utterly inadequate for their purposes. *The Organizer* was a two-page tabloid with a circulation of about 10,000. Though the price of 'one penny' was imprinted below the masthead, people paid what they could for the paper and it soon became self-financing.

Salespeople hawked the paper around Minneapolis, carrying cans which were often stuffed with dollar bills. People who sold *The Organizer* on a regular basis developed sales routes, including news-stands, beer taverns, beauty parlours and other establishments patronised by workers. Copies were sold at factory gates and in railway yards.

The employer-backed Citizens Alliance, concerned at growing community support for the strikers, demanded the paper's suppression based on 'criminal syndicalism' charges. They brought pressure to bear on the various print shops in town. The strikers were forced to go from shop to shop, until they finally found one printer which did the job until the end of the strike.

The Minneapolis Teamsters faced the constant threat of repression of their daily *Organizer*. As linotype operator Ace Johnston said, there was always a 'good chance of having our presses smashed [and] the building wrecked'. Company goons did jump a truck carrying

The Organizer one night – but their attack was repulsed, and not repeated. *The Organizer* continued to appear as a daily for a time after the strike, though it eventually became a weekly and then halted publication for lack of funds.

Others unions have published other newspapers while on strike. Strikers in Kohler, Wisconsin produced a *Daily Strike Bulletin* for several years. In Winnipeg, a generation after the 1919 general strike, workers published the *Winnipeg Citizen*. During the *Daily News* strike in New York City, the striking Guild published a newspaper of its own.

In recent years, striking workers have exploited new media to get their message across. During a San Francisco newspaper strike in the 1960s, strikers created a popular nightly television programme called 'Newsroom', which continued for several years after the strike ended. In the early 1980s, striking New York City newspaper workers broadcast regularly on a local radio station, reading over the air stories they would otherwise have put into print.

The 'San Francisco Free Press'

On 1 November 1994, some 2,600 workers from nine trade unions at the *San Francisco Chronicle* and *San Francisco Examiner* walked out of their jobs, beginning an eleven-day strike. The two struck newspapers continued to appear, though circulation and advertising revenues fell drastically.

Several days after the walk-out began, both papers decided to launch their long-awaited online editions on the World Wide Web. But they were beaten to the chase by the striking workers, who created their own online newspaper, the *San Francisco Free Press,* which appeared within 24 hours of the strike's beginning. It was the very first daily labour newspaper on the Internet.

News of their achievement went out quickly on the net. A delegate to the San Francisco Labour Council wrote a message to Internet discussion groups urging 'those of you who would like to see the possibilities of the Internet for the labour movement' to check out the strike paper. The enthusiasm for the strike newspaper was shared by a Chicago trade unionist, who wrote: 'Score one for the electronic community *and* the labour movement!'

For those without access to the Web, copies of articles appearing in the strike paper were posted to Internet mailing lists. There were some disgruntled remarks made by participants in one of the academic lists, but the moderator emphasised the importance of archiving this material electronically for the future. Solidarity messages were also sent out, as well as calls for action.

Looking back more than a year later, one of those who worked building support for the strikers, Steve Zeltzer of the San Francisco

Labour Video Project, calls the ten editions which were published 'historic firsts for labour communication'. But he doesn't consider these to be 'strike newspapers' in the same way as the *Organizer* was back in 1934. Apparently, some of those who were involved in the *Free Press* effort shared this viewpoint, and wanted the paper to have more of a trade union focus, rather than be what Zeltzer calls 'pro-labour'.

But was the *Free Press* just another newspaper? The strikers' message came out loud and clear in its pages. In an editorial entitled 'Why We Walked', striking journalists told their side of the story in a way that would have been impossible had they not had their own medium. According to the article, 'management's bottom-line negotiating strategy had become union-busting' – thus prompting the walk-out. The article talked about 'hired goons in rent-a-cop uniforms' strutting around the newsrooms. It pointed out the issues behind the strike, including wage increases, job security and pay equity (for example, wage disparities between librarians – mostly women – and editorial staff). Without an online newspaper, how could the union have got this message across? The traditional tactic of a printed strike newspaper would have cost thousands of dollars. Instead, the strikers opted to create what they called 'an independent journalistic voice' on the Internet.

When necessary, the strikers augmented their efforts with more traditional printed materials. Four printed editions of the *Free Press* were produced during the strike in addition to the ten electronic ones. These were distributed by members of the striking Teamsters union, and they included paid advertising from businesses which supported the strike. And on the morning following important national and state elections, the *Chronicle* had no final results – but the striking workers produced a one-page printed 'Election Newsletter' with summaries of key votes. They distributed 30,000 copies of these in downtown San Francisco before dawn. (Complete results and analyses appeared in the online edition.)

Though a typical daily edition of the online *San Francisco Free Press* included Arts, Sports, Business and other columns one would find in a normal newspaper, it would also include items like Jon Caroll's column, 'My Strike Diary'. In one such column, Carroll suggested a number of ways strike supporters could help, including cancelling their subscriptions to the struck newspapers. 'You've probably done that, but do it again', he advised. 'Cancel every day, sometimes twice a day. Be polite, but in a rude way.'

I think that the most interesting column to read was the Letters page, because it revealed the extent to which the *Free Press* was building up support for the unions. Nearly all of the letters were encouraging. Readers wrote in to praise the quality (and indeed the very existence) of the online paper; they also wrote in to express their support for the strikers and their demands.

Some of these readers identified themselves as trade unionists. George Datz wrote: 'Your first edition contradicts the old saw. There is now a way to fight those "who buy ink by the barrel!"' Geoff Miller, who identified himself as 'a one-time labour Organizer and picket captain' who knows 'what it is like to be walking the line' encouraged the strikers: 'I also know how scary it is to be without a paycheque. Don't give in.' Curt Milton, a journalist and trade unionist from the state of Washington wrote: 'Just wanted to send along support from here for your efforts to get a decent contract. We've been following your negotiations (or lack thereof) closely. It's unfortunate that management insists on turning this process into a pitched battle. We survived a similar situation during our prolonged contract talks last year, and I wouldn't wish it on my worst enemy. Give 'em hell and don't give in. We're all pulling for you.'

But many more solidarity messages came in from ordinary readers who did not identify themselves as trade unionists. 'Your readers are with you', wrote Hal Plotkin, 'Keep fighting for your rights.' Elliott Fabric added: 'Keep up the good work. Make sure those underpaid librarians get more dough.'

Another category of mail published in the online daily were letters regarding the stunning technical achievement of the strikers. Some of the letters came from techno-experts of various stripes. Scott T. Boyd, editor of *MacTech Magazine*, wrote: 'While it's harder to read over breakfast or on the bus, your online paper is great. Add in links to previous stories, some searching and indexing capabilities, and some pictures, and you'll have a terrific paper.' He suggested that the strikers 'find a way to continue this on a permanent basis. ... Don't miss the opportunity that you all have to lead the way.'

But most letters expressing amazement at the new technology came from ordinary people and not experts. 'Your use of the new technology is really exciting', wrote Adele Framer, 'Hang in there. I hope the result is better reporting and better working conditions for all of us.' A touching letter came from Don Coco, who wrote, 'As a Totally Blind Person I'd like to thank you for your WWW Service. Without this service, I wouldn't be able to read newspaper articles and I just want to let you know how much I appreciate it.'

More than a year after the strike ended, all ten editions of the *San Francisco Free Press* are still available on the World Wide Web. They are a reminder of what was done, and what can be done in other places and other times. Rather than yellowing in some dusty archive, the pages of the world's first online daily strike newspaper are still fresh and available for all to see.

In summing up the strike, which the unions won, *Free Press* staffers wrote that it would not have been possible to 'secure a fair contract with our employers without the support and encouragement of our community'. That was the whole point of the strike paper: to build such support. And it worked.

The 'Detroit Journal'

Eight months after the San Francisco workers made labour (and Internet) history by launching the first online strike newspaper, they were followed by the workers at Detroit's daily newspapers – the *Detroit News* and the *Detroit Free Press*.

Using a format similar to that of the San Francisco workers, they provided an alternative to the 'scab' newspapers produced by the dailies in the online *Detroit Journal*. The *Journal*'s attractively designed front page included colourful icons for News, Sports, Business, and Features columns, as well as 'Union Postings', a 'Strikers' Journal', and the Editorial page.

By early 1996, the *Journal* was recording some 12,000 'hits' (accesses) on the World Wide Web every week. According to Gary Graff, the *Journal* co-coordinator, the paper 'was born about five days after the strike started. Hiawatha Bray, a *Free Press* business writer, purchased the cyberspace, and a handful of journalists – mostly from the *Free Press* but also a few from the *Detroit News* – began meeting on July 16. Our first edition went up seven days later.'

But the original staff did not hold together during the many long months of the strike. 'Ironically, only myself and our copy chief, Ginger Pullen, remain from that original group', says Graff, 'the rest have either taken other jobs or have crossed the [picket] line and returned to work.' Another exception was features reporter Toni Martin, who makes sure that printed copies of the daily online *Journal* are distributed to picket lines and other union offices. 'Currently I would say we have about ten folks who work on the *Journal* regularly, plus writers who contribute irregularly', says Graff.

Like its California counterpart, the *Detroit Journal* reflected – and helped produce – an extraordinary display of labour-community solidarity. In reading its columns and in particular the Letters page, one recalls the golden age of the American labour movement. One letter after another from local residents of Detroit and its outlying suburbs conveyed a message of hope and solidarity. Solidarity messages also came in from trade unionists in Britain, Mexico and elsewhere.

'I think the strike paper has helped to build support for the strikers, particularly early on', says Graff. 'But it's not broad-based support; rather, it's from a particular sector of the community – local and international – that is keyed into the Web. ... One thing it has allowed us to do is spread the word a little farther and get other folks active in prosecuting the strike.'

'We answer as many of the letters as we can', says Graff, 'always those that ask what they can do; generally we offer suggestions about fund-raisers and awareness raising events, even encouraging those who have written to picket at advertisers in their community (KMart, for instance) who continue to advertise in the scab papers.'

The Strikers' Journal contained an eclectic collection of articles. One was a poem by a nine-year-old girl whose 'Mommy' was on strike. Another was a call on readers to submit recipes for strikers – putting the emphasis on low-cost meals. Another described a prayer service conducted by priests and a rabbi which attempted – unsuccessfully – to reconcile the two sides in what had become a bitter dispute. One article was written by a veteran of the 1994 San Francisco newspaper strike.

One significant difference between the *Detroit Journal* and the *San Francisco Free Press* has been that the Detroit strikers have been regularly producing, in addition to the online daily paper, a weekly Sunday printed newspaper, the *Sunday Journal*. The entire contents of the Sunday paper are made available online in the daily edition. The relationship between the two efforts is 'a solid one', says Graff. 'We also use the *Sunday Journal* offices as a headquarters for the daily *Journal*.'

But there's a downside to publishing both print and online editions, as the Detroit strikers found out. 'So much energy is put into the Sunday edition that it sucks up time (and energy) from some folks who were regularly contributing to the daily.'

I asked Graff if the *Sunday Journal* was earning a profit. It wasn't yet, he said, and that had him worried. There was an advertising staff consisting of strikers, but it wasn't particularly successful in its efforts. One major appliance store chain and some unions bought ads. Until the newspaper becomes profitable, the money earned from the ads goes into paying for its production. If a profit ever turns up, it will go into the strike fund. Efforts made to sell advertising space on the *Journal*'s World Wide Web site were even less successful.

The Detroit strike was quite different from the San Francisco one. The California workers were back in their jobs within two weeks of the walk-out. A year after the Detroit strike began, it was still raging. As early as November 1995, the *New York Times* was already pronouncing defeat for the strikers – but the strikers weren't listening. In mid-July 1996, the Detroit newspaper strike entered its second year – and the online *Journal* with it. As the strikers themselves wrote in their Web-based publication, 'This is one anniversary we hoped we would not see. But here we are. About 2,000 newspaper workers are still on strike. Despite financial hardships and grinding uncertainty about our future, we remain as determined as ever to secure a fair contract.'

Both strikes featured online, World Wide Web-based, daily strike newspapers. In both cases, suggestions were made by readers to turn the papers into permanent ones. In the case of the *San Francisco Free Press*, the strike ended so quickly that nothing was ever done. I asked Graff if the Detroit strikers were thinking about turning the *Journal* into a permanent institution.

In the beginning, he recalls, 'I don't think anybody considered it. Now with no end in sight, it's something to mull over. The key is money – making it. For the *Journal* to be effective, it needs a full-time staff. For that, it needs to make money to pay people – people who were used to good salaries and benefits before the strike. Right now, even the *Journal* principals are involved in a number of freelance projects and other jobs, so I can't say there's been any real discussion of it lately.'

Meanwhile, the strike dragged on, and as more and more workers crossed the picket lines or took other jobs, the strike effort faced a manpower shortage. The Detroit Council of Newspaper Unions was 'dragged kicking and screaming into giving strike pay credits for work' on the *Journal*, says Graff. In the eyes of more traditional trade unionists, strikers should be picketing or leafleting. The union continues to put out its own one-page publication, *The Alliance*, with strike news. Sometimes union officials forget to tell the *Journal* when things happen. 'So when you talk about these efforts being premature', says Graff, 'it's also premature for the union leaders, who don't realise what it is we're doing.'

It is not clear from the experience of the two strikes precisely how effective a weapon the online daily strike newspaper is. We do know that printed strike newspapers have been useful, and sometimes even *decisive*. (According to James Cannon, who worked on *The Organizer*, that was the case in the 1934 Minneapolis strike.) One reason why *The Organizer* may have been such a potent tool – and the *Detroit Journal* a less effective one – may have to do with the universality of the medium. As Gary Graff admitted, the *Journal* couldn't build 'broad-based support' because its readership – no more than a couple of thousand per day – needed access to the World Wide Web.

Another example of an online effort by striking journalists was the *Irish X-Press*, produced by the locked-out members of the National Union of Journalists at the Irish Press. Unfortunately, it is no longer accessible on the World Wide Web.

My conclusion from all this is not that efforts like the *Journal* are pointless, but that they are – perhaps – premature. As tens of millions more people go online in the next few years, the online daily strike newspaper will take its place in labour's arsenal.

Trade Union Use of Existing Employers' Networks

One interesting way trade unionists have been using computer-mediated communications has not been widely reported, nor broadly discussed in the labour movement. I'm talking about the use of existing employers' networks. Long before the Internet was a household word, hundreds of thousands of working people (perhaps millions) had access to electronic mail, online databases, and the like. And they had this without any personal investment in a microcomputer at home. People working for universities and certain giant corporations were using local area networks to communicate with one another, sometimes about union business.

In addition to exploiting the technology of computer communications for immediate benefits, they were learning tools which would become vital as the global Internet expanded. Even now, many of the active voices in online labour movement discussion groups are people who have been using email for many years, in their universities, and feel comfortable with the technology. They are the very opposite of 'newbies', those annoying newcomers to the Internet who know none of the unwritten rules and break all of them.

Probably some of the earliest trade union use of the networks was done this way. But we will never know, because it was probably done quietly. Universities and corporations didn't invest millions of dollars in sophisticated internal computer networks in order to empower their employees. And yet, as we'll see in the examples which follow, this is precisely what happened.

At Michigan State University, the Clerical-Technical Union (CTU) created a local trade union BBS using the existing university network. The CTU represents some 2,000 employees of the university and has been at the job for 20 years. 'We're not affiliated', says CTU programme director Laura Sager, 'although [we are] very much part of the labour movement!'

The CTU publishes a printed newsletter twice a month, running six to eight pages. It operates an information line and has a fax network to media in the state. It also publishes brochures on 'hot topics' which are distributed by union representatives. And it holds monthly training conferences and bi-weekly meetings of its board.

The CTU's Solidarity Committee conducts negotiations with the university. 'To facilitate rapid communications to a broad spectrum of members', Sager explained, 'the Solidarity Committee set up an electronic bulletin board.' Many – though not all – union members have access to email (all the union staff do), and this allowed the Solidarity Committee to use the new technology, as well as the old one of making phone calls, 'to alert members to events and ask for help and ideas'. The BBS's manager posted announcements, information about district meetings, and general union information. Other union committees also have access to the bulletin board, which continued to raise contract questions and to complement information published in the CTU newsletter.

Some of the information they're putting online includes 'news, committee meetings, letters, immediate election results, lists of union reps, contract Q & As, community service info, our union's baseball team scores, and meeting reports', reported Sager.

The CTU encourages its members to use the university's email system, though they caution members not to put confidential information on line – one of the clear disadvantages of using the employer's network.

Halfway around the world from Michigan is Singapore, an island country hot to get on the Internet. Singapore promotes itself as 'the intelligent island'. A few years ago, its National Computer Board adopted a plan called IT2000 which aimed to make the country into the information technology capital of Asia. To encourage transnational corporations to do business in Singapore, the national computer networks connect companies directly to various government agencies involved in import and export, thereby eliminating paperwork and speeding up the movement of goods, services and financial transactions. The government had its qualms about allowing individual Singapore residents access to the Internet, but by the beginning of 1995, there were already 52,000 Internet users there. By year's end, there were 85,000. All the major newspapers in the country already have online editions.

Back in 1992, in his report to the Manchester conference on labour networking, Thomas Thomas, the General Secretary of the Singapore Shell Employees' Union recounted a story that might be typical of many local unions which travelled the road from word-processors to modems. In the end, this union took advantage of a corporate – not an academic – network.

Thomas's union (which represents 97 per cent of the Shell workers in Singapore) began working with computers in 1985, using them to update membership records – which 'used to be done manually over many agonising hours'. This was done in order to save on very limited manpower and funds. The union decided to use the mainframe computer of the national trade union centre's insurance cooperative.

At this very early stage, the union was using a modem to access data which sat on a mainframe computer – using a personal computer in the office. Because there was a PC available in the office, union staff began using it for other purposes, including word-processing and maintaining financial records – the classic early office uses of such computers. 'Within a short time, we got "hooked" on the convenience and benefits of the computer', said Thomas. Unionists learned how to use spreadsheets, began to store more information on benefits members receive from their union, and found that their records were more up-to-date than ever before. 'Information for collective bargaining was stored and tabulated for effective use' in dealing with the giant transnational.

What began as a local trade union modem link-up to the national centre for the very specific purpose of transferring membership data was transformed into something radically different and larger when the Shell Employees' Union joined up with the International Federation of Chemical, Energy and General Workers' Unions. As we have already mentioned, the ICEF was on the cutting edge of trade union telematics by the mid-1980s and, as Thomas explains, 'They did not have to work very hard to convince us to link-up.' That electronic link through GeoNet, becoming part of the ICEF's global network, made communications with the ITS much faster – also made the ICEF 'more valuable to us', according to the Singapore unionist. Eventually, the union bought an IBM-compatible PC, which they linked up by modem to both the national trade union centre (NTUC) and the ITS (ICEF).

By 1989, Shell itself had begun extensive use of computer communications; 'electronic mail replaced paper', explained Thomas. 'As almost all our officials *and members'* were using Shell's system, Thomas continued, 'we also got connected to be in touch, not only with them but also with the management.' Thus was a local trade union network born – using the corporate network, following years of experience with modem-to-modem contacts.

These two examples only scratch the surface of what is certainly an important part of labour telematics. Its scope is hinted at by a new British trade union, the Information Technology Professionals' Association (ITPA), an autonomous section of Britain's fifth largest union, the MSF. The ITPA has an online network which includes 'recruitment and communication to potential members using company email systems'. In other words, using corporate networks as an organising tool. We'll return to the ITPA experience in the next chapter.

Independent Trade Union Networks

The very idea of an 'independent' trade union network almost sounds antiquated. The days when computer communications pioneers would string together cables, connect modems and create networking tools from scratch seem long gone. Today, when it seems as if everyone has a PC, and anyone can hook up to the Internet, what's the point of independent labour networks?

But as we can see in the two examples which follow – both of them from Canada – there is still a point to all this. One provincial union with a well-educated and computer-literate membership, with a decade and a half of networking experience, created a 'virtual network' using such Internet tools as LISTSERV, Gopher and the World Wide Web. The other followed a route startlingly reminiscent of the Danish experiments of the late 1980s, mentioned in the previous chapter. Both unions offer examples of successful networking over large geographic areas, serving thousands of trade unionists on a daily basis.

British Columbia Teachers' Federation

As we explained in the previous chapter, the BCTF established the very first labournet in the world, based on dumb computer terminals, back in 1981. By the decade's end, most union locals had already purchased personal computers and the era of paper-spewing, bulky and not-very-smart terminals was over. In September 1990, the union switched over to Solinet, the nation-wide trade union network established by Marc Belanger and the Canadian Union of Public Employees. The BCTF acquired some 300 Solinet accounts, replacing the 150 machines of the old network. At the same time, the union bought a fax machine for every local, thus creating a province-wide labour fax network.

By the mid-1990s, the BCTF had already outgrown even Solinet, and was ready to work directly on the Internet itself. Its province-wide network still exists; in fact, it's much larger than it was in the past. Only now, people can connect to it from whatever computers they want, from their homes, offices, and schools. They can use the educational system's network, or private Internet access providers, or even freenets which have sprung up in the province. Even those of us who are not BCTF members can access it too – or at least the parts that the BCTF wants us to see.

The new BCTF network is a virtual one, subsumed by the broader Internet and based on Internet tools we've already described in Chapter 2. For those people with email access to the Internet and not much more, the BCTF is offering up a number of online mailing lists, using the powerful LISTSERV program. Five such lists are already up and running:

- BCTF News: This includes short summaries of BCTF activities and issues, as well as the text of news releases.
- BCTF PD Issues: These are focused reports and summaries of BCTF actions and positions related to professional issues, including curriculum and assessment.

- BCTF Research: This list contains information about BCTF research projects and reports.
- BCTF Bargaining Update: Here users will find summaries of current information on collective bargaining. This list is only open to those who are authorised to use it because of their role in the union.
- BCTF President: This too is a closed list, aimed at local presidents and Federation officers.

This collection of online mailing lists represents (to my knowledge) the most extensive and intensive use of this tool by a trade union at any level.

There are certain disadvantages to the LISTSERV model, among them the fact that an archive is not always accessible, and documents may not necessarily be searched by keywords. The BCTF is considering copying the messages from these lists to UnionNet conferences, which are keyword searchable and are archived. (UnionNet is a joint effort by Solinet and the Canadian APC affiliate, Web.) In addition, the messages are available through the BCTF Gopher. In the long run, they want to run a conferencing system directly from the Web page, says Kuehn.

The Gopher includes more information about the union, including most of its printed documents, research reports, information on grievances, the professional development handbook, information about pensions and salary, a guide to the union, and a 'Lessons Aids Catalogue'. Documents available through the Gopher can even be emailed to users who can't access this Internet tool – a good example of backing up a system and allowing those with only limited access to the net to still use the information.

In the last year, the BCTF launched its own Web site, and this is qualitatively different from some of the Web sites we'll be discussing later in the chapter. Rather than just some flashy brochure about the union which no one is actually going to read, the BCTF Web site is part of an integrated network of online information with deep roots in the union. The BCTF Web site includes not only everything mentioned so far, but other material as well. Users will find things like pages from the union's publication, *The Teacher*, and other materials with graphics and colour.

Larry Kuehn, who started up the BCTF network back in 1981, is still around, working for the union, helping adapt this proven tool to meet the ever-changing Internet. These days, the union faces new challenges as a province-wide collective bargaining system is introduced. That change obligates the union to get information distributed more widely than ever before, and quicker too. The BCTF network allows the union to meet this challenge as well.

United Nurses of Alberta

The United Nurses of Alberta (UNA) is a trade union representing 13,000 working nurses in this sprawling western Canadian province. Those nurses in hospitals, health units, nursing homes and blood banks are spread out in 140 locals over the vast spaces of the Alberta prairie. In 1991, a computerisation project was launched and today more than 90 of those local unions are connected to each other and to the provincial offices using a network based on Apple Macintosh computers (which were picked because of their ease of use – just like the Macintoshes used by Danish trade unionists in their experiments in the late 1980s). Today, UNA members who don't have Macintoshes but just ordinary personal computers can also access the network. Secure conferencing for Executive Board members and negotiating committees is also offered.

The UNA's network manager is Florence Ross, who denies that there is a 'gender gap' in computer networking, proudly pointing out that more than 90 per cent of the UNA's workstations are operated by women. 'Most of our local Executive Committee members are women', she adds, 'and many are middle aged; not a group one would expect to be eager to move into the age of technology. I have seen many reluctant users overcome their fears and become keen and competent.'

Ross recently launched the UNA's Web site and says ,'It is very new and limited at this time, but we plan to have many of our documents available for downloading soon, and to use the home page as a tool for lobbying' – using forms embedded in the Web page which will be directly linked to government officials. At the present time, the UNA Web site includes an account of what the union is and what it does for its members; a copy of its Constitution; a critique of Alberta's Premier; and copies of the union's monthly newsletter.

Not content with her success in Alberta, Ross has been encouraging other nurses' unions elsewhere in Canada to go online. 'It is a slow process', she admits. 'Technology is far, far ahead of where people are.'

Dial-up Local Trade Union Bulletin Boards

In his biting critique of all the hype surrounding the Internet, *Silicon Snake Oil,* author Clifford Stoll ends on a curious note. Instead of unplugging his PC – or demonstratively smashing it before the eyes of the press, like journalist Kirkpatrick Sale – Stoll decides to withdraw from the global Internet. But he doesn't abandon computer communications entirely. He remains active, indeed in some sense becomes more active, in his local community online network, San

Francisco's WELL. Stoll finds in the WELL what he cannot find in the vast and all-embracing Internet – warmth, friendship, and community.

We should not study dial-up local trade union bulletin boards as if they were merely a transitional phase before unions link up to the ever-expanding, all-encompassing global net. It is true that for some of us, this author included, the local BBS was a kind of apprenticeship in computer communications, and we did move on from there to 'the real thing', the Internet. But there is something to be said for local trade union BBSs, particularly in places where Internet access is expensive.

At least in North America, many BBSs (and there are 65,000 of these in the US alone) have already linked together using the inexpensive (and somewhat slow) FidoNet system. FidoNet is a means of sending messages from one BBS to another, relaying them by cheap, middle-of-the-night telephone calls from one computer to another, across the whole continent. FidoNet also works quite well in a number of countries of the world's South, where the high-speed, fibre-optic data transmission cables of the Internet simply do not yet exist, and where modems use ordinary telephone lines to pass on messages.

Local 1220 IBEW BBS

One example of a successful local trade union BBS is the one used by Local 1220 of the International Brotherhood of Electrical Workers (IBEW), in Chicago. Its system operator, Bob Kastigar, told me that the BBS was launched in 1988 'to serve our members and other labour members in the Chicago area, as well as invite others to participate and learn a little bit more about the labour movement'.

Kastigar is a 32-year veteran of the labour movement. He works as a technician at WGN television in Chicago and has been at the job, and a member of Local 1220, all those 32 years. Only in the last year has he been an Executive Board member in his local, though he does actively participate in union activities. Kastigar also 'started and ran the electronic Bulletin Board – providing the computer, modem, and printer because I thought it was important'.

When he first proposed the idea, back in 1987, few understood what he was talking about. Those who did understand greeted the proposal without enthusiasm. At the time, there was a two-station network in the union office. There was also a 1,200 bps modem. Kastigar suggested that the union use one of the computers on weekends and during evening hours, existing phone lines, and free software. In other words, he suggested making no investment of money at all. The union agreed.

There was some reluctance to use the new technology by the union leadership, says Kastigar. 'The openness of the BBS is a real threat ... Having members communicate directly with each other, without the control and discipline of a union meeting, was not viewed as a good thing.'

The founders of this local BBS drafted a 'mission statement' expressing their seven goals. It is general enough to serve as a model for other union locals, including those outside of North America, to consider:

- To provide an open channel of communications with emphasis on the labour viewpoint to everyone, both union and non-union participants.
- To provide an open channel of communications among members of the labour community: labour leaders and labour union members – and also researchers, teachers, arbitrators, lawyers and others concerned with labour/management relations.
- To provide a communications channel directly from member-to-member.
- To provide a forum to espouse and further the goals of the International Brotherhood of Electrical Workers.
- To encourage participation by the Local 1220 members of the IBEW.
- To encourage communications of ideas without getting overly concerned with the technical aspects of computers and computer communications available on other bulletin board systems.
- To provide an attractive, interesting, friendly and enjoyable atmosphere that encourages others to participate via this medium of information and idea exchange.

Over time, the BBS began attracting more union members; the equipment got better; and eventually the union even spent some money on the project. (They finally paid for the BBS software.)

Local 1220 was approached by two other union locals – one from the IBEW, and another from the Society of Broadcast Engineers – who asked to have conferences set up for them on the BBS. Kastigar obliged them, not asking for anything in return. 'Our BBS became more attractive to more people', he explained.

'One area where we've tried to make our BBS unusual', says Kastigar, is the long list of files available for downloading. The emphasis is clearly on files trade unionists will want to use. The first file new users will probably want to look at is a long list of all files served by Local 1220's BBS, updated once every day.

As I looked through the list of files available, there was much one would find on any BBS. But there were also many things unique to a trade union BBS. There's a history of Local 1220 since its founding in 1941; electronic versions of its newsletter; texts of reports made to the union about its BBS; a number of files dealing with the broader issue of trade unions and computer communications; information on the loose network called Solinet, linking local trade union BBSs in the US (more on this in a moment), as well as on the AFL–CIO's LaborNet; a file on the 1994 'LaborTech' conference held in Minnesota; and an article entitled 'Labour network established in South Africa'. The file list for the San Diego, California Labour Council's BBS also appears. There are some articles which remind unionists using this ultra-modern technology of labour's past, including an article on the history of the US 'Labour Day', a review of several recent labour history publications and a historic monograph on the Ludlow, Colorado strike and massacre.

The interest in international labour matters is, as one would expect, somewhat limited. We've already mentioned the one article on a labour network in South Africa. And the collection of speeches at the 1993 AFL–CIO convention includes one by the head of the International Confederation of Free Trade Unions. An article by a Japanese trade unionist is also featured. Articles on 'foreign labour trends' for China, Denmark, France, Mexico and Taiwan also appear. The (almost) complete text of the *Communist Manifesto* appears on the list, but seems quite out of place among all the very practical and very American texts which surround it. One article on NAFTA (the North American Free Trade Agreement) appears on the list.

There are a number of lists, updated frequently, of union-made products and the union labels which mark them. These include a file containing information on union-made computers, as well as lists of union-made household appliances, cars and light trucks, coffeemakers, dishwashers, fans, garbage disposals, microwave ovens, and union hotels in Illinois. There are even two *poems* about things being union-made.

There are many files which one wouldn't find anywhere but on a trade union BBS, including:

- Articles reprinted from *Labour Notes*.
- Texts from *CPU*, an electronic publication for workers in the computer industry.
- Bulletins of the AFL–CIO's Lawyers Coordinating Committee.
- Newsletter of the Regional Players Orchestra Association, a union that represents symphony orchestras.
- Recommendations of the Dunlop commission on US labour law reform, plus other articles about US labour law reform. The full text of the National Labour Relations Act, with

commentary. US Court and National Labour Relations Board decisions affecting workers and unions. Names and contacts at the US Department of Labour. A biography of the US Secretary of Labour. A brief article by the new head of the US National Labour Relations Board.

- Articles about women and minorities in the workforce, and articles about health care programmes, actual and proposed.
- Labour-related videos available for locals.
- Text of the General Motors–United Auto Workers labour contract at the Saturn plant in Tennessee, which contains new and innovative approaches to labour-management relations.
- Texts of arbitration briefs and labour contracts.

In addition to all the labour texts, the Local 1220 BBS provides a range of other types of files which members and visitors can download for their education and pleasure. There is no charge for using the BBS other than the cost of a phone call. Nearly all the regular callers are from the Chicago area.

Meanwhile, Bob Kastigar is not optimistic about the survival of local trade union BBSs and their nerwork, Solinet. 'I think some of the labour BBSs are hanging on by sheer determination', he writes. 'The availability of the net is drawing people away from closed, iconoclast BBSs – unless the BBS has Internet access. The Local 1220 BBS gets about 7–10 calls a week. It isn't costing anything to maintain it, so I'll probably hang on a long time. The Solinet LabourChat Network is another matter. Its distribution is dwindling, not growing. And there is much less messaging than in the past.'

TradeZone BBS

Jerry Fray was born into the labour movement. Both his parents were union members; his mother was a telephone operator and member of the Communication Workers of America and his father was a truck driver and member of the powerful Teamsters union. He's a member of Local 919 of the International Union of Electrical Workers in Connersville, Indiana. His union has some 3,500 members, all of whom are employed at the Ford Electronics and Refrigeration Corporation, which supplies the Ford Motor Company with air-conditioning components, including air compressors, radiators, and condensers.

Fray has played an active role at all levels of the union. He's been a shop steward, acting chief steward and chairman of Local 919's Committee on Political Education (COPE). He's served as a delegate to the Whitewater Valley AFL–CIO Central Labour Council, and later as Vice President and President (for five years) of that body.

He founded the Union Label BBS in 1988, in his own time, with his own money. Fray asked the AFL–CIO Union Label Department in Washington DC for permission to use the name, and received it. (The name was later changed to the TradeZone BBS.) 'I started the BBS solely as a hobby', he says, 'and the union aspect was only a natural outshoot of my union activities.' The BBS was always intended to serve a local audience, despite its more ambitious name.

He runs the BBS using a perfectly ordinary home computer – a 486DX4-100 Mhz with 8 MB of memory and a hard drive with 1 GB. In the US, this is the kind of system that people purchase for their homes, and would hardly break the budget of an organisation. He uses only one phone line and a relatively slow (14,400 bps) modem. The additions that turn an ordinary home computer into a local trade union BBS are a dedicated phone line (only one in this case), WildCat software for running an electronic bulletin board, and three CD-ROMs online (soon to be upgraded to seven).

Like the Local 1220 BBS in Chicago, Fray's system has a number of text files with trade union information (including lists of union hotels, union-made products and the like – appropriate for a network server once known as the Union Label BBS). Unlike Bob Kastigar, Fray includes computer games which users can play online. Fray calls his BBS 'a general public' one; it is not officially linked to his union, and receives no support from it, financial or otherwise.

The BBS is used, says Fray, by a wide variety of people, from supervisors to Executive Board members in his local union. Not enough members use the BBS – no more than 50 members of his union local – at this time, but once Fray adds Internet access to it, that will probably change. One concrete result of the BBS has been that the AFL–CIO Boycott list reaches the editor of the local union newsletter.

It 'doesn't look very good from this end', he says, looking back at all the time and money he's put into the effort. 'I am a union activist', he says, but his 'union related BBS ... has no support from my own local.'

Labour Board BBS

In 1986, Mike Lostutter was working as an International Representative for the International Union of Electrical Workers (IUE) in southern Indiana. Like Bob Kastigar and Jerry Fray, he decided on his own initiative to attempt to link together several of the local unions he serviced using an electronic bulletin board – 'for the purpose of exchanging information and dialogue', he says.

The 'Labour Board BBS' was not a wild success, at first. Lostutter started modestly, using an IBM-compatible personal computer (XT) with only a 20 MB hard disk and 1 MB of random access memory (RAM). The BBS had only one phone line and during the first year only about 30 users. Of these, only ten were connected in any way with the trade union movement.

Lostutter set out to build two databases which would be useful to IUE members. One consisted of offers and counter-offers made during collective bargaining; the other was a database of grievance records. This was not a surprising choice, considering that contract negotiations and grievance handling are the bread and butter of local trade unions in the US. The company and union proposals were entered into computer database and spreadsheet programs. Lostutter encouraged IUE locals to buy personal computers and helped them get the programs off and running. The stored data became more and more useful over the years. 'Patterns developed', says Lostutter. It became possible to *predict* what a company would offer.

As for grievances, the new database allowed the union to track the decisions – published and unpublished – of professional arbitrators, who are used to settle disputes between unions and employers. Lostutter developed a base of information on arbitrators in the midwestern US. Unions could – and did – access this database in order to receive 'thumbnail sketches' of arbitrators *before* agreeing to use them in disputes.

In 1992, Lostutter moved east to New Jersey to begin work with the IUE Pension Fund. The Labour Board BBS moved with him – growing all the time. Today, Lostutter's BBS is still free of charge to users, still running on one phone line, and still working on a voluntary basis. But it's running on a much more powerful computer – and has grown from 30 to nearly 500 users.

Solidarity Network

The US Solinet Labour Network (not to be confused with Canada's much larger Solinet) is an 'echo network' linking local trade union bulletin boards in North America. All the messages are forwarded and shared among the participating BBSs – but the network doesn't allow private, routed, messages like FidoNet does. It began operating around 1988 as a link between two existing trade union bulletin boards – the International Union of Electrical Workers (IUE) BBS, run by Mike Lostutter, and Bob Kastigar's Local 1220 BBS. Later, other union BBSs joined the network. The hub of the network is still Local 1220's BBS in Chicago. Mike Lostutter is Solinet's administrator. Jerry Fray's TradeZone BBS is the Indiana state hub.

'It's been a very slow-growth process', says Kastigar, 'because it's all volunteer work and not usually sanction[ed] or supported by the local labour organisations.' By mid-decade, Solinet included a dozen local trade union BBSs from California, Illinois, Indiana, Minnesota, New Jersey, and New York in the US, and from British Columbia and Ontario in Canada. The Canadian BBSs represented hospital workers in Victoria and public service workers in Toronto. The US bulletin boards included the San Diego Labour Council, the Trade Zone BBS, two locals of the International Association of Fire Fighters, Locals 110 and 1220 of the International Brotherhood of Electrical Workers, and the national bulletin board of the International Union of Electrical Workers, based in Secaucus, New Jersey. Also involved are the Empire State Labour BBS, the Gull BBS, and the Peacock BBS.

Local Trade Union World Wide Web Sites

The Internet is not the World Wide Web. The Web is one tool among many which trade unionists can use to create the global labournet. Until now, we have devoted attention to several other tools being used by local and regional trade unions, including online discussion groups, email, and databases. It is only by using a *combination* of those tools that a local trade union creates a real local labournet.

Nevertheless, the Web is a powerful tool for getting local trade union messages across, especially in times of crisis – like during a strike. Many of the local labour Web sites which have been launched in the last few months are 'strike sites' used to promote public support for trade union struggles.

An example of this is the Web site set up by three locals of the Service Employees International Union in San Francisco. The 'Hillhaven Nursing Home Workers' Web site contains nearly four pages of information about the struggle between health care workers and the management of the Hillhaven Nursing Home. In addition to telling the workers' side of the strike and lock-out, the site gives out the union's telephone number to those who want more information or would like to volunteer and help; it allows users to send messages by email telling about personal experiences at the Hillhaven facilities; and it contains updates on the struggle, including an invitation to a demonstration in front of the nursing home.

Better-known labour struggles in the US, including the long and bitter struggle at the A.E. Staley company in Decatur, Illinois (known as the 'war zone'), have their own Web sites. The Staley company produces corn sweeteners, which are used by beverage manufacturers like Miller Beer, Pepsi Cola and Coca Cola. The more than two year lock-out of 763 Staley workers was punctuated by police violence against peacefully demonstrating workers and their supporters. Union and community pressure convinced Miller to stop using Staley. To increase pressure on Staley's other customers, the Web site offers access to Coca-Cola's email address. Users are encouraged to drop Coca-Cola's management a note, suggesting that they buy their corn sweetener somewhere else. As more corporations go online, offering up flashy Web sites and email addresses, this simple device can be a powerful tool in the hands of unions engaged in struggle.

The modest Staley Web site also promoted 'war zone' t-shirts (graphical files showing these in full colour were available for downloading) and allowed users to 'adopt a Staley family' by pointing their mouse at the right hyperlink.

Another major struggle which was the subject of a local labour Web site was the 1995 Boeing strike, involving some 32,500 machinists in the US states of Washington, Oregon and Kansas. It was the largest sustained strike in the US in the 1990s – and the workers won thanks to 'unity, militancy, determination and effectively stopping production', according to the Web site. They also built community support – in part, using the Internet.

The organisation 'Washington State Jobs With Justice' produced a Web site, which includes information about the issues, links to excerpts from the Boeing shop newspaper, information about a mass rally which was led by the new AFL–CIO leadership, links to another union currently negotiating with the giant manufacturer, and even the Boeing corporate Web site itself. 'Do you think Boeing would let their readers check out our page?' they ask. 'Click here if you think they should!' says an underlined phrase – clicking on it sends mail to Boeing. (This raises an interesting point. Maybe trade unions should demand in their contract negotiations reciprocal links between corporate and union Web sites; that would allow workers to always tell their side of the story.)

The International Union of Gas Workers (IUGW) in the city (not state) of Washington set up a detailed, seven-page Web site devoted to its struggle with the Washington Gas Company. Though their site included detailed information about the strike, it used no Internet tools. The union encouraged individuals to write letters to the heads of the company, providing a street address (but not a fax number or email address), and to those who wanted to contribute money to the union's 'Campaign to Fight Corporate Thugs' it provided a form which could be printed out and mailed with contributions and copies of protest letters sent to Washington Gas. There was no way to send the form by email, nor any way to contribute money online. The IUGW had simply posted its printed brochure online.

Not all local trade union Web sites are linked to an immediate struggle. Some exist as online brochures describing a union. The

Coalition of University Employees (CUE) at the University of California has just such a site, which addresses issues like why the workers should drop their current union (the American Federation of State, County and Municipal Employees) and join CUE – this includes testimonials from four workers. The site explains how a union goes about 'recertifying' – meaning changing which union represents the 19,000 clerical employees spread out over the university's nine campuses. The site also includes a list of campus contacts (including email addresses, but these are not hyperlinks). The new union's address is underlined, so it can be emailed to – but workers who want to join the CUE have to print out on paper the form which appears at the Web site and mail it in with their cheques. The sentence 'Please print out the form below using Netscape' appears, emphasising the hybrid nature of this site, which like so many others makes only partial use of the tools available.

A more established trade union, the Ohio State AFL–CIO, was the first state federation of labour in the US to put up a Web site of its own. (They've recently been joined by the Alska AFL–CIO as well.) This one includes many links to information about the labour movement in Ohio, state politics, consumer information and the like. An online newsletter, *NewsHound*, is available. The site includes links to the national AFL–CIO Web site and many other labour sites. This is a rare feature on local Web sites, which tend to focus on their own organisations and issues.

NewsHound is not the only local trade union publication available online through a Web site. *The Unionite*, published by the United Auto Workers Local 974, is accessible through the Web, as is the *L.A. [Los Angeles] Labour News* (the latter is delivered through Gopher).

Local labour Web sites appear all the time. A handful of these have appeared in Canada, including the BCTF and UNA sites, mentioned earlier, as well as Web sites for the Manitoba Organisation of Faculty Associations and Local 3909 of the Canadian Union of Public Employees. At least five state and local trade unions in Australia have launched Web sites recently.

The vast majority of local labour Web sites are in the US, though these still represent a small minority of the more than 40,000 local trade unions in that country. Among these sites are the following: the Screen Actors' Guild in Dallas, the American Postal Workers' Union locals in Philadelphia and Portland, Oregon, the Atlanta Federation of Teachers, the California Farmworkers' Union, Locals 6143 and 9119 of the Communication Workers of America, Local 14-M of the Graphic Communications International Union, Local 152 of the Hawaii Government Employees' Association (AFSCME), Ironworkers' Local 361 in New York, the Kentucky Association of State Employees, locals of the National Association of Letter Carriers in Colorado and Minnesota, Local 153 of the Office and Professional Employees' International Union, the Seattle Professional Engineering Employees' Association, the California State Council and at least five locals of the Service Employees' International Union, the Southeast Massachusetts Maritime Employees' Association, Local 7837 of the United Paperworkers' International Union, and the Wichita Engineering Association.

From Grassroots to Global Labournet

This book began by talking about the next International. So what do these local projects, some of them quite small, have to do with the creation of an immense global online trade union network? I can think of five reasons to pay attention to this phenomenon, and indeed to encourage it.

- Local labournets *offer examples of an online trade union press*, including daily labour newspapers. In Chapter 7 I'm going to propose in some detail the creation of an international labour daily newspaper/news service on the World Wide Web. I think that the trailblazers of this kind of online trade union journalism have not been the staffs of global labour organisations like the ICFTU but rather the striking newspaper workers who put out the *San Francisco Free Press* and *Detroit Journal*, the first daily labour newspapers on the Internet.
- Local labournets, even when they use closed academic or corporate networks, *teach trade unionists basic computer communications skills*, like how to use email. More than that, those unionists learn something about the culture of communication which flourishes on the networks. They acclimatise to the new information age.
- Local labournets, particularly the independent trade union networks and dial-up BBSs we examined, may *serve as a model for labour movements going online in developing countries* where access to the Internet is prohibitively expensive at this time. Even the US Solinet which connects local dial-up BBSs through a trade union 'echo network' could be a quite useful model in Africa, Asia or Latin America.
- Local labournets, when they do connect to the Internet, *teach trade unionists how to use what we've called 'new tools for a new International'* – including online discussion groups based on LISTSERV and electronic publishing through Gopher and the Web. For example, teachers in British Columbia use the same techniques to access their own provincial LISTSERV

mailing lists as they would accessing global lists like Labour-L or Union-D.

- Finally, local labournets *give trade unionists an access ramp of their own to the global information superhighway.* After all, how did we think the global labournet would work? Most workers aren't going to get up in the morning and log on to their international trade secretariat Web site in Brussels. They are probably going to access their local union's electronic press and discussion groups first, talking about local issues with local people. For the same reason, they are more likely to read a local newspaper than the *International Herald Tribune.* Local labournets also offer the advantage of always working in the local language, which will not always be the case in global networks. Even the very best multilingual Web sites don't work in more than a handful of languages.

People like Larry Kuehn, Gary Graff, Bob Kastigar, Laura Sager and Florence Ross may sometimes be frustrated by the enormous efforts they've put into what are, it seems, just local trade union networks. Often, other unionists (including trade union officials) either don't understand what they've done, or are hostile, or both. Their work is rarely acknowledged or appreciated. It often involves much sacrifice, including large investments of time, effort and sometimes money from their own pockets.

But it is not in vain. For all the reasons I have given above, I think these grassroots efforts are essential to the great tasks facing the international labour movement in the next few years: the creation of a true global labournet and a new International.

CHAPTER 5

National Trade Union Networks

A few short years ago, writing this chapter would have been extra-ordinarily easy. There were already local trade union experiments in networking back then. And some international trade union bodies (like the ITSs) were using telematics. But on a national level there was really only Solinet in Canada. I could have asked Marc Belanger for a few words on that, and the issue would have been settled.

Today, there is no way anyone can write a comprehensive and up-to-date account of national trade union use of computer communications. Too many countries are already involved and the situation is far too fluid. The best one can do is to produce a snapshot of labournets at the national level, which is what I have done here. This is the situation in the middle of 1996 in seven countries spread out over four continents. (At the end, I make brief observations on ten other countries as well.)

The material cannot be comprehensive even within a country. In some countries, not only does the national trade union centre have an online presence, but so do many trade unions. I will make no effort to report on all those unions, and will instead focus on a few examples in each country. Nor will I make a special effort to be comprehensive when it comes to other institutions connected to the labour movement (such as labour parties and workers' education associations), though some of these will be mentioned in passing.

One trend which has become clear recently is the increasing involvement of national trade union centres (particularly in the UK, US, Australia, New Zealand and South Africa) in the process of going online. Some of these centres previously had nothing more than a single email address; today they are offering Web sites, online mailing lists, conferences, databases – and support for affiliated unions.

What the future will bring is already pretty clear: *more* online discussion groups, *more* electronic publishing, *more* use of email in internal and external trade union communication. We begin with the country whose trade union movement's founder once summed up the programme of organised labour in that one word: 'more'.

US

When the Internet was created in the United States in the late 1960s, the American labour movement was at the peak of its strength. Union membership had grown in the 1960s from 18.1 to 20.7 million. Never before nor since have trade unions been as large and powerful. In the intervening three decades, the Internet grew exponentially – and the American trade unions declined just as rapidly.

Today the US is a country gone Internet-crazy. According to an October 1995 survey, no fewer than 24 million people in the US and Canada use the Internet. A more recent survey puts the number of US users at a 'mere' 9.5 million. The majority of these began using the net in 1995, confirming very fast Internet growth in the country where the global network of networks was first launched.

Meanwhile, the trade unions suffered disastrous losses of membership through the many long years of conservative Republican rule, as well as a loss of influence, political muscle, and self-confidence. In the last few years, there has been a small increase in the absolute number of trade union members. More important, at the end of 1995, a new leadership was elected in the national trade union centre, the AFL–CIO, which promises to organise millions of workers into trade unions and restore labour's power and prestige.

To even begin to do that, the labour movement in America, more than anywhere else in the world, is going to have to use computer communications effectively and intelligently. In the previous chapter, we saw some good examples of how this is being done on the local level, including online daily strike newspapers, local trade union bulletin boards, local Web sites and use of corporate and academic networks. Here, I want to focus on the use of computer networks at the national level by the AFL–CIO, the national trade unions, and other groups (most notably, LaborNet@IGC) which work in the field.

I'll divide up this section into four parts reflecting the four ways US trade unions use the networks:

- Dial-up national electronic bulletin boards.
- Conferences on commercial networks.
- Internet-based email discussion lists and USENET newsgroups.
- Gopher and Web sites.

In a moment, I'll discuss the advantages and disadvantages of each method, and give examples at the national level in the US. But for now it's important to define what I mean by each of the four terms.

A dial-up national electronic bulletin board is usually a single computer one accesses by dialling a particular telephone number using a modem. This is just like a local trade union BBS, as described in the previous chapter, except its audience is intended to be national, not local.

Conferences on commercial networks use existing computers, software and often vast user bases, but to access them, union members have to pay to subscribe to the particular commercial service, such as LaborNet@IGC or CompuServe.

Internet-based email discussion lists and USENET newsgroups are accessible by nearly everyone connected to the Internet, whether that be through academic or corporate networks, FidoNet, commercial online services or local Internet access providers. Of the two, email-based discussion lists potentially reach the larger audience, including those users who only dial in to local trade union BBSs.

Finally, Gopher and Web sites (and the later increasingly dominates and replaces the former) are means of both publishing information and, more recently, holding online discussions.

Dial-up national electronic bulletin boards

In the previous chapter, I discussed local trade union electronic bulletin boards. Such BBSs can be effective tools for networking and for strengthening local unions. One of their advantages is their low cost. Trade unionists who have access to personal computers with modems (at home or at work) can network with their brothers and sisters online for the cost of a local telephone call. Unlike commercial online services, or even the Internet (when the service is offered by access providers) there is no charge for the time online, other than what the telephone company charges.

In the United States, several trade unions – or individuals in such unions – have set up national trade union electronic bulletin boards. These require the payment of long-distance phone rates, unless one happens to live in the city in which the BBS is based. This is obviously a very expensive way to be online, and is therefore the opposite of the low-cost local trade union BBS described earlier. One way to cut costs for users would be to use toll-free phone numbers, but only one of the five national trade unions with BBSs that I know about has done this.

Three of the five are based in Washington DC, which is where many national unions have their headquarters. One was set up by the American Federation of Government Employees (AFGE), and includes a file server and a number of discussion areas. Because many AFGE employees work in and around the US capital, for them the BBS is only a local phone call away. The National

Association of Broadcast Employees and Technicians (NABET), on the other hand, does not have a primarily Washington-based membership, and its BBS was actually originally based in Chicago. This national union, whose BBS is considered quite lively, does have a toll-free number for its members to use. The Washington headquarters of the International Union of Operating Engineers (IUOE) also runs a national BBS, but without offering, as far as I know, a toll-free access number.

Two other national unions in the US have their BBSs based outside Washington. One is the American Postal Workers' Union (APWU) whose bulletin board is located in Grand Rapids, Michigan. The other was set up by the Communication Workers of America (CWA) and it operates out of Ohio. The CWA service is a first for the American labour movement: it's designed to help with the union's organising drive at the giant NCR corporation.

Even if all these national trade union BBSs were to adopt toll-free telephone numbers, they appear to me to be transitional media which will be displaced over time by Internet email and the World Wide Web. As it stands, each one uses different software presenting different interfaces to users. And even to know about their existence, unionists would have to read about them somewhere – as opposed to just clicking on them at a Web site. These BBSs, unlike labour Web sites, cannot easily link into each other. Each connection demands a separate telephone call.

For these reasons, I would expect national unions in the US to increasingly follow examples like the Sheet Metal Workers (with their Web site) or the International Association of Fire Fighters (with their Internet-based email discussion list). One of the five examples I gave here – NABET, the only one with a toll-free access number – has already launched a Web site.

Union Conferences on Commercial Networks

Back in 1992, before Internet hysteria swept the US (and the world) the AFL–CIO launched its 'electronic forum' – LaborNET – on the CompuServe network. At the time, that probably seemed like a good idea. CompuServe was then the largest online network in the United States. (Today, with an estimated 3,000,000 members, it's still pretty big.) Internet access was largely closed off to ordinary people who were not academics. And CompuServe was not expensive; it cost less than $10 per month to access its basic package of services. Unlimited access to LaborNET cost another $3 each month. LaborNET included four main sections:

- A library. This section includes AFL–CIO position papers on key issues, fact sheets, public policy statements, and the like.

According to LaborNET, 'to many users, the library is LaborNET's most valuable component'.

- Messages. This is LaborNET's online discussion group, including person-to-person email, requests for information, and continuing discussions.
- Conference. These are online 'chat rooms' where live conversation takes place between trade unionists. Sometimes a guest speaker is involved.
- Announcements. This is where LaborNET informs members about online conferences and changes in the network.

Individual unions could have their own message forums, libraries and chat rooms.

The AFL–CIO went about signing up national unions to use the network, and though this began slowly, today a significant number of such unions are already using it. But LaborNET's strength back in 1992 – its availability on CompuServe – had become its weakness by mid-decade. Trade unionists who were online through America Online, or the Microsoft Network, or any other commercial network, or directly connected to the Internet, could not access LaborNET without first joining CompuServe. The AFL–CIO partly fixed this with the launch in 1995 of its site on the World Wide Web – more on this in a moment – but remained committed to using the forums on CompuServe.

Meanwhile, the AFL–CIO Executive Council adopted a statement in May 1995 on 'the Information Superhighway' calling on 'all affiliates, state federations and local central bodies to explore ways that the labour movement can use the new communications technologies to promote labour's historic vision of a greater voice for working people on the job and in their communities'. Apparently, someone was listening – or natural processes of change were taking their course.

In mid-1994, LaborNET had only 360 subscribers. A year later, the number of LaborNET subscribers had quadrupled to 1,400, and was 'growing by leaps and bounds', according to David St John, Assistant to the AFL–CIO President.

The Communications Workers of America and the International Brotherhood of Electrical Workers, two national unions affiliated the AFL–CIO, 'have brought hundreds of their members into LaborNET', St John told me. Each union using the net would get its own private forum, in addition to access to everything else LaborNET had to offer. 'We're getting dozens of new sign-ups each week ... several other unions are now beginning the process of bringing large numbers of their own members on-line', he said.

In January 1996, LaborNET claimed 2,500 subscribers. Nevertheless, some trade unionists were critical of the AFL–CIO's decision to use a closed, commercial network when the Internet had already opened its gates to the masses. One of these, according to an article published in *Information Week*, was the founder of Canada's Solinet, Marc Belanger. Belanger argued that this decision limited LaborNET's value to the rank and file; he urged AFL–CIO leaders to follow the Canadian model and set up their network independently of the commercial online services. 'There is power in knowing how the networks work', Belanger was quoted as saying.

In a recent posting to the USENET newsgroup alt.society.labor-unions, a member of the Communications Workers of America – which uses LaborNET to provide collective bargaining reports to members – complained about the decision to use CompuServe. 'It would be nice', he wrote, 'if CWA and other unions would use something different from CompuServe for this. There are a lot of us out here that don't use this service. ... Why can't I find a means to get updates using the service I have without having to buy two additional services? It appears to me most of the labour force has been locked out of any updates or forms of dialogue.'

A sharper criticism came from trade union organiser Rand Wilson, who said that the AFL–CIO *deliberately* limited access to LaborNET from the beginning. 'They want to control the information just like everybody else.' LaborNET coordinator Blair Calton said that the network was aimed at shop 'stewards and above from the 600 city central and 51 state labor federations' which led one journalist to deride the network as 'primarily a means for union bosses to talk to other bosses'. But rank-and-file trade unionists who use LaborNET didn't agree. Bill Richards, a member of the International Brotherhood of Electrical Workers Local 640, wrote that 'the AFL–CIO's forum on CompuServe does *not* exclude the rank-and-file – if it did, I wouldn't be on it. In fact, I gather that the attitude there is "the more the merrier".'

A couple of years before the AFL–CIO launched its LaborNET on CompuServe, a group of movement activists had already begun LaborNet on the APC-affiliated Institute for Global Communications (IGC) network. (The name 'labornet' is obviously not copyrighted.)

The IGC network includes a number of new social movements using computer communications, among them PeaceNet, EcoNet, and WomensNet. All of these have been larger and more successful – so far – than the LaborNet effort. Though LaborNet@IGC (as it is now known) was created in 1990, it had only 350 online subscribers by early 1995, according to an article by one of its steering committee members, Doug Ohmans. By the end of the year, membership had more than doubled, but still did not reach a thousand.

LaborNet@IGC defines itself as 'a community of labour unions, activists and organizations using computer networks for information-sharing and collaboration with the intent of increasing the human rights and economic justice of workers'. The LaborNet@IGC Web site, which we'll come to in a moment, is extraordinarily useful, and probably constitutes the core of the emerging global labour Internet, with the most comprehensive list I've seen of labour Web sites and email addresses. If there is any one place to start touring the labour Internet, this is it.

LaborNet@IGC is run by a seven-member steering committee including activists in the teachers', chemical workers', and service employees' unions, as well as representatives from such pro-labour organisations as the Labour Video Project and Holt Labour Library. Its coordinator is Steven Hill, a community organiser and trade unionist.

What LaborNet@IGC offers that is not available from their Web site is a long list of online conferences. These are broken down into five broad categories; the following are just a sampling of the online conferences available:

- Trade and Industry: auto workers; rail workers; teamsters; nurses, hospital and health care workers; maritime workers and longshoremen; postal workers; transit workers; hotel employees; petrochemical workers; workers in publishing and printing; construction trades; garment and textile workers; airline industry; teachers.
- Global: international labour issues; Mexico; Canada; Asia; the former Soviet Union; the UK; Middle East; Brazil.
- Privatisation and the Public Sector: global and US privatisation issues; labour and the public sector; work hours; health and safety; the environment; employee rights.
- Labour News and Resources: news and analysis; labour events; labour calendar (for the US); discussion about a proposed labour party in the US; video and print resources for labour; labour movement videos; trade union organising; labour education; labour and technology; labour newspapers.

Two of the conferences are not in English – 'sindicatos' (which is a discussion of labour solidarity in the Spanish language) and 'pt.brasil' (which comes from the Workers Party of Brazil, in Portuguese). Even though we've placed this discussion under the heading 'US', it is important to note the presence of many non-US trade unionists in these discussions. When looking at the 'labr.cis' conference, one is listening to, and exchanging views with, Russian trade unionists. (The conference originates on GlasNet, the Russian APC affiliate.) The 'labr.uk' conference features a number of British trade union participants. Most of the information in the 'labr.asia' group comes from trade union activists in places like Hong Kong and Japan.

The LaborNet@IGC conferences also 'mirror' a number of LISTSERV email mailing lists, including Publabor, United, and Labor-L. One does not need to separately subscribe to these, and mail from these groups need not fill up one's mailbox.

Conference postings are available from their very beginnings, sometimes going back several years, making them valuable research tools. While looking up information on trade unions and the environment, for example, I was delighted to discover the 'labr.environment' conference with its dozens of postings going back over the years.

The conferences vary in quality and liveliness. Some of them are really just a single person conveying news from time to time. Others are daily barrages of messages and responses to messages. I was told that LaborNet@IGC has no way of knowing how many people access each particular conference, but that the number of messages might be a good way of telling just how active a conference was.

If we compare the two US labournets we can see that each one has its advantages and disadvantages. For example:

- *Participation:* The AFL–CIO network has many more participants than the IGC one, and this is likely to be the case in the future as more trade unions sign up with the 'official' network.
- *Cost:* The IGC network is also signicantly more expensive than the AFL–CIO one. If one uses the network for one hour per week, the cost of using LaborNet@IGC is roughly 50 per cent more than using the AFL–CIO network. In addition the value added of being on the AFL–CIO network – all the resources available on CompuServe – is impressive.
- *International participation:* This is where the IGC network has huge advantages over the AFL–CIO one. As labournets are created around the world, many of them using the APC network, there will be an ever-increasing number of non-US members of LaborNet@IGC's conferences. The AFL–CIO LaborNET will remain a place where US trade unionists meet to exchange news and views – alone.
- *Content:* Now that the AFL–CIO has launched its Web site, including the full text of its weekly newspaper, the *AFL–CIO News*, one does not need to sign up to LaborNET to know the federation's positions on issues. Meanwhile, LaborNet@IGC with its dozens of conferences on a wide range of issues seems to offer the greatest potential for global information sharing and discussion.

Each labournet has something to offer trade unionists and each has its drawbacks. It would be helpful here if the two could try to work together a little more closely, maybe initially 'mirroring' conferences.

But the fact that *both* of them require trade unionists to join a network – when many trade unionists are *already* paying to use the Internet – is a drawback to both networks. A study done in early 1996 showed that 30 per cent of Internet users in the US were connecting to the net using America Online – not CompuServe, nor IGC. Those millions of Americans include many trade unionists – and unless they also pay up to join CompuServe or IGC, they are cut off from *both* established national labournets.

One solution would be for both LaborNET and LaborNet@IGC to offer their conferences as LISTSERV email-based mailing lists. Another solution would be to offer the conferences as USENET newsgroups. Offering the conferences through World Wide Web sites is probably the most elegant solution, but until most people with Internet access have access to the Web – and this is not yet the case – this solution too would exclude most people.

In addition to the two labournets which are designed to serve trade unionists regardless of their particular union affiliation, a number of national trade unions in the US have used existing commercial networks to provide services to members. Among these are the International Brotherhood of Electrical Workers, which has used the both the AFL–CIO's LaborNET on CompuServe and its own 'chat room' on America Online. The Service Employees' International Union and the Communication Workers of America have stuck with CompuServe. Teachers unions were reported to have used the Prodigy online network for their own purposes.

Even the GEnie network hosted a trade union – the National Air Traffic Controllers' Association (NATCA). The 10,000-member union has a 'dedicated area' on GEnie, which is used as a forum for ideas, group discussions, and as an information resource. As NATCA member Janice Kusher told me, 'We have found this to be extremely useful in disseminating information both up and down the chain.' In fact, she added, NATCA does this today 'always with greater speed and efficiency than management'.

Though GEnie is both one of the smallest commercial online services – with only 55,000 subscribers by early 1996 – and is admittedly 'cumbersome', Kushner says that it is the least expensive of the online services. Some NATCA locals are quite small, and keeping costs down is a primary consideration for the union. 'It is strange to me', she writes, 'that people who are at ease with technology still manage to avoid being online.' Though some 80 per cent of the approximately 400 air traffic facilities are online, only slightly more than 300 NATCA members participate in the

online network. 'Only the most computer-comfortable and
outspoken members (and their opinions) are represented.'

Internet-based Email Discussion Lists and USENET Newsgroups

Despite all the hype about the World Wide Web, with its graphics,
full motion video, virtual reality and the like, the traditional
LISTSERV discussion list remains a potent tool for trade unionists.
Though the number of such lists has not been growing exponentially,
it has indeed been growing. In Appendix 2 I list several LISTSERV
lists which serve the labour movement in the US and around the
world. (I also explain there how to subscribe to each one.) Here I
just want to say a few words about some of these groups:

- *Labor-L:* This is the 'Forum on Labor in the Global Economy',
  and is probably the most important trade union LISTSERV
  mailing list. It reaches hundreds of trade unionists and
  academics close to the labour movement, mostly in the US
  and Canada. The list's moderator is Sam Lanfranco of York
  University in Toronto. Discussion on this list focuses on
  current labour topics, and has been an invaluable source of
  information for me in writing this book. An example of how
  Labor-L can be used was demonstrated during the San
  Francisco newspaper strike, when articles from the online *San
  Francisco Free Press* were posted to here. Labor-L postings are
  archived at the Economic Democracy Information Network
  (EDIN) Web site and Gopher, and are mirrored to
  LaborNet@IGC.
- *H-Labor:* This is the labour history discussion list, one of the
  highest quality groups I've ever had the privilege to participate
  in. Most of the participants seem to be US and Canadian
  academics who teach in labour studies or history programmes
  at universities. The list is part of H-Net, an international
  academic network focusing on the humanities. Postings to the
  list are archived. H-Labor's moderator is Seth Wigderson, at
  the University of Maine. I'll give just one example of how I've
  used this list. To write up the history of strike newspapers in
  the US – which you read in the previous chapter – I posted
  a message to the list. More than a dozen responses came in,
  rich in information and pointers to more information. And
  here's the remarkable part: thanks to Wigderson's work as
  moderator, no one repeated anyone else. Each person told
  me about their own town's experience, and each story enriched
  my own account of the history of daily strike newspapers.
- *Labnews*: Nathan Newman of the Economic Democracy
  Information Network launched this list in August 1995. He

subtitled it 'News of Labor Unions and Workplace Organizing'.
Unlike many LISTSERVs, this is not really a discussion list,
but a means of distributing news – labour news – to subscribers.
To those people without access to other online sources of
labour news this is not a bad way to get news out. Even
though Newman was open to posting international labour
news, most of the news is US news, and most of the list
participants are from the US. The discussion list is sponsored
by the University of California at Berkeley's Center for
Community Economic Research.

- *United:* Early in 1994, a notice appeared on the Internet of a
  new 'unmoderated, uncensored email discussion group
  intended for anyone with an interest in the labour movement.
  Subscribers may include members of any union, scholars or
  those interested in organizing a union.' The discussion group
  was called 'United' and it was set up by Len Wilson, a
  member of the International Association of Machinists.
  Wilson invited people to write about the following subjects:
  reports of labour struggles around the world; the decline of
  unionism in the US; bringing unions into the Information Age;
  modern union communications; and the role of unions in local,
  state and national politics. 'United' is one of several labour-
  oriented bulletin boards aimed at rank-and-file workers based
  at the Colorado Cougar in Thornton, Colorado. 'United'
  postings are archived at the EDIN Web site and Gopher and
  are mirrored at LaborNet@IGC.
- *Labor-Party:* This group discusses the question of forming a
  labour party in the US, and is particularly involved with the
  Labour Party Advocates. It is mirrored in the LaborNet@IGC
  conferences.
- *Publabor:* This list, moderated by K.T. Buller, is for public
  sector workers. It is mirrored in the LaborNet@IGC
  conferences and archived at the EDIN Web site and Gopher.

Not all email-based mailing lists are open to the public or even
widely known. Some are internal union projects and have not
received a lot of publicity. An example of this is the online discussion
group of the International Association of Fire Fighters (IAFF).

Lt. David Colee, a fire fighter with the New Smyrna Beach, Florida
Fire Department, is a member of IAFF Local 2271. He told me
about 'a small, non-official mailing list dedicated solely to IAFF
members'. He runs the list manually and says that it has fewer than
a hundred online members – 'but we also have not advertised it
aggressively', he adds. The national union headquarters in
Washington DC is aware of his effort, and at least one ranking
member of the national staff participates in the list. Colee is still

optimistic about the potential, saying that he plans to pressure the union to do more. 'It seems that the Internet would be the ideal place', he says, 'to bring together all our Brothers and Sisters, and to spread the word of what we are about to the world.'

Open any book or read any article about the Internet and you'll immediately come upon the term 'USENET'. USENET is a vast global bulletin board on thousands of topics in which hundreds of thousands of people – perhaps millions – exchange views, share information, insult one another (this is called 'flaming') and do whatever else one can do with a bulletin board.

Though everyone writing about the Internet claims that absolutely *everything* is being discussed, USENET's newsgroups still seem primarily aimed at the audience for which they were originally intended, American university students and faculty.

There are numerous groups discussing technical and scientific issues, arts and music, with a heavy emphasis on popular culture. Politics are discussed by a wide range of newsgroups. But the international labour movement has only one USENET newsgroup, known as 'alt.society.labor-unions'.

The newsgroup was launched by John Baglow, the Executive Vice President of the Public Service Alliance of Canada (PSA). His original idea, he told me, was 'a moderated newsgroup on labour issues' but the freenet he was using 'did not seem to have the capacity to have moderated groups'. Baglow doesn't know if anyone has archived the postings anywhere, and admits that most postings were coming from the US. 'We are now seeing more participation from Canada and the UK', he adds. This may be connected to the fact that the newsgroup has gained publicity by becoming a link on a wide variety of labour Web sites, including those of Bagow's PSA, LaborNet@IGC and the Trades Union Congress in the UK.

Having hung around 'alt.society.labor-unions' for a few months, I noticed the following:

- Very few actual trade unionists, let alone union staff or officials, seem to participate.
- The postings are overwhelmingly from and about the US.
- No one seems to be in charge.

The very fact that the newsgroup is named 'alt.society.labor-unions' means that it has been placed outside of the main newsgroups, in the 'alt' (alternative) hierarchy, which is notorious for its Elvis sightings and pornographic binary files. 'Alt' newsgroups do *not* reach every Internet site, and I myself was unable to access 'alt.society.labor-unions' for a long time as a result. Postings to the group have included reprints of articles from the US Communist Party's newspaper – yes, that still exists – and a discussion of the death penalty.

The Communications Workers of America used the newsgroup as part of its email campaign targetting Bell Atlantic, the second largest provider of exchange telephone service in the US. Their posting to alt.society.labor-unions – which originated in the CWA's America Online account – gave readers basic information about the dispute between union and company, and repeatedly pointed users to the union's Web site for more information. (For those of us reading USENET postings using Netscape software, the Web site address appeared as a clickable link, allowing simple access from the CWA 'action alert' directly to its Web site.) This was good use by a union of several different networks and tools, including American Online and the Internet, email, USENET and the World Wide Web.

Gopher and Web Sites

Trade union Web sites are springing up like mushrooms after a storm. This is just as true of national unions as it is of locals, as I pointed out in the previous chapter. Several of these warrant the name 'megasite' because they include so much material and so many pointers to other locations.

Both of the labournets – at IGC and the AFL–CIO – have impressive Web sites to offer. The AFL–CIO's 'LaborWEB' was accessed less than 200 times per day on average, according to its own counter, prominently displayed on the Web site. This is not an impressive figure for a 13.6 million member federation. Nevertheless, the site is worthy of attention and includes the following main types of information:

- AFL–CIO Policy Statements
- Press Releases
- Boycott List
- The AFL–CIO Organising Institute
- The Stand UP Campaign for America's Working Families
- The current edition of the *AFL–CIO News*

In addition, the site offers a prominent link to the *Detroit Journal* – online daily newspaper of the striking newspaper workers – and many other labour sites. The site promotes subscriptions to LaborNET, though one hardly thinks this will be tempting to someone who already has Internet and World Wide Web access.

It is important to note that at least one of the features now offered by the Web site was previously offered only to CompuServe subscribers – the weekly newspaper of the federation, the *AFL–CIO News*. This is an important step forward, and an excellent use of the Web for online trade union publishing.

NATIONAL TRADE UNION NETWORKS   115

The LaborNet@IGC Web site is, as I've pointed out before, one of the very best labour sites on the Internet. Its list of trade unions and labour-related groups online is probably the most comprehensive one on the Internet. The site also offers an impressive list of 'publications, news services and print materials' related to the labour movement. Among these are:

- Government statistics and publications, including the US Bureau of Labour Statistics and Occupational Safety and Health Administration.
- Online labour publications like *Working People, Union Plus, L.A. Labour News, Labour Centre Reporter, Labour Activist, Industrial Worker* and *The Unionite*.
- Studies and reports about working people and the labour movement.
- Information about labour legislation.
- Labour cartoons, posters, murals, songs and more.
- Several links to 'labour and computers' sites, including a list of labour BBSs, LISTSERV lists, and a specialist in designing labour Web pages.

In conclusion, the site is somewhat eclectic, and includes some old material, but is updated so frequently that it is invaluable. No wonder every major labour Web site in the world contains a link to LaborNet@IGC.

In addition to the two megasites (a third might be that maintained by the Economic Democracy Information Network), several dozen national trade unions already had Web sites up and running by mid-1996. These included the American Federation of State, County and Municipal Employees, Communications Workers of America, United Auto Workers, International Brotherhood of Teamsters, UNITE, National Association of Letter Carriers, Office and Professional Employees' International Union, Service Employees' International Union, Sheet Metal Workers' International Association, Stone Cutters' Union of North America, United Electrical Workers, United Mineworkers of America, United Paperworkers' International Union and the United Steelworkers of America.

Some of these are among the very largest unions in the country; others are quite small. Some of the sites were unusual; for example, the United Electrical Workers were touting an international solidarity project with their Mexican counterparts. Other sites were simply online brochures about the union.

Edward B. Armour, the 'webmaster' for the Sheet Metal Workers, told me a bit about how his union got its site on the World Wide Web. Armour is an organiser for the union in Utah. He attended a course on 'information technology for union leaders' at the

AFL–CIO's George Meany Centre for Labour Studies. 'One of the projects assigned students', he said, 'is to develop an action plan/presentation to convince their local/international decision-making bodies to develop a presence on the Web and also to take advantage of the research opportunities available through the Internet along with the other modern information technologies.'

Armour came back to Salt Lake City and wrote up the union's Web site. Initially, he was met by curiosity and technophobia – but not hostility. Armour wrote to the international union asking for permission to go ahead, got that in May 1995, and on 1 June 1995 the Sheet Metal Workers became one of the first national unions in the US with a Web site. By year's end, the site had a phenomenal 90,000 visits recorded.

As Armour lists them, the subjects the site addresses include: 'Union benefits, how to share in those benefits, workplace rights, workplace safety, pictures of our skilled craftsmen in the US and Canada doing sheet metal work of every description, political education and activism, and why people should use a union sheet metal contractor.' All this, he concludes, costs only a few hundred dollars a year. '*That*', he emphasises, 'is cost effective.'

The union uses the Web site and email in solidarity campaigns. Members write in with information and the union uses email in what Armour calls 'rapid response' communication to get things moving.

'Our membership and the general electronic public have been overwhelmingly in favour of our presence on the Web', says Armour. 'In literally hundreds of email messages, we have never received a negative comment.' The site serves both to educate members and non-members about the union. 'The site has lead to greater participation by our members at the grassroots level (always a positive thing)', Armour commented, 'and has actually generated new members and business for our signatory contractors as people on the web seek us out to ask for help and information.'

Use of the World Wide Web for this union 'continues to change the way we perceive of doing things and ignites not only public interest but serves our membership in a way they never imagined. *Anything* that increases your abilty to communicate, whatever your audience, is a positive thing.'

Canada

Canada is the second largest country in the world. It spans six time zones. For generations, this has made it extremely difficult for national organisations, including trade unions, to function. But not anymore.

The launch of the Solidarity Network (Solinet) a decade ago by Marc Belanger and the Canadian Union of Public Employees has allowed the exchange of email, the holding of permanent and special online conferences, and the transfer of computerised files. It was the first national labournet and remains the most important experiment ever undertaken in large-scale use of computer networking by the labour movement.

Before going into some detail about Solinet today, I want to say a few words about the Canadian networks in general – and the Canadian labour movement. Canada has the third largest number of Internet host computers in the world, right behind Germany and the United States – and ahead of countries like Britain, Australia and Japan. It's an Internet-intensive country, and has been so for some time. FreeNets have sprung up in several parts of Canada, allowing local access at no charge. It is in this context that we should understand the success of local, regional and national labournets in Canada.

The Canadian trade union movement is also relatively vigorous, particularly compared to its southern neighbour. Trade union density in Canada (union membership as a percentage of employed workers) fell by only 1.4 per cent in the 1980s, while it plummeted 28.7 per cent in the US and 18 per cent in Britain during the same period. By the end of the 1980s, trade union density in Canada was more than double that in the United States, and exceeded that of Germany. That this is considered a success was made clear to me by an article I received (for the magazine *Workers' Education*) from Bob White, President of the Canadian Labour Congress, who hailed trade union education as one of the methods used by Canada's labour movement to retain its strength during a difficult period.

Solinet was born and grew up during a time of rapid expansion of computer networks in Canada and trade union successes in retaining their strength. I've already mentioned Solinet's online conferences (in Chapter 2) and the early years of the network (in Chapter 3). Here I want to go into somewhat greater detail about how the network functions today – and what it plans for the future.

Here are some of the things Solinet does today:

- Education: Solinet is used by a number of unions for educational activities. There are four ways it does this: runs courses on the computer system; provides after-course support; links trade union educators; and supplies information through newsletters. We already mentioned in Chapter 3 Solinet's very first course on technological change. Over a hundred trade unionists from all over Canada took part in that. Years later, people still return to the conference to re-read some of the messages. Another example of an online course was one given by a health and safety instructor to about 30 unionists. The instructor was based in Toronto; the students were scattered across the country. After-course support has been critical. During one week-long, traditional face-to-face class on computer basics, students only had one day of hands-on training. But they were able to discuss problems with the course instructor even after returning home. CUPE's fifteen education representatives based throughout Canada rarely had a chance to meet before Solinet was launched. 'They too often learned their trade and resolved their problems in lonely isolation', says Belanger. Using Solinet, they discuss things like setting up schools and problems they're having, both in a private online conference, and using email. Using Solinet's file transfer mechanism, they co-write and edit educational manuals.

• Ongoing, online conferences: These cover international labour, free trade, the environment, women's rights, health and safety, training, pensions, privatisation, workers' compensation, and books.

• *SoliNotes*: This is a weekly labour news service reporting on Canadian labour news. Belanger puts it out every Monday. News is collected from a number of sources, including newspaper databases. (Among these are the *Toronto Globe and Mail*, Canadian Press, Associated Press and Reuters.) Local unions send in news which might not make the national media. Belanger sifts through it all and then writes it up. The result is about six pages of material. 'One of the significant things about *SoliNotes* that I've noticed', Belanger told me, 'is that it reports on a different kind of news. Unions have traditionally put out monthly newsletters. These newsletters, because of their frequency, tend to concentrate on features or long-running issues. What is missed (and what *SoliNotes* picks up) is all that short-time related activity that rarely makes labour publications: a two-day strike, a wildcat, a small demo.' Belanger also pointed out that much of what the labour movement does, it does locally. The national media pays no attention. As a result, 'members of the same union in other parts of the country don't get to hear about activity in other parts of the country'. Solinet members will often take the material off the computer, print it out, and pass around photocopies to those who aren't connected to the net. This has allowed the Canadian labour movement to develop the kind of weekly press service it always wanted but could never have afforded (because of printing and distribution costs). It is also a model of what could be done in the international labour movement, as I explain later on.

- Strike support: Solinet has been used to transfer leaflets from trade union public relations departments out to negotiators in the field.
- Negotiating committee coordination: CUPE has committees which represent workers over wide areas of the country. Members of those committees now keep in touch with each other through Solinet while not negotiating. They also use Solinet as a way of keeping in touch with the union membership during those negotiations.
- Settlement reports: After negotiations are complete, reports on settlements are uploaded to Solinet using electronic forms.
- Grievance tracking: Solinet has a conference devoted to grievances, and this has created a database which can be keyword searched. In addition, Solinet has a real grievance tracking program, but this is not available online.
- Political lobbying: Solinet keeps activists in touch with each other during lobbying campaigns. The network is also used to distribute model briefs which unions can edit and present to government agencies.
- Program support: Solinet distributes software, including a grievance tracking program (mentioned above) and one which produces mailing lists. Using the network's conferencing facility, Solinet gives online support to unions using the software.

Solinet has had to grapple with an audience that didn't always know much about computers or computer communications. One important solution to the problem of training was the development of an easy-to-use front-end program to access the network. Users also receive clearly written manuals. And CUPE provides them with demonstration diskettes that they can use before placing their first phone call to the network.

'By 1995', writes Belanger, 'Solinet was beginning to show its age. The industry had learned how to produce the second generation of computer conferencing systems. Our technology became outdated.'

Solinet's future plans revolve around integrating it much more in the Internet. Solinet plans an interactive site on the World Wide Web which will include conferences, international labour news, and a database on the global trade union movement. According to Belanger, Solinet is working with Simon Fraser University which is writing special software for the project. Belanger has also offered to let Solinet host the proposed International Labour University – but more on that in Chapter 7.

Solinet was the first use by a national union in Canada of computer communications. But other national unions have followed in CUPE's wake, usually with Web sites. Among these are the Canadian Farmworkers' Union; the Public Service Alliance of Canada as well as UnionNet – a joint project between Solinet and Web Networks, the Canadian affiliate of the APC network. The Canadian Committee on Labour History has a Web site with links to its publication, *Labour/Le Travail*. Finally, there are several Web sites of the provincial and federal New Democratic Party, the Canadian affiliate of the Socialist International.

Australia

Australia is one of the most net-intensive countries on earth, with only four countries having more Internet host computers. Its labour movement has also been one of the most powerful, and by the end of the 1980s – despite a significant decline in trade union density – union membership as a percentage of workers was higher in Australia than in Canada, Germany, France, Italy, Japan, the UK and the US. Nevertheless, the Australian trade unions have been slow to get on the network, and had nothing comparable to Canada's Solinet, even though the labour movement in their sprawling country faces some of the same problems encountered by nation-wide trade unions in Canada.

One person pushing for Australian unions to make more, and better, use of the Internet is Adrian Bates. Bates used to work for Poptel in Manchester. After returning to Australia from Britain, Bates went to talk to the Australian Council of Trade Unions (ACTU) about 'labour telematics'. But, as he told me, 'they were a bit behind the times'.

Bates is now working with Vicnet, a state-wide network in Victoria whose main interest is in getting Internet access for rural people facing the 'tyranny of distance'. Trade unions, he admits, are of only marginal interest to Vicnet. Nevertheless, Bates has focused on signing up local trade unions for 'mailboxes' on the network. By late summer 1995, only five unions had done so. They had not set up any discussion lists, newsgroups, or anything like that. But interest did arise within this small group to display information on the net, through the World Wide Web. 'Vicnet is trying to get local unions involved', says Bates, 'but it is hard work.'

Meanwhile, Bates maintains a 'Labour and Trade Union' page on the Web with numerous links to Australian and other – mostly British – sites. Another key site for Australian trade union information has always been the Centre for Labour Studies at the University of Adelaide which had an active Gopher site long before there was a World Wide Web. (To give an idea of how the Internet works, I was able to read back issues of online Canadian labour publications, including *SoliNotes* and the British Columbia Teachers' Federation first on this site in Adelaide.)

The Australian Council of Trade Unions was among the very first to launch a Web site. ACTU is moving in other ways too, including the launching of WorkNet, a collective bargaining system for unions all over the country.

The Labour Council of New South Wales launched its own LaborNet in December 1995 – and the launch included a speech by the state's premier, Bob Carr. (Photos of the launch ceremony are available on the Web site.) The LaborNet Web site includes information about unions, links to no fewer than eleven local trade unions, a couple of online publications (including *NetWork*), a labour library catalogue, and even 'StreetWize' comics. LaborNet also provides email-based mailing lists for unionists.

Other state and local trade unions with Web sites include the National Tertiary Education Industry Union Bendigo sub-branch; the Australian Capital Territory (ACT) branch of the Construction Forestry Mining and Energy Union; the Community and Public Sector Union at the University of Tasmania; the United Trades and Labour Council of South Australia; and the Trades and Labour Council of the ACT. Others are going online all the time.

New Zealand

Another country where one would expect a vigorous national labournet, but which has been rather inactive, is New Zealand. Only in 1996 did unions in this country begin to use the Internet. One must understand this development in the context of the terrifying onslaught of recent right-wing governments against the once-powerful labour movement in these islands.

In May 1991 the Employment Contracts Act was passed, making collective bargaining virtually illegal. Trade union membership suffered a cataclysmic fall from 603,000 at the time the law was enacted down to 375,000 at the end of 1994. In addition, the trade union movement recently split into two national federations. New Zealand's trade unions desperately need to use every tool at the disposal of the labour movement, including computer-mediated communications, if they are to survive.

Peter Hall-Jones in Wellington is one of the people trying to make that happen. He's been working with established unions in New Zealand to get them online through the local APC affiliate. The New Zealand Council of Trade Unions does have an email address. And in early 1996, the CTU did launch an extensive Web site. The site includes many more features than the standard HTML pages found on most Web sites. Among these are a trade union mailing list called 'union-talk', an FTP server offering up union-related documents, and even a link to a USENET newsgroup for New Zealand trade unionists called 'planetnz. unions'. In addition to these, the site includes a directory of the council's 22 affiliate unions, the text of the newsletter *CTU Work*, links to other labour sites around the world, and information on the labour movement's attitude toward the 1996 national elections in New Zealand.

South Africa

When talking about the Internet in Africa, and certainly about trade union use of it, one is really only talking about the Republic of South Africa. There are some other countries in Africa with Internet access, but not many. Countries on Africa's northern fringe, including Tunisia, Algeria and Egypt, are connected to the net through Europe. Universities in a number of African capitals sometimes have some kind of connection. But the vast majority of users of the global networks are in Africa's southernmost country.

There are about 25 million people living today in South Africa, and (at the beginning of 1996) an estimated 150,000 to 200,000 of them are connected to the Internet. There are 27 universities linked to the Internet as well as a couple of dozen Internet service providers. Even the US-based commercial network CompuServe has several points of presence in South Africa. According to *Internet World*, classes in HTML are booked up a week in advance in South Africa's cybercafes. Dozens of new Web sites are springing up every month and more and more ordinary citizens are getting online. And the labour movement too is sharing in the excitement, albeit at its own pace.

Probably at the core of trade union use of the net today in South Africa is SANGONeT – the online network of South Africa's non-governmental organisations founded in 1993 and the successor to WorkNet (whose early years we discussed in Chapter 3). SANGONeT defines itself as 'a regional electronic information and communications network for development and human rights workers'. It is affiliated to the Association for Progressive Communications, and like APC networks everywhere, puts the emphasis on 'the environment, human rights, development and peace' – but not on the labour movement per se.

SANGONeT says that it's no ordinary Internet access provider, but wants to provide popular organisations with the tools they need. SANGONeT delivers relevant information to people working in development; offers an integrated approach to communication and information networking; and promotes open government and access to government information. On that last point, SANGONeT received a special award from *Weekly Mail and Guardian* columnist Bruce Cohen at the end of 1995 for putting various government 'Green Papers' online.

SANGONeT, like its precedessor WorkNet, puts a lot of emphasis on training, including giving courses in HTML, weekly training sessions in computer-mediated communications at both introductory and advanced levels, and free weekly demonstrations showing the power of the Internet. It also specialises in support to non-governmental organisations, and that support includes toll-free telephone numbers, hosting Web sites on SANGONeT's server computer, helping users locate information on the vast Internet, connecting a local area network (LAN) to the net, and much more.

SANGONeT's Web site includes a special labour page, with links to South African unions which have Web sites of their own, plus some other links of interest to trade unionists (including the South African Communist Party). Nevertheless, even SANGONeT staff are not satisfied. 'This is such an important area and it really is a pity that more has not happened', says Anriette Esterhuysen.

South Africa's national trade union centre, the Congress of South African Trade Unions (COSATU), is taking an interest in the new technology. COSATU had been involved with WorkNet from the very beginning. For several years COSATU has also been working together with the Italian trade union centre CGIL on a computerisation project (including email) called 'Metric'. Only in 1993 did WorkNet (by then renamed SANGONeT) switch its software over to one compatible with the COSATU computers' operating system.

In 1995, ten years after it was founded, COSATU announced the launch of its own site on the World Wide Web. Yet several months after its launch, the page was still modest in scope. It included access to fewer than 20 texts of COSATU press statements, and under the header 'COSATU Documents' published only one. Other than a list of local offices and officers, the only real information available at the site is the full text of COSATU's bi-monthly newspaper, *Shopsteward*.

In a 1994 report prepared for the International Confederation of Free Trade Unions and the International Labour Organisation, British experts on labour telematics explained that 'COSATU is well supplied with personal computers and, together with its affiliated unions, is expanding the use of computers and computer communications to regions and branches. There is likely to be a rapid increase in demand for support and training.' Whether that demand was met or not is unclear. What is clear is that two years later, there doesn't appear to be any rapid increase in COSATU's use of computer-mediated communications.

This was confirmed to the author by Celia Mather, an organiser of the two Manchester conferences in 1992 and 1993. Mather, who was then working in South Africa for the International Labour Resource and Information Group (ILRIG), told me that 'not much has yet got off the ground in the unions here in a consistent way'.

The head of COSATU's Information Technology Unit, Charley Lewis, told me of an abortive attempt to use email just before the April 1994 national elections. This effort used donated modems and freeware – and according to Lewis 'was a complete waste of time. The software was clumsy and cruddy to use and kept breaking down. The users were never properly trained ... The result was that it died soon after, having only really been used by a few individuals.'

These days, working with the Metric project, COSATU has now offered to fund an Internet link and training through SANGONeT for each of its affiliate unions. According to SANGONeT, online discussion groups will be set up for COSATU as part of the process. The national trade union centre is also actively promoting email use internally and within union affiliates, beginning with links between the COSATU head office and head offices of affiliate unions. By mid-1996, fourteen of COSATU's nineteen affiliate unions and all eight regions were online. All head office personnel used email as a communications tool. All press statements and key policy documents were published on the home page. COSATU had even begun the use of LISTSERV to distribute press statements by email.

Another South African trade union centre, NACTU, was also discussed in the 1994 report. It had fewer resources than COSATU, 'but has had discussions with local email providers and is keen to develop telematics. It urgently requires trained technical staff and is seeking to establish a modem-linked minicomputer to serve its affiliates and regions.'

Meanwhile, a few of the national unions have begun to use computer-mediated communications on a regular basis. Among these is the 325,000 member National Union of Mineworkers (NUM), a COSATU affiliate. This union represents the vast majority of workers in both the mining and electrical energy industries, and has focused since its founding in 1982 on wages, racial discrimination and health and safety issues.

In 1995, the NUM launched its Web site, which is maintained by and funded by the African National Congress (ANC). The Web site has not been a roaring success so far; in the first four months of its existence, only four people wrote into the NUM offices in response to it. Under 'NUM Documents' only one document can actually be found (a proposal on minimum wages), and the 'Press Statements' mentioned on the home page consist of half a dozen files from a two-week period only. The purpose of the Web site is 'more to get used to using the Internet than to provide information to our own structures', admits Martin Nicol of the NUM. Nicol was frank with me about the sorry state of trade union use of computer communications in South Africa. In the NUM, which has a staff of 157 people, only one (Nicol himself) is connected to the Internet.

Nevertheless, he has been able to use the network to the union's advantage. In a case of union–academic cooperation which has been typical of WorkNet/SANGONeT, Nicol was able to use the Internet while working with the Industrial Health Research Group at the University of Cape Town, collaborating on a complex workshop on the subject of seven-day shift rosters and working time. NUM staffers were able to edit the Research Group's documentation for the workshop using email. This greatly increased the speed with which the report was prepared – 'and its quality', adds Nicol.

In any event, the NUM has plans to improve the situation dramatically in the months to come. These include first of all getting the computer network at the union's head office to work properly. 'It is installed', says Nicol, 'but no one knows how to use it.' Once that is working, NUM staffers will begin using email in the union's internal network. Then the union's network will link up through SANGONeT, with each of its head office 'units' (legal, health and safety, collective baragaining, etc.) connecting as separate accounts. Finally, each of the fourteen regional offices of the union will link up to the Internet.

Nicol is optimistic about the future of South Africa's labournet. 'Internet communication is now easy and possible', he says. 'There are several capable and reliable providers, especially SANGONeT, which is used to dealing with the special training and adaptation problems that unions face.' Nicol even imagines a practical use for the network in the very near future. 'Email could be used', he believes, 'for preparing joint trade union submissions to the new tripartite bodies that take up a huge amount of time and energy in the New South Africa.'

Other COSATU affiliates have also taken an interest in computer communications, most notably the Chemical Workers' Industrial Union (CWIU) and the National Union of Metalworkers of South Africa (NUMSA). These unions are, respectively, affiliated to the chemical workers' (ICEM) and metal workers' (IMF) trade secretariats. Both unions have ambitious plans for using networks.

According to Christian Sellars, a researcher at the CWIU, the union has been connected to the Internet for nearly a decade. Initially the union's account was through Poptel, and email was mainly used to stay in touch with the ICEM. That correspondence usually consisted of press reports on a particular industry or corporation, or an issue like occupational safety and health. Stellars was not around at the beginning. 'I joined the union two years ago', he told me, 'and have since been lumbered with the task of looking after info technology.'

One recent change for the union has been that the CWIU stopped working with Poptel. 'It makes more sense for us to use a standard account from a service provider, in our case the South African non-governmental organisation network, SANGONeT', says Stellars. He called SANGONeT 'the major supplier to progressive organisations' of Internet connections in South Africa today. (Anriette Esterhuysen of SANGONeT blamed Poptel for holding back labour networking in the country. 'Labour networking here was held back for many years by the fact that many unions were on GeoNet, not on SANGONeT/WorkNet, and therefore not part of the APC', she told me.)

To this day, the main use the union makes of the Internet is email. The CWIU is not only sharing information with the international trade secretariat, but increasingly with other South Africa unions and non-governmental organisations. As with the NUM, the CWIU has only one connection to the Internet – the modem on Chris Sellars's computer. But they plan to expand. The union head office has a local area network, and by the end of 1996 everyone on that network should have an Internet address too. Modems will be installed in all CWIU branch offices around the country.

The emphasis is clearly on connecting union officers and staff, to each other and to other parts of the labour movement – and less on the flashy aspects of a World Wide Web site. The CWIU isn't even thinking of such a site now, not wanting to invest the time or money. Sellars adds another reason, which is probably true in many trade union offices around the world: 'I guess fear of being caught "playing" on something that colourful during working hours is a barrier to entry!'

Practical uses have been found for email, both in connecting within the country and outside of it. One example Sellars cited concerned centralised collective bargaining. This is something the union is very keen to implement, particularly in sectors that are hard to organise on a plant-by-plant basis. Employer organisations in South Africa have reluctantly agreed – but they've used the excuse of 'sector demarcation' to delay discussions. 'In the course of negotiations', Sellars says, 'the union used the Internet to get the advice of the ICEM on which unions in other countries have successfully set up centralised bargaining and on how their sectors are demarcated.' The union received a 'very useful response' from the Germany chemical union IG Chemie, which 'demonstrated how a unified centralised bargaining system could be applied to a range of different sectors.' The CWIU put the German information to work. 'Using this experience as an example we have been able to reject employers' arguments about the unworkability of unified bargaining systems', Sellars reports.

Another use of email by the union that produced results took place within South Africa. The CWIU has been quite involved in discussions of a new national policy for South Africa's petroleum industry. 'Our involvement in drafting new policy has been greatly assisted by the use of email and the electronic transfer of files', reports Sellars. 'Working documents have gone through many drafts which have been sent between parties involved over the net.'

The changes in South Africa have shifted the emphasis in the labour movement from the struggle against apartheid to more traditional trade union issues. That means that trade unions need specific information on transnational corporations active in South Africa in order to bargain collectively with them. Access to labour-related computerised databases is required, as are connections with other national and international trade unions (especially the international trade secretariats), union-related research centres and academic institutions, and the International Labour Organisation in Geneva. The need for contact with friendly institutions in the developed countries which was so strongly felt during the years of white minority rule has not lessened with the political changes in the country.

Finally, there is also a continuing need for south-south communication, as South African unions exchange information with other countries undergoing development and democratisation. But South African unions will not limit their information exchanges to neighbouring countries, and might well find common ground for discussion with labour movements far afield.

Britain

'After a little hesitation, the British have taken the bungee-jump into cyberspace', wrote *Internet World* magazine in its special 'State of the Net' survey at the end of 1995. The estimated number of people with Internet access in the UK rose from 200,000 at the beginning of the year to over half a million by the end. Internet editions of a number of well-known newspapers, including the *Daily Telegraph* and the *Guardian* have appeared. The BBC ran an eight-part series on the Internet, with an estimated audience of about a million people per episode. Businesses have gone online, and the first online shopping mall opened in the country. The British even proved to be pioneers in one field of Internet activity: cybercafes. Europe's first cybercafe, Cyberia, opened in London in late 1994, and was followed by fourteen more in the UK and another twenty on the continent.

Several of the 'new social movements' in Britain adopted the new communications technology with fervor – as did some of their enemies, including the far right. The labour movement was not excluded from this, even though net-oriented magazines (with few exceptions) rarely ever note this fact. British labour's 'bungee-jump into cyberspace' includes:

- Online discussion groups
- A permanent training and research centre
- Trade union networks
- Labour Web sites

Union-d

Online discussion groups based on email are one of the simplest, oldest and yet most powerful tools available to trade unionists on the Internet. Now that tens of millions of people have Internet access, this tool is more powerful than ever before. Unlike USENET newsgroups or conferences in closed systems like GeoNet, email-based discussion groups are open to *everyone*. Even people with access only to local community bulletin boards (which are linked to the loose and informal network called FidoNet) can get involved in such efforts.

In August 1995, the European trade union movement finally got its own email-based discussion group on the Internet. Its founders and moderators were Greg Coyne and Jagdish Parikh. They called the group 'Union-d'. (For information on how to join the group, see Appendix 2.)

We've already met Jagdish Parikh several times in this book – working in Hong Kong with the pioneering Asia Monitor Resource Centre in the late 1980s; popping up again to help set up LaborNet@IGC in San Francisco in 1990; representing a Uruguayan network at the 1992 Manchester conference. While writing this book, I tracked him down to Bombay, India. It seems that Parikh is now based in the US – but that's only an educated guess. He could be anywhere. This man is the Scarlet Pimpernel of the global labournet.

Greg Coyne is somewhat easier to pin down. He has served as a trade union shop steward and held other posts in the labour movement, including working full-time on the Trades Union Congress's education programmes. In that capacity, he launched the TUC's computer courses for union representatives in the Liverpool area. He's been deeply involved in the fight against unemployment, and is a senior member of the Merseyside Trade Union Community and Unemployed Resource Centre. He currently works as Education Officer for the centre. Coyne was introduced to computer communications back in 1991, with the launch of

GeoNet's Manchester host. In the summer of 1994, he initiated an informal online discussion group that a year later evolved into Union-d.

The list was aimed principally but not exclusively at the European labour movement. It hoped to promote online dialogue, information sharing and organisation between active trade unionists who have access to an Internet email box. According to Coyne and Parikh, the group's origins lay in a group of 30 to 40 'mainly UK-based trade unionists who had established an email corresponding group to share information and ideas'. Union-d was intended to serve as 'an easy way for trade unionists coming on line in Europe to plug into an established and sympathetic network'. Using the Internet, rather than the Poptel or APC networks, was a strategic decision. 'Trade unionists can participate regardless of which host system they are using, and [this] will obviously assist in drawing online trade unionists into a closer community.'

One problem which Union-d was intended to help solve was 'the isolation that many trade unionists feel when opening a mail box for the first time. They know the potential of online communication, but they don't know who to contact and nobody knows to contact them.' According to Coyne and Parikh, 'all too often, in our experience, trade unionists give up checking their mail box after a few weeks of receiving nothing'.

Six months after the discussion group was launched, Parikh told me that there were already some 130 to 150 subscribers, mostly in Europe. This number is quite small by the standards of email-based discussion lists on the Internet; North American-based lists like Labor-L and H-Labor were several times larger. Participants come from various networks, including the APC and GeoNet/Poptel networks. That was part of the reason for using LISTSERV in the first place, says Coyne.

Subjects being discussed on Union-d include how to use the list to assist organisation; announcements about the UK labour movement; queries about health and safety issues, etc. During the first few months, there were two or three postings per day on the average.

'Solidarity and information is being exchanged all the time', adds Greg Coyne. 'Union-d has recently scored a number of successes in building support for striking Liverpool dockworkers internationally, and in connecting engineering workers in different countries who work for the same multinational' corporation. (We'll talk more about this in the next chapter.) In Coyne's view, the list is too focused on the UK, and he intends to make special efforts to promote discussion of European topics, including possible national sub-lists for the various European countries. Moderators of those sub-lists would then post to Union-d messages of broader international interest.

The Labour Telematics Centre

The Labour Telematics Centre (LTC) was founded in January 1993 as the first and most tangible result of the 1992 conference held in Manchester (which I discussed in Chapter 3). Its goal was 'to support and encourage labour movement organisations in getting access to, and benefits from, computer-based electronic communications and information technology – telematics'.

If in other areas, such as online discussion groups, the British have lagged somewhat behind their North American cousins, this centre is a unique achievement. Though courses on what they call 'labour telematics' are offered elsewhere in the world – for example, at the George Meany Centre for Labour Studies in the US – the LTC is the first permanent training and research centre devoted solely to this subject.

It is located at the GMB National College in Manchester, and this British union (the second largest in the country) has been both far-sighted and generous in its attitude toward labour telematics. The GMB donates the premises and other resources to the Centre. The GMB's General Secretary, John Edmonds, delivered the keynote address to the first Manchester conference in 1992. He told participants that the 'time for experimenting is over', and that the establishment of 'global union networks' were already on the agenda. Edmonds also stressed the importance of the new communications technologies in democratising trade unions. A union branch, he pointed out, could have access to the same quality of information as quickly as senior officers or the executive council.

The LTC lists the following services which it can provide to trade unions and other workers' organisations:

- Communications audits and feasibility studies for organisations considering making use of electronic communications.
- Policy development and research on the impact of telematics on employment and trade union organisation and activity.
- Training in electronic communications and related computer applications.
- Production of training materials for in-house use by organisations.
- Development of online information services specifically for the labour movement (for example, setting up collective bargaining databases and electronic publishing of union reports and journals).
- Technical consultancy.

- Organising seminars and conferences.
- Researching and publishing reports and guides on telematics issues.

Early in 1995, the LTC sponsored a major conference called 'Working on the Infobahn – Teleworking and the Labour Movement'. More than 140 people attended the event, which far exceeded the organisers' expectations. Nearly 20 British trade unions sent representatives, as did the Labour Party, two international trade secretariats, two national trade union centres (Britain's TUC and the US's AFL–CIO), and the International Confederation of Free Trade Unions.

The LTC has organised courses in telematics for a number of British and international unions, including the Trades Union Congress, the National Union of Journalists, the Public Service International, and others. They conduct basically two kinds of telematics courses – an Internet Users Course and a Training the Trainers Course.

The first covers background to electronic communications; the sending and receiving of email; exchanging formatted files (for example, Microsoft Word files); using Internet tools like the World Wide Web; and accessing electronic databases. The more advanced course covers all of those topics plus: technical background to electronic communication; technical troubleshooting (modems, communications software, telephone lines); and providing training and support for the organisation. In addition, the centre offers courses in word-processing and desktop publishing, though this is admittedly 'not the primary focus of the LTC'.

In 1994, the LTC launched its own home page on the World Wide Web, and in early 1995 published (on paper) the first edition of its newsletter, *Labour Telematics News*. It remains closely linked to Poptel and maintains 'bulletin boards' on both Poptel host computers, MCR1 and GEO2. 'Labourtel' features general news items, while 'labourtel-int' and 'labourtel-uk' store the reports and papers from the 1992 and 1993 Manchester conferences respectively.

In early 1995 the LTC coordinated an application to the European Commission in Brussels from an alliance of European trade union federations interested in exploring the impact and future use of telematics in 'traditional' industrial sectors. The proposed Industrial Labour Telematics Education Project involved European committees representing textile and garment workers, food workers, chemical workers, the European Trade Union College and the LTC itself. Similarly, the LTC is supporting national unions in Africa, Asia, and countries of the former Soviet bloc to make better use of online communications.

The centre is also working on a proposal to establish a service for publishing health and safety information on the World Wide Web. Though editorial control would reside within the participating unions, the LTC would ensure the coordination and structuring of the material published in this way.

The LTC is managed by the Workers' Educational Association as a national project. John Atkins coordinates the activities of the LTC on behalf of the WEA. A national Advisory Group comprised of trade union users of electronic communication exists to support the work of the LTC.

Trade union networks

Poptel (the Popular Telematics Project) is not only the first British trade union network; it is one of the very first labour networks in the world. As we mentioned back in Chapter 3, Poptel was founded with the support of the Labour-dominated Greater London Council back in 1986. For a decade now it has provided services to the labour movement in Britain, Europe and around the world.

On its Web site, Poptel sums up its activity as follows: 'Poptel provides Internet access, electronic messaging and on-line information. We collaborate in projects to make telematics widely accessible to the local and global community, and provide on-line information to trades unions, campaigns, agencies, charities and organisations.'

A glance at the list of Web sites Poptel hosts – which include nearly *all* of the British labour sites – shows how much this network dominated and still dominates the British trade union scene. Web sites hosted by Poptel include those of the Labour Party and several major trade unions, including UNISON, AUT, MSF and GFTU (we'll review several of these in a moment). With the emergence of an open Internet by the mid-1990s, Poptel became more of an Internet access provider and less of a network within the network.

If Poptel may be said to have a rival in the field of 'movement' telematics in the UK, it comes from GreenNet, the British affiliate of the Association for Progressive Communications. As we have seen in this chapter, the APC has been playing an increasingly important role in the development of a global labournet in countries like the US, Russia, South Africa, and Canada.

GreenNet describes itself as a 'global computer communications network for environment, peace, human rights and development'. Its home page on the World Wide Web doesn't even mention the labour movement. Nevertheless, GreenNet aspires to repeat the modest success of APC's US affiliate, the Institute for Global Communications, which hosts LaborNet@IGC. Like Poptel, GreenNet offers Internet services plus. The plus includes 'access

to GreenNet-specific public and private discussions and databases'
and email-to-fax service. At its Web site, GreenNet offers nine
examples of how movement activists might find it useful. None of
them refer to the labour movement. Still, GreenNet is now hosting
its own 'LabourNet', set up by Chris Bailey.

Bailey was at one time an activist on Britain's far left. 'I've
mellowed a bit since', he now says. He became a machinist and
got involved in the trade union movement, rising to become a
member of one union's National Committee. Like Coyne, Bailey
got involved in centres for the unemployed and in education. He
helped organise and teach courses on computers for unemployed
people at a couple of those centres. In the mid-1980s he was
involved in an unsuccessful global solidarity campaign using
traditional media. Losing the fight left Bailey with a bitter taste –
'and an awareness of how powerful the transnationals were and how
difficult it is for trade unions to fight them'. Working as a trade
union branch secretary pays little, and Bailey – who became a
computer enthusiast after teaching the courses – also builds, repairs
and sells computers and computer parts. A lot of his work is for
the labour movement, he says. 'Sometimes they pay me.'

Bailey is a regular – sometimes sole – contributor to
LaborNet@IGC's conference on British labour, called 'labr.uk'.
The new LabourNet is intended to be 'a kind of subgroup modelled
on' LaborNet@IGC, says Bailey. 'Besides my own union branch,
the International Campaign for Trade Union Rights has also
decided to take out a Web site within LabourNet and the signs are
that, given some publicity, the overall response will be good. The
rank-and-file union journal *Trade Union News* has agreed to let me
promote LabourNet through them. I have been supplying the
news for their international pages for some time from the Internet.'

So far what the LabourNet page has to offer is only one site –
but what an interesting site it is. The Liverpool Dockers' Lockout
page is the first trade union dispute in Britain to have its own World
Wide Web page. The idea for the page came from the Union-d
mailing list. It was put together over a weekend by trade unionists
on three continents, using email. And the home page was provided
free of charge by GreenNet as part of the embryonic LabourNet
project.

This Web site includes basic information about the lock-out of
some 500 dockers by the Mersey Docks and Harbour Company,
several updates and urgent appeals, the complete texts of the
dockers' newspaper (*Dockers' Charter*) and a page of solidarity
messages. I turned to these in particular, remembering the great
success the online strike newspapers in the US, the *San Francisco
Free Press* and the *Detroit Journal*, had with such messages. But there
were fewer than a dozen messages on the page. And unlike the

solidarity messages one finds in the US strike newspapers, which seem to come from ordinary people, many of them not even trade unionists, these messages come exclusively from labour movement and left – particularly the far left.

One came from the Norwegian group 'Internasjonale Sosialister'. Another was from the defunct Industrial Workers of the World. Another came from 'the theoretical study group Socialist Association' in Japan. Yet another came from the Trotskyist Militant group. Two of the messages came from British trade unionists using Poptel email accounts, and one of these was only one word long ('Cheers', it read).

Greg Coyne says that the Liverpool dockers 'are very pleased' with the Web site. 'They have engaged', he told me, 'in raising major international solidarity in order to get around the restrictive legislation imposed on unions in Britain. Wherever in the world they have travelled to publicise the dispute the Internet got there before them.' When dockers toured Australia and Canada recently seeking support they found they were constantly introduced as 'from the dispute we first heard about via the Internet'. The Japanese dockers' union and the San Francisco longshoremens' union local are both examples of support for the dispute gained through the net.

Coyne admits that the Web site 'was more a stunt than an organising tool. It has not really been a vehicle for raising solidarity messages.' Such messages have travelled the more conventional route of faxes. Nevertheless, the infant Labournet's Liverpool Lockout page 'deserves interest' says Coyne because 'it was the first time in the UK that the Web had been used to raise support for an industrial dispute'.

Poptel and GreenNet do not exhaust the networks being used by trade unionists in the UK. Several unions have their own networks. Two outstanding examples are those of the National Union of Journalists (NUJ) and the Information Technology Professionals' Association (ITPA).

The NUJ's network, called NUJnet, was launched in 1992, using the Manchester GeoNet host computer. One of its initiators, Andrew Bibby, told me that the NUJ (which includes members in Ireland as well as the UK) was 'the first British union to use online services as a way of communicating with members, and encouraging members to communicate among themselves'. The network allows freelance journalists to check rates of pay, exchange information with each other, access databases (such as the union's Freelance Directory), read union publications and circulars, and even take part in international actions in support of press freedom. According to Mike Holderness, another founder of the network, NUJnet was set up to help overcome the isolation of freelance journalists who are traditionally difficult to organise. At its start, it had no fewer than fifteen separate conferencing areas, called bulletin boards.

The ITPA is an autonomous section of MSF, Britain's fifth largest union. It was established in June 1995. ITPA offers advice for employees and freelancers on a wide range of issues, including employment rights, contracts, restraint of trade, pensions and salaries. ITPA maintains a legal clinic which specialises in intellectual property rights.

As should be expected, a union consisting of information professionals makes some very interesting uses of the new computer communications technology. The MSF has a wide area network (WAN) and the ITPA makes extensive use of email, corporate networks, and the like, creating a diverse online network of its own. The ITPA's National Secretary, Peter Skyte, told me that the new network has four tasks:

- Electronic communication amongst members.
- Recruitment and communication to potential members using company email systems.
- Linking up with unions in Europe for passing information in individual companies.
- Linking up with union colleagues world-wide and transmitting information.

The MSF often uses internal corporate systems, usually with the agreement of the employers. It is rare that an employer prohibits such use. 'Using company networks', says Skyte, 'is no different to using other employer facilities such as telephone, fax, photocopier and internal mailing.' But where employer hostility has been encountered, the union has used the networks without agreement.

As we mentioned in discussions of use of corporate and academic intranets earlier, this raises some questions of security. Union email can easily be checked by an employer who wanted to. 'No doubt if someone wanted to monitor the use made of internal networks, this could be done', admits Skyte. 'So far, except where employers specifically prohibit such use, I'm not aware of any occasions where mailboxes are examined.'

Finally, the union is using email and online discussion groups as tools to communicate with other trade unionists in the UK and elsewhere. The ITPA represents workers in a number of transnational corporations such as Digital and Unisys. Skyte uses email to contact his equivalents in trade unions in a number of countries, including Germany, France, Italy, the US, Portugal, Belgium and Scandinavia.

Labour Web Sites

The World Wide Web is growing as rapidly in the UK as anywhere else, and trade unions are often eager to get a piece of the action.

The very first union to set up a Web site in Britain (on 22 March 1995) was UNISON, the largest union in the country, representing 1,400,000 workers in the public sector. Just as CUPE in Canada pioneered the use of computer communications in that country, so UNISON and its predecessors (UNISON is a mega-union, a merger of several smaller unions) have been in the forefront of what the British call 'labour telematics'. Unlike CUPE, UNISON did not set up its own network a decade ago. But the Web site is not UNISON's first, nor only, venture into cyberspace. Sixty local branches of the union had been using Poptel since 1993, and were electronically distributing information about contracts and collective bargaining.

The UNISON site offers union news (including press releases and news of a health pay campaign), the UNISON Guide, UNISON Communications, and UNISON Education and Training. The UNISON Guide explains the origins of the union (a 1993 merger of three unions, COHSE, NALGO and NUPE) and offers further information organised by the sector represented (local government, health care, higher education, etc.). The Guide is accessed by chapter (aims and values, women in UNISON, members' rights, etc.). The Education and Training page consists of an introductory article called 'What we stand for' by UNISON's Director of Education and Training, and links to two other pages, one on trade union courses and one on vocational courses.

UNISON was followed onto the Web a few months later by the national trade union centre in the UK, the Trades Union Congress, which represents 68 trade unions with nearly 7,000,000 members. Its goal was to 'construct the UK's premier campaigning site' and the TUC announced its commitment 'to making available the wealth of TUC advice, publications and campaign briefings ... to anyone with Internet access'. The site was launched to coincide with the 1995 TUC Congress.

According to Nigel Stanley of the TUC's Campaigns and Communications Department, the organisation has embarked on a major effort to use the new communications technologies. The TUC Web site, updated every week, would include all press releases and most research reports. The TUC is also taking advantage of the powerful LISTSERV tool, using it to send out press releases. Other online mailing lists are also planned. Every member of the TUC staff is getting Internet access from their desktop computers.

Meanwhile, the TUC is also beginning to provide a wide range of Internet services to affiliated unions. These include:

- Hosting union Web sites on the TUC's server computer. These will allow updates from the unions via email, so there will be no need for in-house mastery of HTML.

- Hosting union LISTSERV mailing lists.
- Profiling unions through the TUC's Web site and its online directory of affiliates.
- Organising one or more UK-specific USENET newsgroups for the labour movement.
- Helping unions get their own domain addresses on the Internet.

The 275,000 member General Federation of Trades Unions, representing 32 specialist unions, launched its Web site (using Poptel's server) in the spring of 1995 in conjunction with its biennial General Council meeting. The intention of the Web site was to publish conference details – agenda, executive report, press releases, results of elections and motions. Information posted to the Web site would also be copied to a Poptel bulletin board. The site currently offers a three-page guide to the union and a list of affiliates, as well as information on the May 1995 meeting.

Meanwhile, other national unions are jumping on the World Wide Web bandwagon – but not at the hysterical pace one finds in North America, for example. The giant Transport and General Workers Union (TGWU) launched a Web site, as did the Association of University Teachers (AUT), and the Labour Party.

Russia

For three-quarters of a century, the Russian working class (and the workers in other countries under Soviet domination) was not represented in, nor active in, the international democratic labour movement. Independent trade unionism was crushed by the Soviet regime very early on. Independent, democratic trade unionism in Russia revived itself only with the final collapse of the Communist regime in 1988–91. In the process of re-creating an independent trade union movement, both the new and old Russian labour organisations did not neglect the possibilities of computer communications.

Three features of the Russian labour movement's use of telematics seem to be worthy of emphasis:

- The number of trade unions online in Russia is much higher than one would expect, and it is sometimes easier to reach a provincial trade union headquarters there by email than it is to reach a national centre in a Western European capital.
- Using computer communications has been a way to connect to the international democratic labour movement after decades of isolation – and at a time when transnational corporations are becoming increasingly active in Russia (and everywhere else).

- Several Russian trade unionists have gone far beyond the practical, day-to-day thinking about the new technologies that is characteristic of pragmatists in the West, and have begun developing a vision of a global labournet and a reborn International.

Russia's labournet began, as it did in so many countries, with the founding in 1990 of an affiliate network of the Association for Progressive Communications – GlasNet. GlasNet was not exclusively a labour network. Its expressed goal was to promote 'democratic communications among individuals, independent groups and non-governmental, non-profit organisations, including organised labour, in the fields of human rights, ecology, democratic development, etc.'. It put the emphasis on affordable electronic communications.

In Moscow in the spring of that same year, the independent labour education centre KAS-KOR was set up. Its goal was to provide information, technical advice and publishing services to trade unions and other workers' organisations in the USSR.

KAS-KOR and GlasNet would together play a critically important role in linking Russian unions to the emerging labour Internet. The mainstream labour movement was also making an effort to get connected. As Vassily Balog, the Deputy Head of the International Department of the General Confederation of Trade Unions (GCTU), explained, the then-USSR's national trade union centre 'was the first ever national workers' organisation to set up direct interactive online connection with the International Labour Organisation' in Geneva. A modem (probably the first one used by anyone in the Russian labour movement) was purchased in 1990; fortunately, it turned out to be a reasonably fast and reliable one – a necessity for Russia's terrible telephone system. As Balog explained it to me, the 1991 connection between the Russian unions and the ILO was interesting for three reasons.

- No ILO constituent organisation (and these include governments, national trade union centres, and employer organisations) had ever connected electronically before to the organisation's databases.
- It was probably the first international connection at all made by Russian unions using modems. Direct computer-to-computer connections were already being made inside the country, for example from Moscow to Leningrad, but using modems to connect to the outside world was something quite new.
- The connection was made through a commercial network instead of by simply dialling up internationally using telephone lines, which would have been prohibitively expensive.

After a few months, the GCTU stopped using this channel. The ILO then could offer little information online that was not more readily available offline. Nothing was available online then (or now) in Russian. But something was learned from the effort. 'It ushered in an understanding that new, potentially more powerful means of communication were available, bringing down barriers and frontiers', concludes Balog – who now adds that as the ILO and its offices get online, Russian interest in connecting will return.

According to a report in the *New York Times*, during the abortive coup of August 1991, coup plotters 'did not have the foresight to yank out the phone lines' and as a result, 'GlasNet never stopped filing urgent messages to a breathless outside world'.

When the first international conference on labour computer communications was held in April 1992, Anatoly Vononov of GlasNet was already there, and he made a presentation. At that time, as he pointed out, many Russian unions couldn't even afford the inexpensive GlasNet. A year later, two labour-oriented online conferences were set up on GlasNet. One is in English (labr.cis) and it is moderated by Balog. The other is in Russian (glas.trud) and its moderator is Kirill Buketov of KAS-KOR. Labr.cis is available to this day on the LaborNet@IGC network. These two conferences offer 'a reliable first-hand speedy source of labour-oriented information on Russia and other CIS countries', says Balog. 'Their value – both within Russia and beyond – became quite outstanding at the time when our unions and union officials came under direct attack', referring to the arrests of trade unionists in October 1993 (more on that in the next chapter).

They were not only a way to send information out of Russia, but to bring information in. I was surprised and delighted to discover that Balog had posted the text of an issue of *Workers' Education* to one of the online conferences. In any event, an important motivating factor, as in the earlier attempt to connect to the ILO, was the desire to use the emerging global labournet as a two-way channel of information for the new labour movement in Russia.

In addition to online conferences like labr.cis, Russian trade unions are represented in Internet LISTSERV mailing lists, including Union-d, United and Labor-L. Those lists, according to Balog, 'are read – and valued – here'.

In June 1993, at the second international conference on labour's use of computer communications in Manchester, Kirill Buketov of KAS-KOR made a unique presentation. By this time GlasNet and KAS-KOR had been in existence for three years. As Buketov pointed out, there were then fewer than 20 Russian unions involved in any way in email. The problem was partly one of finance – some of the unions were using computers donated by Western unions – but also the underdevelopment of Russia's entire technology base and communications systems. (Though a high-quality ex-military network covering 200 cities did exist.) There was also a critical lack of information on the subject of computer communications in Russian and the other languages of the Commonwealth of Independent States (CIS), he said. KAS-KOR intended to translate such materials and make them available.

Russian trade unions were using two different networks, GeoNet and APC, each with its own advantages and disadvantages. Though GeoNet boasted of its multilingual capabilities, for some reason this was not the case with its Moscow host computer. GeoNet was therefore mostly used for contacts with European and international trade unions which used that network. The APC-affiliated GlasNet, which was far more affordable – and which didn't demand payment in US dollars – became the *de facto* trade union network within the CIS countries, offering them the full range of Internet services.

By October 1993 the Russian labour movement was ready to host a major international conference in Moscow on the subject of computer communications. The emphasis was then, as always, on connections both within the vast CIS and with the international labour movement. KAS-KOR, an American group called Labourtech Communications, and GlasNet sponsored the event. Russian unions endorsing the conference included unions of fisherman, the nuclear industry, miners, auto workers, and construction workers. Unions from Ukraine, Belarus, Kazakhstan, and various regions in Russia were represented. It was a rare moment of trade union unity, commented Balog, as 'representatives from various – and at time rivalling – unions met' to share their experiences and hopes.

As Balog put it, the conference had two goals:

- To speed up the development of trade union information networks in Russia and other countries of the former USSR.
- To make it possible to promote integration of trade unions and other labour movement organisations of the countries of Eastern Europe into international information networks.

More than 80 trade unionists attended the conference. Foreign participants included a number of key labournet pioneers, among them Solinet's Marc Belanger, the ICEF's Jim Catterson, LaborNet's Steve Zeltzer, Malcolm Corbett of Poptel, and Peter Waterman. (Waterman wrote a very detailed account of the conference; details of this are in my bibliography.)

Greetings were received from both the ILO and ICFTU. Plenary sessions focused on the information society and the international labour movement; new communications technologies; the problems of the integration of the Eastern European labour movement into international trade union networks; and finally, the labour movement and public opinion – using mass communications. Workshops were devoted to radio and television; email and electronic bulletin board systems; computers and unions; the labour press; and labour videos.

Since the conference was held, the development of those networks and connections has proceeded, albeit not as quickly as Balog and others would have liked. By March 1994, GlasNet was claiming 1,500 regular participants in its network. By mid-1995, Balog estimated that some 30–35 trade unions in the CIS countries were connected to the networks. These are not just national offices, but unions with branches that are online. The mine workers' union has branches all over Russia and quite a few of these are computerised. The loose network of BBSs called FidoNet is also used by trade unionists in the CIS; Balog sent a megabyte of data to Donetsk in the Ukraine to the local union node there. The actual number of trade union Internet users could therefore be 20 or 30 times the number of unions mentioned, says Balog. In addition, representatives of Western and international trade union organisations posted to Moscow, Kiev and elsewhere were also using email – and not only to connect to their home offices, but with local trade unions as well.

There is much talk of the future among the Russian trade unionists online and this talk focuses on two projects. One is the creation of a national trade union network with sub-networks for various sectors of the economy. The other is the urgent need for the strengthening of the emerging global labournet. Balog has been thinking about the former since the early 1990s, and organisations like KAS-KOR have been lobbying to raise funds outside of Russia to set up such a national network. But when Russian trade unionists appear at international events, they put the emphasis on the latter.

Kirill Buketov makes it clear that the new trade union internationalism has its roots in new economic realities. 'Drawn into the international economy as never before', he says, 'the Russian trade unions need a greater exchange of information, and direct contacts with kindred union organisations in other countries.' He points out that the mining of low-cost coal throughout the CIS is linked to mine closures in Britain, for example. 'It is essential', he says, 'that Russian labour organisations maintain continuous and direct contact with international partners, to strengthen and broaden the links between trade unions. This is possible *only* through electronic communications.'

Vassily Balog has been promoting the idea of an organised, formal global labour network. As he told a 1995 conference sponsored by LaborNet@IGC, such a network would peform at least five functions:

- Ease and speed up the distribution of labour-related news and documentation.
- Collect and archive labour-related information, making this accessible to all users.
- Provide unions in various regions with a channel of multilateral communication.
- Promote development of information infrastructures in the workers' organisations.
- Promote communications links among various trade unions.

Balog believes that LaborNet@IGC, Canada's Solinet, the GeoNet/Poptel network, the Labour Telematics Centre, and participants in the Labor-L mailing list could serve as a backbone for such a network.

Other Countries

In this chapter, I've focused on seven countries spread out over four continents, hoping to show something of the emerging global labournet as it stood in the mid-1990s. I haven't mentioned some of the most powerful labour movements in the world, even though a number of these have been making interesting uses of computer communications. If I decided to cover the whole world thoroughly, that would require another book – and one of much greater length. Nevertheless, there are just a few more examples of national labournets that I want to mention here before moving on in the next chapter to international trade union use of the Internet.

France is one of the countries most resistant to adopting the Internet, partly for fears of Anglo-American cultural domination, and partly because of a commitment to the existing national network, Minitel, established in the early 1980s by the socialist government. As *Internet World* magazine put it, 'Cyber-France is sparsely populated', estimating the number of those online at only 150,000. This is reflected in the French labour movement, which has no significant Internet presence to speak of. However, the French Socialist Party did launch an attractive World Wide Web site during its unsuccessful campaign for the presidency in 1995.

Even though Germany also lags behind many other countries in its use of the Internet, German trade unions and institutions associated with them are increasingly using the net and the World Wide Web. An important German Web site is the one maintained by the Friedrich Ebert Stiftung (FES), a foundation maintained by the German labour movement with offices (and projects) around the world. Their Web site contains a whole book (in English) on how to use email which is an excellent primer on the subject.

Probably the most important feature of their site is the online access to their library catalogue – but more on that in Chapter 7.

In addition to maintaining Web sites, an interesting use of the Internet has been made by the workers' education group Arbeit und Leben. They have used email as an educational tool in their efforts to train trade unionists for working within the European context – for example, in language instruction.

The Austrian Social Democratic Party launched its Web site with great fanfare in 1995, including an online chat between the Austrian Chancellor and Portuguese Prime Minister. The party has posted the full text of its newsletter, *Social Democratic News from Austria*, at the site. The Austrian national trade union centre OeGB also has a Web site.

Holland is a country where the Internet has really taken off. There are freenets, free ISDN lines, and very cheap connections to the Internet. It has one of the highest computers-per-capita counts in the world and a large percentage of the Dutch speak and read English. The 1.1 million member Netherlands Trade Union Federation (FNV) maintains a lively Web site, as does the Dutch Labour Party (PvdA). As early as March 1995, the latter was transmitting an average of over 1,250 files per day. They were able to reach relatively large audiences outside the country. The Dutch Labour Party site, which included much material in English, was being accessed by hundreds of North Americans and others.

The Nordic countries are all heavily involved in the Internet to one degree or another. The Swedish and Finnish social democratic parties both have Web sites. Finland is, in fact, the world leader in terms of Internet penetration. Access to the net there is extremely cheap. The social democratic government in Sweden has plans to link all ministries and ministers to the Web.

Norway was one of the very first countries with an Internet connection (thanks to its membership in NATO). Its Labour Party government is working hard to provide online information to citizens. It is possible to 'sit in' on live sessions of the Norwegian Parliament, hearing the speeches as they are given, over the Internet. The Norwegian trade union movement and institutions connected to it have been showing an increasing interest in the net recently, according to Aslak Leesland of the workers' education association AOF. He told me of several examples:

- The Labour Party used the Internet in the September 1995 municipal elections in Oslo.
- There is increasing cooperation between the People's Correspondence School, the European Trade Union College, and the AOF (Norway's workers' education association)

concerning the use of Internet in trade union education, though the trade union centre LO has been cautious.

- The Norwegian People's Aid, the labour movement's humanitarian organisation (with offices in 20 countries), has begun actively using the net.
- The AOF, which will soon have a Web site of its own, uses email for internal communications as well as links to its Danish and Swedish counterparts. Local AOF offices will be connected during the course of 1996.

According to *Internet World*, Nordic citizens and officials – more than in other parts of Europe – 'are calling for universal access to the Internet and an educational system that teaches all people to master it'. Such an approach is precisely what one would expect from a part of the world dominated by the social democratic labour movement for generations.

Trade union Web sites and online discussion groups continue to proliferate around the world. The National Trades Union Congress (NTUC) in Singapore was possibly the very first national trade union centre with a Web site of its own, early in 1995. But a couple of visits to the site didn't find much there – and this is surprising considering Singapore's famous commitment to the Internet. But according to the Singapore newspaper *Straits Times* in January 1996, the NTUC 'is turning to the Internet to reach its members and attract new ones'. The NTUC's Deputy Director of Planning and Research said that the Internet would be used to allow Singapore trade unionists to get legal advice on labour matters, give feedback on issues, and even book vacations.

In the neighbouring country of Malaysia, unions have also begun to go online. The National Union of the Teaching Profession (NUTP) in that country joined the Internet at the very end of January 1996. 'We hope to become a centre of information on the teaching profession' for the Asia-Pacific region, said the union's President, quoted in a Malaysian newspaper, the *Star*. The NUTP emphasised that the network would be used to keep in touch with international issues concerning teachers.

An interesting recent development was the launch in late 1995 of an online discussion group in the Spanish language for Latin American trade unionists. The group is being sponsored by Peru's Programa Laboral de Desarrollo (PLADES). No doubt other intitiatives will follow.

As I live in Israel, I think it wouldn't be entirely fair not to at least mention what is going on here. The answer is, apparently, very little. On the one hand, the Tel Aviv-based International Federation of Workers' Education Associations has done a good deal – which

I'll discuss in the next chapter – but what it's done has had little to do with Israel.

The Histadrut national trade union centre has a single email address, recently acquired. There is to my knowledge no plan to use email, discussion groups, the Web or anything else. The one interesting – indeed, unique – use of the Internet by the Israeli labour movement so far has been the Histadrut's campaign to get individuals and organisations to buy sweaters from the 'Oman' factory under threat of closure in the town of Ofekim. As part of the campaign, a World Wide Web site was set up, and email messages were posted to Israeli Internet addresses warning that 'a large percentage of the population of Ofakim are heading for a "cold winter" unless the rest of the country bands together to help'. The message informed readers that each one of us could 'personally help to keep the people of Ofakim employed and Oman open' by ordering 'at least one sweater from Oman'. If this appeal to national and labour solidarity wasn't enough, the message reminded us that Oman's 'sweaters are of superior quality' and that they were being sold 'at COST PRICE!' (emphasis and exclamation marks from original).

One of Israel's two social democratic parties, Mapam (the United Workers' Party), launched a Web site in 1995; it was the first political party in Israel to do so. During the first three months of the site's operation, it recorded nearly 17,000 'hits'. A breakdown of the accesses was published in Mapam's newspaper. As someone who was active several years ago in Mapam's efforts to produce foreign language (i.e. English) publications to get the party's message out to the international democratic left and labour movement, it was remarkable to see how the new medium distributed the party's message far and wide. Hundreds and in some cases thousands of accesses were reported from the US, Canada, Britain and Australia (in addition to over 6,000 hits from within Israel – and remember that the Web site is entirely in English, not Hebrew). Users from more than 30 countries accessed the Mapam site during its first few weeks online.

A number of kibbutzim – collective agricultural-industrial settlements closely linked to the labour movement and left-wing parties – have launched Web sites of their own. Most of these simply offer various products and services for sale, but some are beginning to talk a little about kibbutz itself as a social experiment. These sites, if developed in a political and social direction, could themselves contribute something interesting to the international labour movement.

Meanwhile, the small right-wing trade union centre, Amit, which is linked to the Likud party, launched its own Web site – correctly pointing out that it was the first workers' organisation in Israel to do so. The Amit Web site consisted of about ten pages of information, including details of Amit's services to members, particularly in the fields of labour relations and legal assistance. Amit openly admitted that its site was aimed primarily at young Israelis who were online – an audience which is being missed by the Histadrut as well.

CHAPTER 6

The Emerging Global Labournet

So far, I've used the term 'emerging global labournet' a few times, but all the examples I've given have been local and national. A new internationalism isn't going to be created from the BBS of an electrical workers' local in Chicago or even a province-wide network of teachers in Canada. Those are important efforts to introduce computer communications into the labour movement. They have had positive effects, including democratising ones in the unions themselves. But they cannot by themselves create a global labournet, let alone a new internationalism.

In this chapter, I want to focus on two approaches to international labour computer communications. One is what we might call the 'vertical' global labournet. This is the one involving the existing institutions of the labour movement, including the International Confederation of Free Trade Unions, the various international trade secretariats, and other groups, like the International Federation of Workers' Education Associations. The other is the 'horizonal' global labournet. By this I mean the contacts being made and coalitions being built between individuals and organisations in different countries without the intermediary of an international organisation.

Some early observers of the emergence of 'labour telematics' in the 1980s thought that the 'horizontal' net would bypass or even replace the traditional international trade union structures. They were wrong. Thanks to computer communications, those structures have become stronger, not weaker.

The Vertical Labournet

Dan Gallin minces no words when he writes about the International Confederation of Free Trade Unions. In his 1994 article for *New Politics*, 'Inside the New World Order: Drawing the Battle Lines', Gallin calls the ICFTU 'a directionless giant'. (It is certainly a giant; by mid-decade, the organisation had 188 national affiliates in 134 countries representing no fewer than 126,000,000 members.) Those ICFTU officials who saw its primary function as fighting the Cold War are disoriented. 'The obvious alternative', writes Gallin, 'does not occur to them: that now is the time to pick up where the serious labour internationals of the past left off.'

Such a reinvigorated international labour movement is 'beyond the imagining' of those ICFTU officials who 'are largely ignorant of past experience, contemptuous of history and theory, and afraid of struggle'. Gallin explains that the ICFTU's Executive Board consists of officials from national trade union centres who 'have a vested interest in believing that there are national solutions for their members' problems and are caught in structural constraints which obstruct a global vision'. Such centres are now often bypassing international trade union structures like the ICFTU and giving aid directly to unions in developing and post-Communist societies. 'Such bilateral assistance', says Gallin, 'creates chaos, increases the danger of corruption and weakens international trade unionism at the time it most needs strengthening.' On the other hand, he admits, such bilateral aid 'plays well for the home audience'.

The ICFTU, says Gallin, should be on the cutting edge of the defence of trade union rights, supporting unions in developing and post-Communist countries, and (in cooperation with the ITSs) taking action on the transnational corporations. Instead, what little the ICFTU does is 'underfunded and undervalued'. The organisation, he concludes, 'lives far too much in a bureaucratic and abstract world where form takes precedence over substance and preoccupations with turf, jurisdiction and status overshadow the original purpose of the exercise'.

Early in 1995, the ICFTU declared that one of its top priorities for the year was to participate in the United Nations Social Development Summit in Copenhagen. The organisation planned to put its campaign for a 'social clause' in international trade agreements on the agenda of world politics. But, as Peter Waterman observed, the ICFTU activities at the Summit 'made less public impact than did such tiny NGOs as Oxfam'. Waterman concluded that the ICFTU 'is marked less by any Free World triumphalism' and more by 'confusion, ineffectivity – and criticism from its own allies'.

In April 1994, the ICFTU (together with the ILO) funded a Labour Telematics Centre report on 'The Opportunity and Challenge of Telematics'. The ICFTU sent out a detailed questionnaire to all its affiliates. Many of them replied. Several asked for assistance. Hopes were raised. In a foreword to the report, ICFTU General Secretary Enzo Friso (who retired later that year) wrote that 'there is a great potential for telematics to be used to contribute to equity, social justice and sustainable development'. The international trade union movement, he wrote, 'must develop a cohesive and proactive international approach in this field'. It looked like the ICFTU was about to do something.

Two years later, the organisation continues to have a single email box on GeoNet. Very recently, its Asia/Pacific regional organisation – which is based on the Internet-intensive island of Singapore – launched a Web site of its own. But in June 1996 the ICFTU finally launched its own global site on the Web – and what a site it was to be. The home page opens up in no fewer than four languages (English, French, Spanish and German) and is rich in ICFTU material. But the site seems to be no more than a spin-off from the organisation's Congress, which was held at the end of that month, and not a permanent communications tool. It includes daily updates of Congress news, but no more than that. When clicking on a link which should have told me more about how the ICFTU deals with the problem of transnational corporations, I received an error message. Clearly the sleeping giant is awakening – but slowly.

Another important institution slowly awakening to the significance of the Internet has been the International Labour Organisation. Only in 1996, and following international pressure, did the ILO launch a serious Web site. The ILO site, in English, French and Spanish, is rich in information of the organisation's concerns – which are often those of the labour movement. Among topics covered by the new ILO venture in cyberspace are the following:

- Child labour
- Employment
- Equality for women
- Human rights
- International labour standards
- Social security

The ICFTU lags far behind other trade unions in developing online databases, discussion groups and electronic publishing. Even the moribund WFTU has more of an online presence. (Its press releases appear in LaborNet@IGC conferences.) The ICFTU's monthly publication, *Free Labour World*, largely ignores the whole question of computer communications. The one article on the subject published in 1995 – and this in reaction to the G7 Brussels Summit on a global information superhighway (so much for a 'proactive' strategy) – was headlined 'The Information Superhighway – Road to Nowhere?'.

Meanwhile, the international trade secretariats, pioneers of the labournet as early as 1984, continue to move forward. They are continuing and expanding their use of online databases. They are beginning to create sites on the World Wide Web. More affiliate unions and more branch offices of the ITSs are online. Fax and email networks are increasingly integrated. And they are slowly breaking away from the old GeoNet network, switching over in some cases to direct links to the Internet.

ICEM

In November 1995, two giant ITSs – the miners' and the chemical workers' internationals – merged, creating the International Federation of Chemical, Energy, Mine and General Workers' Unions (ICEM). The new ITS includes 402 affiliated trade unions in 112 countries, representing over 21,000,000 million workers.

In the ICFTU's coverage of the merger in a page one article in *Free Labour World*, it noted that 'both organisations are coming to the merger congress in a position of strength'. The miners pushed through an ILO Convention on Safety and Health. And the chemical workers? Listen carefully to the ICFTU's evaluation of their strength: 'The ICEF has been a trail-blazer for trade unions in their use of information technology, and has come to be seen by its affiliates as a premier source of online information.' Even the net-challenged ICFTU put the ICEF's achievements in the field of computer-mediated communications at the very top of the organisation's list of achievements.

Jim Catterson, the ICEF's Research Officer who helped bring the organisation online back when few trade unionists (or anyone else) had ever heard of computer networks, is still at his post in the new secretariat. The research staff still consists of only three people, though it may soon increase to as many as five. (By contrast, Amnesty International's paid staff at its London secretariat is about 300 people.)

Though Catterson is glad that more and more affiliates use email, those online number still little more than 10 per cent of the total number of ICEM unions. But the majority of ICEM affiliates now have fax machines. Email is now used extensively where it could not be used at all a decade ago – in contacts with ICEM affiliate unions in the former Soviet Union. 'Nearly all of our affiliates in Russia now have email', says Catterson, 'and I can communicate via Internet with the Independent Miners of Kazakhstan (NPG) region in Karaganda.' Ironically, trade unions in the developed countries are the ones with cold feet when it comes to adopting the new technology. 'It's a pity I still rely on fax for a lot of our European affiliates', Catterson adds.

The ICEM continues to subscribe to the databases that it began using in 1985. These include Datastar, Dialog, Reuters, and Infotrade in Belgium. The organisation uses CD-ROMs especially for occupational safety and health material. Meanwhile, the number of requests for information from affiliates to the secretariat in Brussels continues to rise. In 1995, the ICEF processed some 1,700 such requests – a 30 per cent increase since 1991.

In 1996 the ICEM launched its own extensive and highly professional Web site. It includes *ICEM Info* (the organisation's magazine), a cartoon series and five murals created for the ITS's Founding Congress. Like other labour Web sites, the ICEM pages include links to other sites, a brochure describing the organisation, ICEM Update (an international labour news service), and other publications.

But once again, the ICEM went way ahead of everyone else, as it has been doing since the 1980s, with its 'cyber-campaign' against the tyre giant Bridgestone/Firestone. The ICEM home pages showed Web surfers how to email Bridgestone officials and other ways to bombard the company with protests during a global 'day of outrage' in July 1996 to commemorate two years since the launch of a bitter strike. The ICEM encourages visits to the various home pages of the transnational corporation and its subsidaries around the world, supplementing the picket lines and protests that were happening outside of cyberspace.

Finally, the trade secretariat is also working on building a global database of contract information – a project discussed many years ago by the ICEF.

ITF

The London-based International Transport Workers' Federation unites more than 400 unions in about 100 countries representing over 5,000,000 workers. It was one of the first international trade secretariats to adopt email and online databases back in the mid-1980s. A decade later, it continues to play a pioneering role. While other organisations still pat themselves on the back for having purchased access to email through GeoNet, the ITF has gone far beyond that. The organisation now has its own leased line connection to the Internet. The result, says Richard Flint, is 'desktop electronic mail, Web and FTP access at *blistering* speeds'. In fact, the ITF can now act as an Internet service provider itself.

The ITF made the decision to connect directly to the Internet – which costs more than simply buying the right to access email on networks like GeoNet – in order to provide Telnet access for the organisation's maritime inspectors to an online database on ships covered by ITF agreements, and other information. (Telnet is an Internet tool allowing remote access to computers.) Those inspectors work in ports all over the world. Today, they can directly access the ITF's computer and get the information they need. The database is closed to everyone else.

The ITF became the first international trade secretariat with its own World Wide Web site. They were not yet recording 'hits' to the site, so there is no way of knowing if anyone is accessing it.

The ITF's monthly publication, appearing in five languages, *ITF News*, is available for downloading. But instead of creating a simple

HTML or text file, the organisation chose a more sophisticated route. They created, using the Adobe Acrobat software, a 'portable document file' (PDF) which allows sophisticated graphics. This is (to my knowledge) the first trade union publication to do so.

In addition to making the *ITF News* available, the site also offers access to the organisation's constitution, an article about what the ITF is, its press releases, and much more. When there is a need for urgent action – as occurred in the Liverpool dockers' case in January 1996 – the appeal is blazoned across the front of the home page.

The organisation is also experimenting with an FTP server, which will allow the transfer of files from computer to computer. (FTP is the Internet's 'file transfer protocol' – the fastest and most efficient way to move files around the net.) The advantage of such a technique, as I discovered myself, is that it allows users to download very large files quickly and easily.

'We have big plans and hopes for on-line communications in the future', says Richard Flint. 'As an organisation we can be proud of the fact that we were very early proponents of the use of email and computer communications. It now seems that everyone is getting on the bandwagon and suddenly discovering the advantages that we were going on about for years.'

An important development for the ITF is the discussion taking place within the International Maritime Satellite Organisation (INMARSAT) about the possibility of linking up the Internet with the INMARSAT Satcoms network. This would allow email and Web access to virtually every cargo ship in the world. Rank-and-file seamen (or at least their shop stewards) would have access to their unions and their trade secretariat in London *while at sea* – as a matter of right. This would end the isolation and vulnerability of merchant seamen which has been the case for centuries, and would empower them for the very first time *vis a vis* ship officers and owners. This would strengthen not only the individual seamen and their national unions, but their international trade secretariat as well. 'Obviously, this will be very good for us', says Flint.

FIET

FIET is the International Federation of Commercial, Clerical, Professional and Technical Employees – the only international trade secretariat known by its French initials. It represents some 11,000,000 private sector employees in about 400 trade unions in over 120 countries. More than half of those unions joined FIET in the last decade and a half, making it one of the fastest growing international trade union organisations.

The Geneva-based trade secretariat was one of the first two ITSs to launch a Web site. It did so on 10 July 1995, coinciding with the opening day of FIET's World Congress, held in Vienna. The union expected the Web site 'will be of particular interest to the growing number of employees who work online', many of whom are represented by FIET affiliated unions.

One positive feature of the Web site – which appears in English – is the publication online of *FIET Info*, the organisation's newsletter. Only two issues were available when I looked, but each one offered dozens of articles which are not only easy to access, but easy to incorporate in other publications. Without re-typing, FIET affiliates around the world can now take articles easily from the ITS publication.

Another nice feature is headlined 'FIET Documentation'. International trade union organisations often produce printed pamphlets and even books. The Web is one way to boost interest in these. The FIET site lists all available publications (these are free of charge) and using an online form with check boxes, allows users to mark the publications they'd like to receive, and record their snail-mail addresses. Rank-and-file members of trade unions which are affiliated to ITSs usually know very little about those international organisations. They are probably unaware of publications the ITSs put out. With its Web site, FIET is encouraging direct contact between the ITS in Geneva and the eleven million affiliated workers out there, around the world.

IUF

The Geneva-based International Union of Food, Agricultural, Hotel, Restaurant, Catering, Tobacco and Allied Workers' Associations (IUF) has a membership list long enough to justify the length of its name. The IUF represents some 2,650,000 workers organised into 312 trade unions in 110 countries.

The IUF went online several years after the pioneering trade secretariats in the chemical and transport sectors. Only in 1989 did the organisation connect its secretariat in Geneva and regional offices in Sydney and Hong Kong to the GeoNet network. The three offices continue to use email today, mostly to transmit and receive reports. A year later, the Latin American office in Montevideo connected. This allowed the organisation to do its Spanish-language translations from Uruguay. This remains a key use of email for the IUF today. Translators all over Europe work for the organisation, sending and receiving materials by email. In 1993–94, the IUF's North American office in Washington went online too, but instead of linking up to the GeoNet network, they opted for the APC network (now LaborNet@IGC). In addition to internal communications, the

IUF uses email in its contacts with other trade secretariats and organisations like Amnesty International.

The IUF uses the Poptel bulletin boards (in particular, the one called 'Labour') to send out the organisations's frequent press releases. These are often of general interest, and reflect not only the practical day-to-day work of the IUF, but its views on major world issues like Bosnia, French nuclear testing, and human rights in China. In one particular case, the IUF was contacted by a very helpful non-trade union group which had picked up a solidarity appeal on one of these bulletin boards.

Only in 1995 did the IUF begin the use of online databases, using those which were available through Poptel. IUF staffers say that while this is very useful in investigating transnational corporations and their subsidiaries around the world, it's also very expensive. A much cheaper source of information has been the World Wide Web. But as one IUF staffer told me, 'the only problem is sifting through all the information in the Web to find what is relevant'.

IUF plans for the near future include launching a Web site focusing on one particular transnational corporation in the food sector. The aim of the Web site is to 'encourage our affiliates to start taking advantage of email and all the opportunities the Internet offers'.

The organisation is also planning to assist unions in developing countries to get online. Very few of the IUF's affiliates were online by early 1996, and those who were seemed to be reluctant to adopt the new technology, still preferring to use fax and mail. Finally, the IUF is considering the establishment of online networks of unions within a particular company – or what might be called 'virtual company councils'. (More on this in the next chapter.)

PSI

Some of the most interesting and important experiments in labour's use of computer communications have taken place among public sector trade unions. Among these are Canada's Solinet and Britain's MSF–ITPA network. Those unions are affiliated to the Public Services International (PSI), which represents more than 20,000,000 workers in over 400 unions all over the world. Its membership is composed of personnel employed in national, regional and local governments; electricity, gas and water workers; health, environmental and social services; educational, cultural and recreational services; and other bodies whose function it is to provide services to the public.

Its secretariat is located in France, on the outskirts of Geneva. The PSI staff numbers nearly 30 people, of whom only three are today connected to the Internet (the Research and Information

Officer, Alice Carl, and two technical people). But plans are afoot to connect all staff members to email in the near future. Outside of the secretariat, the organisation has a staff of several dozen more, including some 20 'education coordinators' and representatives in a number of countries. Nearly all of these are connected by email to the office in France, and to each other.

The PSI connected to the Internet, as did nearly all the international trade secretariats, using Poptel. A representative from Poptel even spoke before 1,000 delegates representing PSI-affiliated unions at the organisation's 1993 World Congress, introducing them to the idea of global labour networking by computer. GeoNet's labour bulletin boards were consulted on a daily basis, and 'Urgent Action Campaigns' and four regional PSI news bulletins were posted to those boards. The secretariat also used Poptel's FIND database, and considered subscribing to other online sources of information. (Today Carl uses other databases, including FT Profile.)

Late in 1993, Solinet's Marc Belanger paid a visit to the PSI secretariat, and deepened the organisation's understanding of the importance of using the new technology.

In 1994, when the Labour Telematics Centre undertook its survey of international trade union use of the networks, PSI affiliates turned in 60 replies, which was the second largest number among the organisations surveyed. According to the LTC report, the PSI's use of telematics 'has dramatically improved their internal communications capabilities'.

In early 1995, the organisation decided to probe existing information held by affiliates on privatisation of public services, mainly by transnational companies, and at the same time investigate members' use of computers in a survey entitled 'PSI Global Network on Multinationals and Computer Communication'. Even though the secretariat had copies of the answers to the 1994 LTC survey, a broader and more up-to-date survey was needed.

Affiliate unions were asked if they had regular electricity supply, the conditions of telephone lines, if they possessed personal computers, modems and communications software, if staff were trained in email usage, etc. By the end, over a hundred replies had been received. Carl concluded that 'although many affiliates are working with computers, use of computers for communication and research purposes is still limited, as is the use of outside online databases'. The exchange of information, she wrote, 'will have to include paper' for quite some time to come.

The survey is quite important in that it is one of the most extensive, and yet sector-intensive, research efforts ever made into trade union use of telematics. In a breakdown prepared when nearly 70 responses had been received, some trends had already emerged:

- Among the organisation's thirteen African affiliate unions which responded, nine had fax machines, and only one owned a personal computer. None used email.
- Of the thirteen Asian unions which replied, all but one had personal computers, three of those had modems, but not a single one used email.
- The European affiliates and those in the Americas were not in much better shape, even though nearly all had personal computers and fax machines. No fewer than 20 of these affiliates owned modems, but the only ones with email – in fact the only PSI affiliates at all which answered that they had access to email – were one union in Canada (CUPE, of course), two in the United States (AFT and AFSCME), and one each in Sweden (ST) and the UK (GMB).

It seems as if CUPE's Solinet is still slightly ahead of its time.

Meanwhile, PSI plans for the near future include a Web site, online databases and an online discussion group. Through its own research network, Carl got technical support and ideas for the Web site and is working carefully to produce one which concentrates on selected issues of concern to the PSI's unions. As for databases, subjects expected to be covered include water, electricity, waste management, health services and others. The online discussion group will devote its initial efforts toward discussing a World Bank water policy paper. The final document to be prepared by that group will then be used in the PSI's water campaign as a means of assisting unions, and will be submitted directly to the World Bank itself.

IFWEA

Dan Gallin writes that 'the vast edifice of the pre-1930s social-democratic labour movement in Europe lies in ruins'. Nevertheless, 'there is evidence of life in these ruins ... The labour movement in all its vastness still has immense resources at its disposal.' Those resources include 'social and cultural organisations, women's and youth organisations, educational associations and schools, hiking and touring clubs, sports clubs, travel agencies, consumers cooperatives, banks and housing cooperatives'. Gallin is particularly interested in international organisations which work in the fields of workers' aid and workers' education. The labour movement's educational needs today, he says, 'are *immense*. The whole political culture of the labour movement has to be passed on to millions of people who have been cut off from it for several generations.'

The International Federation of Workers' Education Associations (IFWEA), he writes, is 'the only organisation of the labour movement that combines trade unions ... party institutions, think tanks and workers' education associations' at the international level. 'It is uniquely well placed to become the laboratory where the labour movement develops its new ideological instruments, provided that this is perceived as its principal priority.' Gallin ought to know. In 1992 he was elected President of the IFWEA.

A word is in order here about the IFWEA itself. This little-known organisation was founded in the final days of the Second World War by the British Workers' Education Association (WEA) and other groups involved in labour education. It was formally constituted in October 1947 at a meeting in London. By the early 1990s, the organisation was relatively inactive, yet (as Gallin pointed out) it included in its membership some very powerful and vibrant labour education organisations, including the Swedish ABF, the Norwegian and Danish AOF, Germany's Arbeit und Leben, as well as national trade union centres like the DGB in Germany and Israel's Histadrut. With the election of a new leadership at the IFWEA's 1992 Congress, the organisation made a concerted attempt to revive itself.

At that congress, John Atkins of the Labour Telematics Centre in Manchester made a presentation to delegates on the subject of computer communications. Upon the initiative of British delegates the organisation decided to join up with the GeoNet network, and encouraged affiliates to do so as well. A few months later, the new IFWEA General Secretary visited the Labour Telematics Centre himself, where he was given a short course in the subject.

The IFWEA also decided to launch a quarterly magazine after 45 years of existence without a regular publication of any kind. That journal, *Workers' Education*, began appearing in May 1993. I was hired earlier that year to serve as its editor. In its December 1993 edition, devoted exclusively to the subject of 'Computer Communications and the Labour Movement', it was announced that the journal itself would be available online.

With the assistance of John Atkins, copies of that issue and several subsequent editions were posted to four labour bulletin boards around the world (all of them linked to GeoNet). But the electronic publication of *Workers' Education* didn't stop there; copies were made and posted elsewhere as well. Bob Kastigar posted the whole issue both to his own local union bulletin board and to the AFL–CIO's LaborNET. Seth Wigderson, moderator of the H-Labor discussion group, announced the existence of the publication and sent out copies by email to those who asked for them. ('Many wrote back to me telling me how much they liked it', he told me.) Vassily Balog posted the full text to the APC conference 'labr.cis'.

Meanwhile, all subsequent issues of the magazine devoted a full page, usually the back cover, to a column called 'Online'. No other international labour publication had done this – so far.

By April 1994, the Labour Telematics Centre was reporting that the IFWEA 'has decided to use electronic communications and is encouraging its affiliates to do so. Already, IFWEA is making use of telematics to help with the production and printing of its quarterly journal.' As I explained in an article in the magazine, the text of articles was typed into a personal computer (using the QText word-processing software) and then transmitted using a 2400 bps external modem from my office to the electronic mailbox of a graphic designer in Tel Aviv (using Telix communications software). The intermediary was Israel's largest electronic bulletin board, Rudy's Place. The graphic design was then done using Ventura Publisher desktop publishing software.

Over time, the technicalities changed – instead of using a local bulletin board, we began working directly through the Internet; Telix was abandoned in favour of the Internet Chameleon software suite; we began using much faster modems; the word-processing and desktop publishing software went over to Windows and Macintosh products. In just two years, nearly all the software and hardware involved were changed. (Compare this to the 1980s, when the British Columbia Teachers' Federation was able to use the same software and hardware for nine straight years.)

And increasingly, article submissions have come in via modem, and through the Internet. Articles for the magazine from England, Canada, Norway, New Zealand, the Philippines, the US and Switzerland have reached the editor this way. The journal is now translated into Spanish and French, with the English text reaching the translators through the Internet. (The French translation is done in Europe.) And the process of editorial review, involving the IFWEA's General Secretary (in Tel Aviv), and its President (in Geneva), is also done via modem.

The Internet was also a research tool in the hands of the IFWEA staff. An early use made was an effort to produce an introductory bibliography on the subject of May Day, the international labour holiday. This was done by accessing a major university library in the US, and searching by keyword. Issues of the magazine on the subjects of women workers and labour videos were largely researched on the net. One negative side effect of all this was an increasingly heavy 'American' focus to the magazine, which resulted naturally from relying on Internet resources.

In March 1995, *Workers' Education* made Internet (and labour) history by becoming the focal point of the IFWEA's brand new Web site at the Economic Democracy Information Network in Berkeley, California. Not only were all the issues of the publication (full text) transferred to the computer in Berkeley using the Internet's file transfer protocol (FTP) and then posted for all to see, but the eighth issue, not yet published in its print version, was instantly made available on the Web. It was the first international labour publication to go completely online (while maintaining a print edition).

News of the transformation of *Workers' Education* into a full text e-journal quickly spread through the Internet. Notices were posted in USENET newsgroups and LISTSERV lists. Key individuals in the Solinet and Poptel networks were informed. Conventional means of informing the Internet community as a whole were also taken up, including a posting in the widely read NCSA Mosaic 'What's New' page. The magazine was even listed in the 'Internet Mall'.

But the results were initially disappointing. After about two weeks online, it turned out that fewer than 100 readers had accessed the site. Interest in the site slowly picked up, and after a few months nearly 1,000 accesses per month were being recorded. Though this did not compare well with such popular sites as the Internet index, 'Yahoo', with its reported 3 million accesses *per day*, it wasn't bad for a magazine that was printing only 2,000 copies on paper (English edition).

To boost interest in the site, in early April the IFWEA began offering online users the chance to order free of charge its first book, *Fighting Unemployment*. Dozens of trade unionists and academics wrote in asking for copies. A number of these came from developing countries, including Brazil and Peru, where the IFWEA traditionally had few contacts. Within a few months, a Peruvian group which made contact this way was formally applying for membership in the international organisation.

A key factor in the dramatic increases in the number of 'hits' (accesses through the net to the site) was the introduction of a US Federal Budget simulator at the EDIN Web site. This attracted thousands of people to visit the EDIN site, and in turn, several thousand of them checked out the IFWEA site. Meanwhile, the IFWEA site was increasingly listed as a link at other key labour sites throughout the net, including the important LaborNet@IGC Web site.

The IFWEA site was demonstrated to the organisation's Executive Committee for the first time at its meeting in Namur, Belgium in May 1995. 'Neat', was the response of one member, while others sat open-mouthed in awe. Poptel founder Dave Spooner, just elected General Secretary of the IFWEA's European regional organisation, while appreciative of the work done, felt that the site had to include material in the organisation's other official languages, and not only English.

In early July, the site underwent a major transformation, as the ninth issue of *Workers' Education* went online. It, and the previous issue as well, were converted into full hypertext files. What this meant was that the various regular columns, different articles, and keywords were turned into hyperlinks, and by clicking on them readers could jump around the issue as if they were turning pages, instead of scrolling down more than a thousand lines of text. Graphics were deliberately not introduced at this stage because of concerns that many potential readers of the online magazine would not be able to see them, and others would download them at tortuously slow speeds.

If *Workers' Education* was something of a success story, the IFWEA has still not realised its hopes of using computer communications in other ways. It continues to use regular mail, international telephone calls, and faxes to communicate between the secretariat and the various affiliates.

Even the members of the Executive Committee, a small group which could easily have been linked by email, have largely not done so – despite the prodding of the IFWEA staff. At least one member of the Committee told this writer that though she had access to email, she refused to use it because of all the junk mail which filled up her electronic mail box.

As a result, the only interaction between Executive members takes place at the semi-annual meetings, usually held in Europe. Decision-making moves at a snail's pace. Executive members are sometimes out of touch with the secretariat, and each other, for months at a time. It is impossible to react to events at this speed, or to build consensus before taking decisions at meetings. Only a small number of the organisation's nearly 100 affiliates use email, making it an ineffective medium for distributing information to them.

Even though the IFWEA Executive officially committed the organisation as early as 1993 to using the Internet, nothing has concretely been done other than hooking up the secretariat and, of course, the use made in writing, editing and distributing the organisation's magazine. In this sense, the experience of the IFWEA is not very different from that of international trade secretariats, as described elsewhere in this chapter.

The IFWEA experience has not been the only attempt at some kind of international labour education using the net. Others have included Solinet courses and the TUDIC project. A word on both seems appropriate here.

In May 1994, Solinet ran what was described as 'the first ever international trade union class'. The subject of the class – one of Solinet's many special conferences – was the Russian labour movement, and the 'lecturers' were activists in the Russian trade union movement. Once every week, trade unionists in Moscow would upload to Solinet (using Telnet) texts, which would then be discussed by the Canadian unionists and their Russian counterparts.

But more than three years before that, the Danish and Swedish trade union centres, working together with the British TUC, started a project in distance learning within the trade union movement using computer communications. The courses, which began in the autumn of 1990, were aimed at shop stewards in each of the three countries. Subjects included the trade union movement and Europe, word-processing programs, and spreadsheets.

The Horizontal Labournet

The Internet is being used by individual workers and local organisations every day to promote international trade union solidarity. Most of the stories of how it is used are unknown to us. But every once in a while, we hear of one, and from this we learn what is going on.

As early as 1989, the Internet was being used to promote international labour solidarity under the most arduous of conditions. The autonomous workers' movement in China, facing brutal repression, was able to get its messages to the outside world using the new communications technologies, including email and fax.

In the years that followed, use of the Internet by trade unionists for international solidarity has increased. This activity is not always coordinated by established international bodies like the ITSs. It does not always go through what were once the 'proper channels' – national trade union centres. Our evidence of this activity is therefore entirely anecdotal. Three examples follow.

'The Calls Seemed To Be Coming from Everywhere'

In 1993, one of the most extraordinary (and best documented) uses of the 'horizontal' global labournet took place. The story was told by Renfrey Clarke, the Moscow correspondent for Australia's *Green Left Weekly*, and was posted to the LaborNet conference 'labr.cis' under the headline: 'E-mail helps win release of political prisoners'.

Late on the evening of 3 October, during Russian President Boris Yeltsin's armed assault on the Duma (the Russian parliament), three leaders of the tiny Party of Labour (PT) were arrested. They were Alexander Segal, Boris Kagarlitsky and Vladimir Kondratov. The latter two were former members of the suppressed Moscow City Council. Kagarlitsky is well known to the left in the West; he writes for the *Russian Labour Review* (KAS-KOR's magazine, which appears in English) and many other publications. All three men were associated with the major ex-Soviet trade union confederation, the Federation of Independent Trade Unions of Russia. The men were picked up by police as they stood on the pavement outside the offices of a local council in the southern part of the city. They had just returned from preventing a potentially disastrous and bloody attack by pro-Duma crowds on the Shabolovskaya television station.

For a whole day, no one knew what had become of the men, nor of several others who had been arrested with them. Meanwhile, the PT leaders were beaten up by the police, who were trying to get them to confess to killing two policemen and stealing police vehicles. Only on the night of 4 October, when a criminal prisoner was released, did news reach Kagarlitsky's wife of their whereabouts. She called Vasily Balog, who we met in the last chapter. Balog, you will recall, is Deputy Head of the International Department of the General Confederation of Trade Unions. He was also an early email buff.

Within minutes, Balog began what Clarke called 'a swift international campaign to secure the prisoners' release' using email. He posted messages to several online conferences, urging anyone who was listening to call the Moscow police station where the men were held. 'I was so agitated that I couldn't remember the English term "police station"', Balog later recalled, 'I think I called it a "police house". But the message did the trick.'

Kagarlitsky recounted what happened next. 'We were watching from the cell as the phone calls came in', he remembered. 'One of the first was from Japan. The police didn't seem able to believe it. After that the phone ran hot. The calls seemed to be coming from everywhere – there were quite a few from the Bay Area in the US In the end the police started saying we'd already been released. But we were shouting through the bars, "No! No! We're still here".'

Most of the detainees were released within a few hours, and the frame-up charges against them were dropped. As Clarke summarised the story, 'With labour and political activists in Russia increasingly hooked into international email systems, repression in the country will never be as easy again.'

Cross-border Solidarity

Another use of computer networks by trade unionists in different countries took place during the recent struggle by the labour movements in North America against the North American Free Trade Agreement (NAFTA). Though not as dramatic as other stories, this example is important for a number of reasons. It involves both mainstream trade unions and groups on the margins of the labour movement. And it took place in the most Internet-intensive part of the world, North America. (Though Mexico is not especially Internet-intensive; only 17 per cent of Mexican families have telephones.) If cross-border solidarity using computer-mediated communications won't work in North America, it won't work anywhere.

Joe Brenner did a fascinating study of how Mexican, Canadian and US unions used various communications technologies, including computer networking, in the period leading up to the adoption of NAFTA. Brenner cited several examples, beginning with US–Canadian computer networking in 1987.

By the early 1990s, US groups concerned with NAFTA began dialogues online with such Mexican groups as the Red Mexicana de Accion Frente al Libre Comercio (RMALC), also known as the Mexican Free Trade Action Network. RMALC, which includes trade unions like the Frente Autentico del Trabajo (FAT), published English-language summaries of Mexican news stories and posted these on APC networks, including PeaceNet and EcoNet. Another Mexican group making use of the progressive APC networks was SIPRO (Servicios Informativos Procesados) which also provided training to grassroots groups.

One of the US groups close to the labour movement which was actively online during the NAFTA debate was the monthly magazine *Labour Notes*. It sent electronic and print mailings on a regular basis, and used the network to solicit information. By August 1992, *Labour Notes* announced online the formation of North American Worker-to-Worker Network. The emphasis was on *direct contact between workers*, hailed by the new network as 'the strongest form of education toward effective international solidarity'.

Other US groups linked to the labour movement which used computer communications during the NAFTA debate included the American Labour Education Center, which publishes the magazine *American Labour*; the Mobilization on Development, Trade, Labour and the Environmment; the International Labour Rights Education and Research Fund; and the Development Group for Alternative Policies. These groups transmitted information online about NAFTA, including materials in Spanish. Ongoing publications like *NAFTA Thoughts* had online editions.

One example Brenner cited of a concrete call for cross-border solidarity came on May Day 1991, when a message posted to LaborNet described the abduction of Braulio Aguilar Reyes, the brother of a leader of petroleum workers. LaborNet participants were urged to send requests for urgent action to other groups online, using the APC-affiliated PeaceNet, Canada's APC affiliate Web, or the Solinet or GeoNet networks. Brenner did not report whether there was any result to these calls.

Cross-border trade union cooperation increased in the years following the adoption of NAFTA by the US Congress in November 1993. An example may be found in the Web page set up jointly by FAT and the US electrical workers union. What we have described above were just the first, halting efforts of trade unionists and networks close to the labour movement. As Brenner himself noted, many of the key players in the labour movement, and not only on the Mexican side of the border, were simply not yet connected to the networks.

Please Tell the Internet ...

Chris Bailey of Britain's LabourNet also serves as Branch Secretary of the Cambridge and Newmarket District Committee of the Amalgamated Engineering and Electrical Union (AEEU). The union was considering calling a strike at PreStar, a company owned by the German transnational Krupp. The local managers at PreStar told the union that it would immediately fire the entire workforce if it went on strike and that 'it has the full support of the parent company' (meaning Krupp in Germany) for this.

Bailey decided to put out an appeal on the Internet, looking to talk with other workers employed by Krupp. 'We feel that for us to be able to confront such blackmail', he wrote, 'we need to establish links with the workforce throughout the Krupp company particularly in Germany.' He sent the message out to the LISTSERV mailing list Union-d, and posted it to two conferences on LaborNet@IGC, labr.uk and labr.global. The message produced several responses from Germany, which put Bailey's union in contact with IG Metall (the German metal workers' union) at both Krupp-Hoesch in Dortmund and Krupp in Duisburg.

Faced with the threat of being sacked, the workers at PreStar decided not to strike. Bailey sent out a thank you note (via the net) to all those who replied. But the story didn't end there. 'We are not sure what has been happening at the German end', he wrote, 'but it seems clear from the reaction of the management here that IG Metall has been asking questions in Krupp about our situation. The personnel manager who made the original threat has been phoning our district office in an agitated state demanding that we announce the resolution of the dispute "on the internet". He has apparently been sent a copy of our original message by Krupp in Germany.'

Bailey commented that 'this must be the first time such a demand has been made as part of the resolution of a dispute'. In his opinion, this episode 'shows the potential of computer communications for the labour movement in tackling the power of the transnationals.

It is clear that the PreStar management is worried about the contacts we have now established with IG Metall at Krupp.'

The *practical* result was a strengthening of the links between the British and German Krupp employees – and a strengthening of the union's commitment to using computer-mediated communications. The union in Cambridge accordingly decided to sponsor a Web site for the local trade unions and plans to pressure the Cambridge city council to link it to the city's official home page.

CHAPTER 7

The New Internationalism

Until now, I've been talking about the past. Every book about the Internet is necessarily a work of history. When I look at the 'Guaranteed Timely and Accurate' symbol on the back of one of my 1993 Internet books, I smile. 'Timely' is not the adjective that jumps most readily to mind.

In this final chapter, I'll return to the theme with which this book began. I'll discuss the construction of a global labournet and the next International. I'll begin by discussing the good news (and the bad) about the emerging global labournet. The bad news is that there is no real global labournet. The good news is that serious efforts are being made by trade unionists and others to overcome all the obstacles standing in the way.

Some fascinating proposals are being made for the next few years – including online company councils and an international labour university – and we'll look at each of these. Then I'll 'push the envelope' and go further, with a handful of radical proposals for the labour movement to consider in the years ahead.

The Bad News and the Good

Everyone who has written about or spoken about labour use of computer networks has come up with a list of the obstacles to expanding and intensifying that use. Those obstacles are very real, and a global labournet is not yet a reality. But it will become one because for every problem we are able to define, a solution is already in sight. Even as I write these words, some of the 'classic' obstacles to an international online labour network are crumbling.

Where Is Everybody?

It is agreed by nearly everyone that for the Internet to have any relevance at all for working people and their institutions (trade unions and labour parties), it must reach them by their thousands and tens of thousands in their homes and workplaces. So far we have seen a few examples of this in this book. The British Columbia Teachers' Federation seems to have successfully brought the net right into the homes, classrooms and offices of teachers, allowing it to serve the purposes it was designed for. But as we have seen, their experience is not typical.

The international trade secretariats, for example, though pioneers of computer networking in the labour movement, have not successfully brought all (or even most) of their national union affiliates on line. We're not talking about the average worker, or unionist, or shop steward. Most national trade union organisations are not yet online.

Even if the Internet connects 50 million people (and that's the highest estimate current), we're still talking about *less than 1 per cent* of the world's population. One result is that some of the international discussion groups concerning the labour movement are infinitesimally small. The European trade union forum had fewer than 150 participants. The 50 forums available at LaborNet@IGC are accessed by fewer than a thousand trade unionists. Even networks which are sponsored and supported by huge national trade union centres are microscopically small. The AFL–CIO's LaborNET on CompuServe has, as we have mentioned, only 2,500 participants. So long as the Internet is used by only a tiny percentage of trade unionists, we cannot have any illusions about its impact.

Time will solve most of these problems by itself. The Internet is more-or-less doubling in size every year. The estimates vary of when 100 million people will be online, but almost no one doubts that the number will be reached. Even the most serious researchers toss around various dates – including as early as the year 2010 – when *one billion people* will be online. So the natural growth of the net will sweep in tens of millions of working people and trade unionists, at least in the advanced industrial countries. But the developing countries are another story.

To Be Online, First of All, You Need a Line

The precondition for getting online is, of course, a line. But if you live in a part of the world where there is no telecommunications infrastructure – and this is the case in many developing countries – cheap little computers and modems are not going to be very useful to you. A secretary of one of the international trade secretariats told me the story of how Japanese unions generously donated the very latest computer equipment to the labour movement in Nepal, but the equipment is still sitting in its original boxes years later, unused. A similar story was told by South Africa's WorkNet. Of course trade unionists in the developing countries need computers, modems, and training. But without inexpensive telecommunications, all that will be worthless.

The problem of expensive telecommunications is not confined to the developing countries. Using a telephone is a much more expensive proposition in Britain and France than it is in the United States. This is one of the reasons why Europe lags far behind North America in Internet use. The labour movement should be demanding cheaper telecommunications for everyone, everywhere.

It might be argued that the information gap between developing and developed countries will grow, but that the labour movement need not concern itself with this. We could decide to use the new communications technologies *where they exist*, to strengthen trade unions – where they exist. The result would be an online, high-tech 'communications International' linking Western European and North American unionists, with maybe some Japanese or Australian unionists thrown in as well. That wouldn't be as good as a real global labournet, but it's better than nothing. And to a certain degree, this is what is actually happening.

Yet the changes in the global economy, with the shifts of capital away from the developed countries, are also shifting the centre of gravity of the labour movement away from Western Europe and North America, and towards the world's South. If trade unions want to take on some giant transnational, they are going to have to do this together with workers in the South – or they will fail. It is not merely a question of solidarity, but of survival. To create a global labournet without African, Asian and Latin American participation is not only unfair and unjust, it is also pointless. Unless and until the developing countries become connected – and that means low-cost communications available to the general public – a new workers' International can only be a dream.

The free market is obviously not racing into Africa to set up Internet connections, though some companies like AT&T have kindly offered to do all kinds of nice things (including a fibre-optic undersea cable around the African coast) if only someone would pay. Some labour movement activists think that one approach is to lobby and pressure the venerable International Tele-communications Union (ITU). Maybe.

Another approach would be to lobby and pressure national governments in the rich countries to include a computer communications infrastructure as a top priority in aid to developing countries. In the past, progressives lobbied to get rich countries to give appropriate forms of aid – including low-tech agricultural assistance – rather than building steel plants in the heart of the jungle. Today, we must lobby for the installation of satellite and ground-based fibre-optic and microwave communications networks throughout the developing world. This must be high on the list of labour movement priorities, right up there with protection of trade union rights in those countries. Because if we can get those young labour movements online, we can protect them better.

Tower of Babel

The World Wide Web is a proud creation of European scientists based in a Francophone city, Geneva. Yet their creation, like much else in the world of computers, exists primarily in the English language. The Web, even more than the Internet itself, is English-language dominated. I mentioned this in passing in Chapter 2; let me return to it once again in some detail.

With other Internet tools, like email, language is increasingly a non-problem. One software company (Accent) is offering free 'decoders' for dozens of languages for use in Internet email. Write a letter using that program, make sure your recipient has a decoder program, and you can correspond in Korean or Urdu, if you want. An earlier, but still effective solution, is to send text files which are not written in English as encoded binary files, via email. If I can send a picture of my baby son in glorious colour by email, I can certainly send a text file in the French language.

The World Wide Web, however, is an entirely different problem. Despite all the talk about interactivity, the Web is a lot more like printed matter. A Web page which has been written in English *stays* in English, and no software currently existing can, with a simple click of the mouse, translate such a page into Danish, Swahili, or Arabic. (There is a company offering automatic translation of Web pages to and from English – but there's a catch. There are only a couple of languages involved and the translation is poor.) What some sites offer – and these are almost always *not* sites in the US – are different versions of the site in two or three languages. Each additional language means additional translation costs, and if the material is updated frequently (as it should be if one wants people to return to a particular Web site), those costs can become substantial.

This is not a problem for giant, US-based transnational corporations. Their sites are maintained in English, period. Matters are not so simple for the labour movement, which is supposed to respect cultural differences. Publications of international trade union organisations usually appear in several languages. (The ITF even has a newsletter in *eleven* languages.) There was a time when the labour movement showed an interest in the international language, Esperanto, though that proved unsuccessful.

To produce a publication in a second or third language today requires not only that the material be translated, but also typeset, printed and mailed. Once publications go online, all those other costs drop to zero. Money can be diverted to translation costs. An international organisation that wanted to stop publishing its newsletter on paper and go for an online edition might find that instead of publishing the information in just *one* language, it can now afford to publish it in *ten*.

I want to say a few words about automatic translation software, which is in its infancy – but which exists. One can go into a store today and buy a program which will translate text, for example, from English to Spanish. Professional translators need not panic; their jobs are in no danger. Such programs provide only a rudimentary translation. It will be years before really first-rate programs are available. But there is a huge potential market for such software, particularly as the global system of production expands. It is only a matter of time until automatic translation software becomes both effective and inexpensive. And when this happens, it will represent *the* solution to the biggest obstacle to the creation of a true global labournet, which is the barrier of language.

A Question of Quality

When training people to use the Internet, more than once the questions come up: How do you know this information is reliable? Can we trust the information we're getting here? Who wrote this? It's usually not difficult to answer, because one uses Internet-based information the same way one uses any other kind: *carefully*. There are Web sites and online databases which seem to be more reliable than others. Common sense should tell us that.

The problem is not so much the *reliability* of the information, but its *quality*. Too much is headlines, synopses, digests – and too little substance. There is lots of news, but very little analysis. And this is also true on the labour Web pages.

People do not like to sit for long hours reading from computer screens. And for those of us paying for Internet use by the hour, this can cost a lot of money. Articles offered up on the World Wide Web are either going to be short or they are not going to be read. Instead of news, we get news bites.

In the United States, there is a newspaper which was launched in the 1980s which reads very much like a page on the World Wide Web: *USA Today*. It is colourful, there are lots of graphs and charts and photos, and articles run to about 150 words in length. There is lots of sports coverage. That describes the Web as well as it does the newspaper, and it is not certain that this medium is ideal for advancing labour's cause, with its complexities and shades of grey.

On the other hand, certain very serious media, the very opposites of *USA Today*, are publishing their material on the Internet, through the World Wide Web. I'm thinking particularly of low-circulation scholarly journals. For them, the cost of producing the material on paper is so high, and that of publishing on the Internet so low, that simple economics are forcing a shift to online publishing.

What this means is that over time, more and more scholarly publications will be made available online. Those of us who don't enjoy reading from a computer screen (and who does?) are going to have to point their mice at the printer icon on their computer screens, and print out copies of articles which interest them. What is happening is not that printed material is disappearing, but rather that individuals are selecting which items interest them, and printing out those. The costs of such printing have been shifted from the information *suppliers* to the information *consumers*.

Some Web Sites Are More Equal Than Others

The World Wide Web may have started as a project at a physics laboratory and its pioneering software may have been written by a student, but behind the image of informality lies a growing corporate presence. The Web is increasingly becoming a corporate Web and this has ramifications for the labour movement.

One example: it is becoming harder to find one's way around the Web without help. The 'What's New' page now includes hundreds of new sites each time. The 'Yahoo' index includes tens of thousands of sites. Digital's 'Alta Vista' search program indexes some 20 million Web pages. Ordinary people without a lot of time on their hands are looking for ways to find information on the Web quickly and easily. And corporations – not non-governmental organisations and certainly not trade unions – are arriving on the scene with their ready-made answers.

One of these is preparing 'hot lists' for information consumers. The Netscape Corporation, whose home page is accessed by thousands of Web surfers, has generously prepared lists of 'What's New' and 'What's Cool' – but none of these are labour sites. The same is true of other popular Web sites, such as Yahoo, which point users to corporate-sponsored Web sites for information.

As the number of people accessing the Web grows from year to year, sites which are based on small budgets and small computers will increasingly answer incoming calls with busy signals – while giant corporate sites will always be open for business. The idea that all Web sites are somehow equal is an illusion, and labour Web sites are going to have to fight for survival just as the labour press today fights for survival in a corporate-dominated culture.

Big Brother on the Electronic Frontier

A couple of years ago, writers like Howard Rheingold (author of *The Virtual Community: Homesteading on the Electronic Frontier*) were positively giddy about how the Internet was going to blow apart the corporate monopoly on information. Everybody could be their own publisher on the Internet. Every person could write whatever they wanted into newsgroups and discussion lists. Free speech was blossoming everywhere; nothing could stop it now. 'You can't control it, it's uncontrollable', said MIT's Nicholas Negroponte, the author of *Being Digital*.

Well, that was before the Exon bill and CompuServe's decision to shut down some 200 newsgroups. That was before *Time* magazine did its panicked cover story on 'cyber porn' and before certain authoritarian governments, including China's, began making menacing noises toward the free flow of ideas on the net. (New Chinese regulations forbid users 'to produce, retrieve, duplicate or spread information that may hinder public order'. That presumably includes trade union publications.)

While it is true that at the present time much of the attention is focused on pornographic newsgroups, even CompuServe's move didn't only shut these down. Among the groups the giant commercial online service decided to ban were several on gay rights and AIDS.

More threatening than these first few attempts to impose censorship on the net have been the technological and political changes which now make censorship possible. Programmers are working overtime to create 'filtering' programs which parents can use to screen out dirty pictures and offensive words. Just tell the programs to cut out 'sex', for example, and little Johnny won't be able to access the *Playboy* Web site.

But the same techniques can also be used by governments, which can filter out words like 'labour' and 'freedom'. It was no accident that the Chinese government (probably the most anti-labour regime on earth) was the first in the world to hail CompuServe's decision to ban pornographic newsgroups. The dictators in Beijing certainly see the potential in all this.

The labour movement today is fighting battles all over the world to protect and expand trade union and human rights. The flow of information to and from all countries, including many with repressive regimes, must continue uninterrupted if trade unions will be able to use the net to their greatest advantage.

There are organisations, perhaps foremost among them the Electronic Frontier Foundation, which are working day and night for a free and open Internet. It seems now as if they're fighting a losing battle, as right-wing politicians grasp the potential of using the pornography issue to clamp down on the unruly and wild Internet.

The labour movement should be in the thick of this fight, building alliances with civil libertarian groups, understanding that no one has more to lose than working people if the fight is lost. But this is not the case. Even those trade unionists who use the Internet are barely heard from on the issue of censorship. Labour Web sites almost never mention it. Wouldn't it be tragic if the Internet grows to include a billion people, but its content is completely controlled by governments and corporations?

The List Continues

We know that the Internet needs to reach 'critical mass' before it becomes really useful for popular organisations; this is already happening. We've pointed out that the developing countries must get online for the net to be useful to the labour movement; this is happening too, albeit more slowly than we would have liked. We've discussed the problem of English-language domination of the networks; this problem, too, is taking care of itself, particularly as Europe gets connected. We've mentioned the problem of getting quality material online; the increasing corporate dominance of the World Wide Web; and the battle against censorship. And this doesn't even begin to exhaust the list. But it does exhaust me, so I'll just toss out a few more problems and their possible solutions.

- The lack of *support and training* has been noted by labournet pioneers everywhere. Everyone who has taught anyone how to use email or the Web understands just how big a problem this is. But two developments are solving the problem for us. One is that software is getting much easier to use all the time. The other development is the emphasis placed by trade unions and their allies on training. We can see this clearly in Canada's Solinet and South Africa's SANGONeT, but perhaps the best example of a solution in practice is Britain's Labour Telematics Centre.
- Another problem often pointed out in the past has been the general *resistance to technological change* in the labour movement. There are many stories of hours spent trying to persuade trade union executive committees to invest a small amount of money in a modem. This problem too is sorting itself out as the mass media blitz about the Internet finally seeps down to the level of the local trade union official. Today, practically everyone has heard of the net and many want to connect, without necessarily understanding why. Here too, one cannot place enough emphasis on the heroic efforts made by those hardy few who worked for many years trying to persuade trade unionists to go online.
- Some concern was expressed a few years ago about the possible rise of a *new class of trade union techno-experts* who would become indispensable in the information age. I think that this

danger has largely disappeared with the increasing popularity of tools like the World Wide Web. One doesn't have to be a rocket scientist to use the Web; one did a decade ago to use the email program of the European Space Agency, which was tested by the founders of Poptel.

• The *rivalry between groups* working toward the creation of a global labournet, while not as vicious and crippling as most in-fighting on the left and labour movement, has taken its toll. Often the bickering seems petty to outsiders – and maybe to insiders as well. Though some veterans of the APC–Poptel wars may understand the point of all this, most trade unionists don't, and couldn't care less. Fortunately, far away from the battlefields, labour movement activists in places like South Africa and Canada have steered clear of the conflict, giving their members access to both networks.

Are there even more obstacles and problems that I've forgotten to mention? Of course there are. But without minimising their importance, I think that trade unionists will find solutions to all of them. One by one the obstacles to a global labournet are falling. Let us now discuss what comes next.

What Comes Next?

Some of the trade unionists involved in networking have on occasion spelled out their visions of the next steps, pointing to a future in which working people in different countries can exchange views, share information and work together in ways which have not been possible before.

I won't be able to review here every prophecy and every prophet. Practically everybody who has anything to say about the Internet, has something to say about the future. I've decided to take just a couple of things some of the more prescient labour movement people have been saying in recent years.

Online Company Councils

In 1992, Jim Catterson had just completed a decade working for the chemical workers' trade secretariat, the ICEF. He was speaking to the first international conference on labour telematics, in Manchester. We must remember that Catterson was coming from Chip Levinson's union – the same Levinson who raised the possibility, back in 1972, of a global labournet. Levinson was also a proponent of 'company councils'. As Catterson summarised the proposal, workers 'must be organised at the same level as the company' if they are to negotiate successfully on an international level. This demands 'the establishment of some form of world company council bringing together trade union representatives'.

The idea was first broached in the 1950s, and the ICEF leadership, as well as other ITSs, pushed hard for it in the 1970s. But the attempts failed. No parallel structure to the transnational corporation was ever set up by the international labour movement. Why not? According to Catterson, the problem was 'lack of finance'. In order to 'realistically carry out a programme of world council meetings able to meet frequently enough to develop policies rather than simply share initial information would require resources well in [excess] of those realistically possible for the ITSs in the foreseeable future.' But the Internet could change all that.

Catterson ended his 1992 presentation by suggesting that as soon as some kind of critical mass was reached, virtual online company councils could be created. Email, he said, 'makes face-to-face meetings redundant if their only purpose is to share information'. Such meetings – 'with their enormous travel and interpretation costs' – would be held only when necessary to handle a particularly acute issue, or to develop policy.

Toward that end, the ICEF was already considering setting up company-specific bulletin boards on the net. Every few months, the ICEF would post there a brief review of the company's finances, investment and disinvestment decisions. This information would be largely based on commercial databases already in use by the organisation. Catterson imagined a situation in which individual unions engaged in negotiations with a transnational corporation would access such information electronically, post information of their own, tell others about disputes taking place and request solidarity actions when needed. They could ask other ICEF affiliates online questions about contract provisions, for example. The secretariat would coordinate the activity, providing translation services, for example. The result of such activity, beginning with company-specific bulletin boards, would be 'a fully functioning genuine permanent world council of trade unions' for each transnational corporation. Of course face-to-face meetings would take place as well. But these would focus on policy development and decision-making.

An International Labour University

Solinet's founder, Marc Belanger, put a message out to the net in mid-1995. It was brief and to the point. 'I dream of the day', he wrote, 'when we can run courses from an international labour university.' Such a university – which everyone was quickly calling 'ILU' – would 'teach classes either via email or Internet newsgroups' and would have to 'recruit instructors from around the world'. To move such an initiative forward, Belanger proposed that the first tasks would be to 'find instructors who would be willing to teach (for free at the start) and a certifying body'. Belanger admitted that the project would probably take a few years to organise, but 'if we don't start now, it'll never be'.

The proposal attracted attention immediately. Not only was it coming from the originator of the first, and still most important, national labournet, but Belanger had already organised transnational trade union courses online, involving Russian, Australian and Canadian unionists. Interest was shown by both trade unionists and labour studies people in the US, Canada, Britain, Russia, the Netherlands and Norway. Among those replying with detailed comments to Belanger's proposal were a number of individuals whose names should already be familiar to readers of this book, including Peter Waterman, Jagdish Parikh, Vassily Balog and Gregory Coyne. The discussion focused on six issues:

- Cooperation with existing organisations
- Accreditation
- Curriculum
- Language
- Delivery Systems
- Funding

As Belanger summarised the discussion, many people mentioned the need to work with the existing international and national labour bodies such as the International Confederation of Free Trade Unions, the International Federation of Workers' Education Associations, and others. Belanger favoured formal, cooperative links with those organisations. But, he added, 'these organisations are understaffed and underfunded. Many, if not all of them, are just now starting to think about the possibilities of electronic messaging. We shouldn't impede the development of an ILU simply because we couldn't get a formal linkage to the established labour bodies. That formal linkage could develop in time.'

The curriculum questions revolved around three basic issues: Is the ILU to be an academic or tool-teaching body? Should its instructors teach only courses that are international in scope? And what sort of courses might be taught? Belanger saw the ILU as a teaching entity that can encompass both academic study and tool-teaching. But in the end, he felt, the ILU should be seen as a academic institute which (in some manner) provides a degree, or at the very least, a certificate. (By tool-teaching, Belanger meant courses such as Grievance Handling or Negotiating an Agreement.) The criteria for judging how academic or tool-teaching the ILU should be would be determined by its audience. The students in such a university should be practising trade unionists and workers.

If that were the case, then a mixture of tool-teaching and academic courses might make sense.

Should the ILU teach courses on national as well as international topics? For example, would the ILU teach courses on Labour Relations in the UK? Or would it be more appropriate to teach courses such as Comparative International Labour Relations? Belanger thought that there may be a danger in teaching courses that relate only to one country. But students could very well need a basic grounding in their own country's labour relations systems before studying others. Also students might be interested in taking courses that teach them in more detail the workings of a particular country. The sort of courses which were mentioned included:

- The International Labour Movement
- Privatisation of Public Services
- Labour History
- Labour Law
- Labour and Technology
- Comparative Labour Relations
- Labour and the Economy
- Unions in the Public Sector
- Theories of the Labour Movement
- Health and Safety for Trade Union Activists
- Internal Union Administration
- Developing a Grievance System
- Negotiating a Contract
- Union Leadership
- Using Computers for Union Work
- Organising Unorganised Workers

Belanger considered it essential that the ILU be linked to a formal university so that the university can be the body which grants the degree or certificate. Without that formal linkage ILU students might not be able to get funding or time off work. And they might not commit themselves to a full programme of studies if they didn't feel they were working towards a formally recognised goal. However, this does not necessarily mean that a bureaucracy has to be established at the accrediting university. Belanger suggested the consideration of the idea (originally proposed by Gregory Coyne) that the ILU not actually teach courses, but act as an accrediting and approval body.

In any event, Belanger stressed that the ILU should act as a multilingual body offering (or accrediting) courses in at least English, French and Spanish. If the ILU becomes an accrediting body it might be possible to have courses in many different languages, depending on what instructors would be available in various countries. Belanger added: 'If the ILU develops into an entity by which knowledge is passed from developed to developing countries, solely, we will have missed our goal. We should aim at developing a multinational entity in which all parties learn from each other.'

Belanger offered Solinet's services to help launch the ILU, including a conferencing base, Web sites, Gopher and Telnet access.

The question of funding remained unsolved. 'In the beginning we might be able to kludge together a system using our current resources', suggested Belanger. 'But eventually we would have to face up to the fact that a successful ILU would need funding for delivery systems, instructor stipends, and course development.'

The proposal continues to be discussed today, and was even placed on the agenda of recent IFWEA Executive Committee meetings. A prototype of the ILU (tentatively called 'Solinet on the Web') was scheduled for launch in late 1996–early 1997. Belanger took the initiative, got the Web conferencing software up and running, and began linking up lecturers from Canada, the US, Russia, Israel and elsewhere. Whether this initiative will lead to the creation of a full-blown online labour university remains to be seen.

Three Crazy Ideas

Virtual company councils and an online international labour university are good, solid ideas. I have no doubt that they will be realised in the near future. But I want to conclude this book with three far-out ideas. Because I don't want to embarrass anyone else, I'll even claim some of these as my own.

An Online International Labour Press

In most countries the national labour press is dead. When I came to live in Israel back in 1981, there were *two* national daily newspapers of the labour movement. One was owned by the national trade union centre Histadrut; the other was owned by one of the country's two democratic socialist parties, Mapam. Over the years, as both newspapers faced the problems of declining circulations and rising deficits, suggestions were made to rescue them somehow, including a proposal to merge them into a single newspaper. By 1996, both newspapers had closed.

The United States has never had a successful national labour daily, and the mass media's anti-union bias is felt intensely by the trade unions. In a recent book about the labour press there, Jo-Ann Mort, the Communications Director of the clothing and textile workers union, proposed the launching of a national labour daily. Over the course of several pages, she carefully explained what such a paper could do, and the void it would fill. But no union or coalition of unions has taken up the idea so far, nor does it seem likely that any one will.

Even in Scandinavia, where the labour press (like the labour movement) thrived until recently, trade union-supported newspapers are in decline. In Denmark, the national labour daily is now defended by the Social Democrats with the very same arguments once used by Israeli leftists in defence of the now-defunct labour dailies. Though the newspaper has a small and declining circulation, they say, it has influence far beyond its readership.

The international labour press is in equally bad shape. The International Confederation of Free Trade Unions publishes every month a small newspaper called *Free Labour World*. It comes out in a few languages, and is read by trade union officials in a number of countries. The international trade secretariats publish their newsletters according to their budgets. For example, the *News Bulletin* of the food workers' ITS, which is supposed to come out every month, has been appearing only about four times a year recently.

There is no way that the labour press can compete with the capitalist mass media under these conditions. But the Internet does offer a way out: the creation of an online daily labour news service or newspaper. There may no longer be a difference between the two concepts. Such a daily newspaper would serve as a news service for countries without extensive Internet access; articles which appear in it could be lifted for use in local publications without any need for re-typing. The very idea of a 'daily' is also largely irrelevant; the Internet newspapers I read are updated all the time, not just once a day. So what I'm suggesting is an online, constantly updated labour news service, in the form of a series of pages on the World Wide Web.

Such a service should be produced by the ICFTU together with the international trade secretariats. Only they have the skills and knowledge to publish a multilingual survey of labour news from around the world. The emphasis must be placed on the importance of multilingualism here. Such a news service should be available in all the major European languages as well as Chinese, Japanese, Korean, Arabic and others. If the cost of such an operation is *entirely* the writing and translating, without paying for paper, printing, typesetting or mailing, it should not be much more expensive than what the ICFTU and the ITSs are paying today for their printed publications.

What would be the effect of such a global labour news service? A daily labour press helps create a *community* of ideas and feelings among its readers. It would be the best organising tool ever in the hands of the international trade union movement, and should be launched without delay.

In fact, a daily online newspaper is only the beginning of what might be done. The latest technological developments are truly stunning – 'streaming multimedia' on the net. These applications basically turn the Internet into a full-blown, real-time global radio and television broadcast medium that also happens to be interactive.

Using an ordinary home computer, equipped with a not-very-fast modem, a couple of inexpensive speakers and a sound card, I have been able to listen in on some local radio broadcasts from around the world. Using a technology like ReadAudio (the client program as well as the encoder are available free of charge), it would be fairly easy to launch what was once an impossible dream: a global labour radio network.

The labour movement wouldn't need expensive broadcasting equipment nor governmental permission to 'broadcast' using a technology of this kind. Such broadcasts could be picked up by trade unionists anywhere in the world, and could be copied and re-broadcast using conventional local radio stations in places where Internet access is expensive. Such broadcasts (actually 'narrowcasts' is a better term) are much harder to censor or jam than ordinary radio.

More advanced Internet technologies available today, such as VDOLive, offer the promise of live television broadcasts (though these do not work with slow modems). Inexpensive colour digital video cameras (which currently cost about the same as a 28,800 bps modem) mean that online labour television broadcasts are only a matter of time. The possibilities for the trade union movement are staggering indeed.

An Online Archive, Discussion Group and Journal

Back during the International's 'golden age', before the First World War, the German Social Democratic Party (SPD) was the flagship of the whole world movement. Debates which took place in that party – for example, between Eduard Bernstein and Rosa Luxemburg on the question of reform or revolution – were echoed around the world. The theoretical publication of that Party, *Die Neue Zeit* (The New Age), was edited by the SPD's chief theoretician himself, Karl Kautsky. It was read not only in Germany but by social democrats everywhere. Articles which were published there, and books or pamphlets produced by the SPD's presses, would be translated into every written language.

Since that time, there has been no single international publication which had that kind of impact. But as the labour movement enters the twenty-first century, with all the dramatic changes taking place in the world of work, in the global economy and in politics, the need for a deeper and more serious look at things is more closely felt than ever before. When I began publishing the *New International Review* back in 1977, I had hopes that it might help by playing this kind of role, but its circulation was so small, and its editors so inexperienced, that such hopes were in vain.

The Internet allows the inexpensive publishing not only of new works which contribute to a democratic socialist view of the world, but also to the reprinting of texts which would otherwise be lost in the archives. This is already being done in some parts of the world. For example, Sydney University and the State Library of New South Wales in Australia are investing half a million dollars in a project to film, digitise and make available over the Internet some 75 Australian publications from the years 1840–45. According to an article in the *Sydney Morning Herald*, 'Although the primary focus is on meeting the needs of researchers ... who currently have extremely limited access to these materials, it is hoped that they will also interest social, economic and family historians.' The same could be said of early socialist and labour publications, with the potential audience including not only historians.

What we should be considering, then, is not only an ongoing journal, which would publish original articles and replies to them (some of this could be conducted in the form of discussion groups located within the Web site). We should also begin the task of digitising the thousands of important books, journals and pamphlets published by the labour and social democratic movements over the last century, and making these texts available through the Web.

Now what *practical* use could this possibly have? I'll give an example. In 1993, we decided at the International Federation of Workers' Education Associations to devote a whole issue of *Workers' Education* to the subject of May Day. There was a debate about this at the IFWEA's Executive Committee, with some voices being raised against the whole idea. But the majority felt that it was important to discuss the meaning of May Day, its origins, how it is celebrated, and what future it has. May Day is one of the labour movement's most potent symbols to this day, and we wanted to publish the best material we could about it.

Using the Internet, we were able to construct a bibliography of books and pamphlets about the holiday, including some material which is long out of print. Unfortunately, archival material about May Day was not available online.

The issue of *Workers' Education* was published and was used to some practical effect by trade unionists in a number of countries. In New Zealand, where the labour movement has been under brutal attack for several years now, the national Council of Trade Unions reprinted portions of *Workers' Education* for its own packet of materials on the holiday. In New York City, a left-wing magazine reprinted the editorial. Part of the issue was reprinted in the Philippines. There was – and is – a hunger for information about labour's past and its traditions.

What we need, therefore, is not only a theoretical journal like *Die Neue Zeit* but a combined *journal* (where original articles could be published), *archive* (where older material could be presented in digital form) and *discussion group* (where readers could easily make comments and ask questions). Such a project could be realised using the World Wide Web.

Who should undertake this task? The answer is not so simple. Probably the library and archive of the Socialist International, the International Institute for Social History in the Netherlands, should play a key role. So should the International Federation of Workers' Education Associations. Institutions like the Friedrich Ebert Stiftung and the Karl Renner Institut, which already print and reprint much material, should be involved. But the labour movement's archives, libraries and research centres, the labour museums and academic journals, should all play a role.

A beginning has been made by the Friedrich Ebert Stiftung in Germany. When I checked out their Web site and clicked on 'Library' my hopes were initially dashed. What is being offered is a single paragraph describing the FES's immense library of trade union and social democratic materials. Access to the card catalogue, for example, is not to be found here.

However, the online catalogue to the FES's phenomenal library *is* available online – through the German menus. I decided to try it out on a subject which interests me – the social democratic republic in Georgia in the years 1918–21. I typed in 'georgie' and the program instantly located a whole bunch of books on my subject. This the first major social democratic research centre, archive or library to make such a service available to all, free of charge, through the Internet.

I can imagine a day when 1 May is approaching, and a local trade union, or branch of a social democratic party, or workers' education group, is looking for some material about the holiday. They can turn to such a Web site and find reams of material, including graphics and sound files, which will enrich their celebration of this key event on labour's calendar.

An Early Warning Network on Trade Union Rights

Trade union rights are under attack everywhere in the world. This is true in the remaining Communist countries (especially China); it is equally true in the traditional right-wing authoritarian regimes;

it is surprisingly true even in some Western democracies, like New Zealand, where several basic trade union rights are now denied.

Often international labour bodies hear about some violation of rights, and using faxes and telephone calls get the word out to their affiliates in different parts of the world. But as groups like Amnesty International have discovered, a more effective way, supplementing but not replacing traditional communications technologies, would be the use of computer-mediated communications.

To a certain extent, the international labour movement has been doing this already, albeit not very systematically. In the early years of the global labournet, the GeoNet bulletin boards were used to post notices of violations of trade union rights, calls for solidarity and the like. But as Jim Catterson of the ICEM has pointed out, it was never clear that these messages were read by anyone. The experience of the IUF was a little different. It regularly posted to the GeoNet bulletin boards information about Guatemala and other places where transnational corporations like Pepsi-Cola were active – and where workers' rights were denied. In one case, an important non-trade union group made contact with the IUF because of these appeals. The APC conferences are also filled with solidarity appeals, usually from the developing countries, often coming through the trade secretariats, but these seem to be mere supplements to conventional forms of communication like press releases and faxes. One of the groups posting to the APC conferences is the International Textile, Garment, and Leather Workers Federation, which went online in mid-1995. The ITF has used its new Web site to publicise solidarity actions.

But the international trade union movement is using the networks sporadically and not systematically. Unlike Amnesty International, which centrally coordinates its campaigns across countries and sectors, trade unions have tended to use the Internet in the same limited, sectoral way they have always worked. The one trade union organisation which spans all countries and sectors, the ICFTU, has not conducted any solidarity actions through the network. And because attacks on trade union rights anywhere are the concern of workers everywhere, information about them should not be confined to a particular sector or country. It is not enough that a union in developing country A phones up contacts in country B, whose labour movement then mobilises. Similarly, it is not enough when one international trade secretariat alone tries to handle repression of trade unions in 'its' sector when this issue concerns all parts of the labour movement.

We should be building a global early warning network, based on three elements:

- Internet-connected computers and responsible individuals in countries where unions are under threat, whose job it is to notify one central address of incidents like kidnapping of unionists, attacks on demonstrators, and arrests and murders of trade union officials.
- A central address, meaning a computer and operators whose job it is to receive the information and process it.
- An 'urgent action network' (that's what Amnesty International calls it) which uses the Internet to get the word out to those who can act quickly and effectively.

The first element requires that the international labour movement supply the computers and skills to maintain at least one workstation in each country where trade unions are under attack. It is true that in some countries, this could be an expensive proposition, requiring the placement of international phone calls to get Internet access. It is equally important that appropriate individuals in those countries be trained to receive information, process it, and send it on to the central address. Presumably the places to start are ICFTU-affiliated national trade union centres. But it is also possible that local human rights organisations may serve the role better.

The second element requires a host computer and staff on call 24 hours a day, seven days a week, presumably at the ICFTU headquarters, or at one of the international trade secretariats. Within moments of receiving news of a violation of trade union rights, the information would be processed, checked, and passed on electronically to the appropriate individuals in trade unions around the world. In addition, groups allied to the labour movement, such as human rights organisations and labour parties, would be informed – also by email.

A global trade union 'urgent action network' based on the Amnesty International model could be developed using a tool as simple as LISTSERV. Mailing lists could be built up based on countries, sectors, languages, or other criteria.

Let me give an example of how this would work. A trade union activist employed by a leading multinational (e.g., Coca-Cola) 'disappears' one day in Brazil. His local union tells their national office, which in turn tells the national trade union centre in Rio de Janeiro. A photograph of the missing activist arrives in the office as well. Using a scanner, a computerised image is prepared. The person responsible in Rio sends on the information by Internet email, using a prepared electronic form so that all the relevant information is included. The photograph is sent the same way.

A minute or two later, the information reaches the central address – say, the ICFTU headquarters in Brussels. After being read by the operator on duty there, the already digitised information, including the photo, is passed on to two LISTSERV mailing lists which are constantly being updated in Brussels. One is for Coca-Cola employees' unions around the world; the other consists of Portuguese-speaking trade unionists on three continents.

Only minutes after the information has been sent out of Brazil, it is in the electronic mailboxes of trade unionists in dozens of countries. Those who work as editors or journalists can immediately incorporate some of the text in their articles. The digitised photograph and articles about the case begin appearing in trade union newspapers within hours. Telephones begin ringing in politicians' offices around the world. A picket line goes up at Coca-Cola headquarters in Atlanta even before the corporate officers know what's happened. Within hours, someone at Coca-Cola places a quiet telephone call to someone in Brazil, and the missing activist reappears, blindfolded and a bit battered, but basically safe and sound.

Such an early warning system would, I believe, do much to speed up response time, prevent duplication of effort, and yet ensure a maximum global trade union response to rights violations anywhere. This, in turn would make a major contribution to strengthening trade unions in the South, which is critical to a rebuilding of the International.

The International Has Been Reborn

I began this book with a brief history of the various Internationals, starting with the one Karl Marx founded in 1864. I described an era, lasting until the outbreak of the First World War, when the International existed not only as an organisation, but as an *idea*, as something in the consciousness of millions of men and women. Those men and women a hundred years ago 'belonged to the International'. Sure, they were members of local and national trade unions and socialist parties. But they also belonged to something much larger. Something of that consciousness has begun to return to our world.

When Marc Belanger in Ottawa and Vassily Balog in Moscow are discussing an international labour university online, *where are they?* One answer Internet users will usually give is 'cyberspace'. That's true, but that's not enough. Because the discussion about Belanger's proposal took place not so much in cyberspace as in a particular part of it which I have been calling the emerging global labournet.

As such an online community grows, it will begin to create some of the institutions I have discussed in this chapter. Online company councils will appear – there is no question about that. As for the international labour university, that too is only a matter of time. My own proposals for an online global labour press, a combined archive/discussion group/journal, and an early warning network on trade union rights are, at worst, premature. Every one of them will be realised, in one form or another, sooner or later.

Peter Waterman writes of a new 'global solidarity culture', which replaces old notions of internationalism, communications and the labour movement with new ones attuned to our changing world. He is enthusiastic about alternative international communications based on the new social movements. When labour's interests and those of such new social movements overlap, he notes, international labour computer communications 'does seem to take off'.

Not long ago, someone asked Bill Gates if he would have been surprised back in the 1970s by some of the new technological developments taking place today, like laptop computers and the Internet. Gates answered, 'No'. Every technological development that has happened since then was foreseen and expected, he glibly answered. And he was right. Similarly, the rise of a global labournet is a long-awaited, long-expected development. Chip Levinson foresaw it in 1972. It is being created out of necessity, by the changing character of global capitalism, and though it can be slowed down, nothing can stop it.

It can also be speeded up. For a decade and a half now, a few dozen men and women from Vancouver, Manchester, San Francisco, Geneva, Johannesburg, Moscow, Ottawa, Brussels, Chicago, London, and other places have been creating local trade union BBSs, regional labour networks, global email networks, and, most recently, Web sites by the hundreds. When they began in the 1980s, they were met with hostility or confusion by their brothers and sisters in the labour movement. Today, we understand that they were, as one transnational corporation puts it, just slightly ahead of their time. Their time has come now.

The 'new world order' is giving birth to a new internationalism. Participants in the international labour movement have begun to transcend their own local and national limitations and feel themselves to be part of a global community based not on language or skin colour, but social class – and a vision of a new society.

Thanks to the Internet, a century-long decline in internationalism has already been reversed. For thousands of trade unionists who log on every day, the International has already been reborn.

APPENDIX 1

Selected Labour Web Sites

The addresses on this list change so frequently, and trade unions are jumping on the World Wide Web with such enthusiasm, that there is no way for such a list to be comprehensive or up to date. I recommend that first-time users of the Web go to one of the mega-sites listed here (for example, LaborNet@IGC) and use that as jumping off point. From sites on this list, one should be able to find all of the local sites mentioned in this book.

International

International Labour Organisation
http://www.unicc.org/ilo/index.html
International Confederation of Free Trade Unions
http://www.icftu.org/
International Confederation of Free Trade Unions - Asia Pacific
  Regional Organisation
http://singnet.com.sg/~icftu/welcome.html
International Federation of Commercial, Clerical, Professional
  and Technical Employees (FIET)
http://www.fiet.org/fiet/
International Federation of Workers' Education Associations
  (IFWEA)
http://www.poptel.org.uk/ifwea
Euro-WEA
http://www.wea.org.uk/eurowea/index.html
International Transport Workers' Federation (ITF)
http://www.itf.org.uk/
International Federation of Chemical, Energy, Mine and General
  Workers' Unions
http://www.icem.org/
Public Services International
http://www.world-psi.org

National

Australian Centre for Labour Studies
http://gopher.labour.adelaide.edu.au/Default.html
Australian Council of Trade Unions (ACTU)

http://129.127.68.34/Unions/actu-home.html
Australian Labour and Trade Union Page
http://www.vicnet.net.au/vicnet/labour.html
Austrian Trade Union Confederation (OeGB)
http://www.oegb.or.at/oegb/
Canadian Farmworkers' Union
http://artworld.com/cfu/intro.html
Canada: Centre for Industrial Relations, University of Toronto
http://utll.library.utoronto.ca/www/cir/bookmark.htm
Canada: Public Service Alliance (PSA)
http://www.psac.com
Canada: UnionNet (Solinet/Web)
http://www.web.apc.org/unionnet/index.html
Germany: Friedrich Ebert Stiftung (FES)
http://www-fes.gmd.de/
Germany: IG Metall
http://igmetall.de
Ireland: IMPACT
http://www.iol.ie/arena/impact
Israel: International Sociological Association, Research Committee
    on Labour Movements
http://pluto.mscc.huji.ac.il/~mshalev/welcome.htm
Korea: Korean Confederation of Trade Unions
http://www.cybercom.co.kr/kctu/
Netherlands Trade Union Confederation (FNV)
http://www.fnv.nl/
New Zealand Council of Trade Unions (CTU)
http://www.union.org.nz/
Singapore: NTUC
http://www.technet.sg/NTUC/ntuc.html
Congress of South African Trade Unions (COSATU)
http://www.anc.org.za:80/cosatu/
South Africa: National Union of Mineworkers (NUM)
http://www.anc.org.za:80/num/
South Africa: SANGONeT
http://www.wn.apc.org/labour/labour.html
UK: Communication Workers' Union
http://www.cwu.org/
UK: General Federation of Trade Unions (GFTU)
http://www.poptel.org.uk/gftu/
UK: LabourNet (GreenNet)
http://www.gn.apc.org/labournet
UK: Labour Telematics Centre (LTC)
http://www.poptel.org.uk/ltc
UK: Media Unions' Website
http://www.gn.apc.org/media/

UK: MSF Informational Technology Professionals' Association (ITPA)
http://www.poptel.org.uk/msf/
UK: National Union of Schoolmasters/Union of Women Teachers
http://www.poptel.org.uk/nasuwt/
UK: Poptel
http://www.poptel.org.uk/
UK: Public Services, Tax and Commerce Union
http://www.poptel.org.uk/ptc/
UK: Trades Union Congress (TUC)
http://www.tuc.org.uk
UK: UNISON
http://www.poptel.org.uk/unison/
USA: American Federation of Labour–Congress of Industrial Organisations (AFL–CIO)
http://www.aflcio.org
USA: American Federation of State, County and Municipal Employees
http://www.afscme.org/
USA: Economic Democracy Information Network (EDIN)
http://garnet.berkeley.edu:3333/
USA: International Brotherhood of Teamsters
http://www.teamster.org/
USA: LaborNet@IGC
http://www.igc.apc.org/labornet/
USA: Office and Professional Employees International Union
http://www.opeiu.org/
USA: Service Employees International Union
http://www.seiu.org/
USA: Sheet Metal Workers' International Association (SMWIA)
http://www.smwia.org/hvac/
USA: Teamsters for a Democratic Union
http://www.igc.org/tdu/
USA: UNITE
http://www.uniteunion.org/
USA: United Auto Workers
http://www.uaw.org/
USA: United Mine Workers
http://access.digex.net/~miner/
USA: United Steelworkers of America
http://www.voicenet.com/~enos/
USA: Workers' Education Local 189/Labour Educators' Newsletter
http://www.erols.com/czarlab/
USA/Mexico: United Electrical International Solidarity Site
http://www.igc.apc.org/unitedelect/

Regional and Local

British Columbia Teachers' Federation (BCTF)
http://www.web.apc.org/bctf
Detroit Journal
http://www.rust.net/~workers/strike.html
Local 1220, International Brotherhood of Electrical Workers
http://www.ecnet.net/users/urkastig/ibew1220
Nova Scotia Nurses' Union
http://fox.nstu.ca/~nsnu/
Ohio State AFL–CIO
http://www.ohaflcio.org
San Francisco Free Press
http://www.ccnet.com/SF_Free_Press/welcome.html
United Nurses of Alberta (UNA)
http://www.ccinet.ab.ca/una/una.html

APPENDIX 2

Email-based Trade Union Discussion Groups and How To Join Them

H-LABOR
The labour history discussion list, based in the US. To join, send a message to listserv@uicvm.uic.edu. with the words *subscribe h-labor yourname yourschool* as the only text in the message.

H-UCLEA
The discussion list of the University and College Labour Education Association (UCLEA). To join, send a message to listserv@h-net.msu.edu with the words *subscribe h-uclea yourname youraffiliation* as the only text in the message.

LABNEWS
A US-based list, launched in August 1995, offering labour news. To join, send a message to listserv@cmsa.berkeley.edu. with the words *sub labnews firstname lastname* as the only text in the message.

LABOR-L
The Canadian-based 'forum on labour in the global economy'. To join, send a message to listserv@vm1.york.ca with the words *subscribe labor-l firstname lastname* as the only text in the message.

LABOR-PARTY
A US discussion group around the question of forming a labour party in that country. To join, send a message to majordomo@igc.apc.org with the words *subscribe labor-party* as the only text in the message.

MUNDO SINDICAL
A Latin American discussion group, launched by Peruvian unionists in late 1995. Discussions are conducted in Spanish. To join, send a message to listasrcp@rcp.net.pe with the words *subscribe sindical* as the only text in the message.

UNION-D
The first European email-based discussion list, launched by British trade unionists in the summer of 1995. To join, send a message

to listserv@wolfnet.com with the words *subscribe union-d* followed by your email address as the only text in the message.

UNITED
The rank-and-file trade unionists list, based in the US. To join, send a message to united-request@cougar.com, with the word *subscribe* as the only text in the message.

Glossary

@: Pronounced 'at'; the part of an email address separating the user's name (to the left) from her computer's domain address (to the right).

Access: To reach, connect or interact with a remote resource.

Address: A unique alphanumeric sequence used to identify a computer transmitting or receiving data.

America Online: One of the two largest online services in the US.

Application: Software which does productive external work, as opposed to system software which is internal to the computer system.

Association for Progressive Communications (APC): A global network linking non-governmental organisations, including such networks as GreenNet (UK), the Institute for Global Communications (US), Web (Canada), GlasNet (Russia) and SANGONeT (South Africa).

bps: Bits per second; the speed at which a modem communicates.

Browser: A program, like Netscape, for accessing pages on the World Wide Web.

Bulletin board system (BBS): Dial-up online systems from which users can download programs, leave messages for other users, and the like.

Comintern: The Communist, or Third, International.

CompuServe: One of the two largest commercial online services in the US.

Cyberspace: The place where you are, when you use the Internet.

Data: Literally, 'that which is given', data refers to raw facts, measurements, numbers, and so on. Data can exist in any form, but is commonly identified with electronic digital signals.

Database: A collection of information organised in electronic form.

Dial-up: Method of accessing online services using ordinary telephone connections.

Digital: Using numbers to represent quantities or symbols. An electronic digital signal consists of countable pulses of fixed size.

Downloading: The electronic transfer of information from one computer to another. The opposite is uploading.

Email: Electronic mail – the use of computers and modems to send text and other data from address to address.

FidoNet: A global network of local bulletin boards.

File: Data which has been organised, stored and named. In computing, files are usually stored on disks.

File transfer protocol (FTP): A protocol (and program) that allows transfer of files from the user's computer to a remote computer.

FreeNet: Networks that allow free access to the Internet.

Freeware: Software which is distributed (legally) free of charge.

GEnie: A small commercial online service in the US.

GeoNet: An international communications system which originated in Germany, with links to Poptel in Britain and many European and international labour organisations.

GlasNet: The Russian network affiliated to the APC.

Gopher: A document retrieval system on the Internet considered quite sophisticated and friendly until the arrival of the World Wide Web.

Histadrut: Israel's national trade union centre.

Home page: see *Web site*.

Host: A central computer which provides services, such as database access, to users across a network. Also known as a server.

Hypertext markup language (HTML): A simple computer language for creating pages (files) for display on the World Wide Web.

Hypertext transfer protocol (HTTP): The transmission protocol used for sending World Wide Web data over the Internet.

Infobahn: The European term for an information superhighway.

Information superhighway: One of a number of media-hyped terms for the Internet.

Integrated services digital network (ISDN): Digital telephone systems capable of transmitting data much more quickly than conventional analogue systems.

Interactivity: The characteristic of systems which accept user input as well as delivering output.

International trade secretariat (ITS): Global organisations of trade unions, organised by specific industries.

Internet: The global network of networks, founded as ARPANET in 1969, and today linking several million computers and tens of millions of people.

Internet Relay Chat (IRC): A real-time chat system, developed in Finland.

Internetworking: Linking networks to make a bigger network.

Leased-line: Communications line reserved for private data communications.

LISTSERV: A program to run online discussions using email mailing lists.

Local area network (LAN): A medium-to-high speed network restricted to a room, floor or building.

Log-on (also, log-in): To connect to a network and identify yourself. To disconnect, one logs off.

Mapam: Israel's United Workers' Party.

Mirror: A copying of files which appear on one computer to another computer, or a copying of messages from one discussion group to another.

Modem: Derived from the term 'MODulator/dEModulator', a modem is a device which 'listens' to your computer, then translates computer-talk into telephone-talk so that what your computer says can travel over an ordinary telephone line. Internal modems are cards you stick inside your computer; external modems sit in a metal box and are connected by cable to the computer.

Mouse: A pointing device one connects to a computer.

Network: A collection of linked computers which can exchange data, share resources, or even make use of each other's software.

Newsfeed: The process by which Internet access providers obtain newsgroup messages.

Newsgroup: A discussion group in USENET.

NUJnet: The National Union of Journalists' network in the UK and Ireland.

Online: To be actively connected to a network.

Password: A code which authorises access to protected networks, systems or files.

Poptel: The Popular Telematics Project, launched in 1986 in Britain, to promote trade union use of the net.

Prodigy: One of the large commercial online services in the US.

Program: A set of coded instructions to a computer.

Protocol: A set of rules by which each computer interprets what the other is saying. When one computer talks to the other, they must be using the same protocol.

Real time: Refers to applications which perform tasks without delay.

Scab: Strike-breaker.

Shareware: Computer programs which are distributed for free. Users pay the companies which make such software only if they like it and decide to continue using it. The prices are usually very low.

Snail mail: What Internet users sneeringly and accurately call mail delivered by the postal services.

Software: Computer programs. (The opposite of hardware, which consist of the various physical parts of a computer, like keyboard or screen.)

Solinet: (a) The nationwide computer communications network set up by the Canadian Union of Public Employees in 1986; (b) the loose confederation of local trade union BBSs in North America, mostly in the US.

Surfing: Accessing a number of different Web sites, one after another.

Telecomputing: Interaction with any computer from a distance.

Telematics: The interaction of all types of data-processing, electronic information and communication.

Telnet: An Internet protocol that allows a user to log in to a remote computer from the user's local computer.

Terminal emulation software: The programs to set up your modem, control its operation, connect to other modem-equipped computers, to interact with them, and to exchange files through modems.

Transmission control protocol/Internet protocol (TCP/IP): The set of protocols which forms the basis of the Internet; a kind of Esperanto that allows different kinds of computers to talk with each other.

USENET: Originally, the Unix Users Network; today, a global bulletin board containing thousands of newsgroups.

User: Anyone using an information technology or telecommunications system.

User-friendly: Software or hardware that is easy for human beings to use.

Videoconferencing: Interactive communication using video and sound transmitted over telephone lines in real time.

Virus: A program that replicates itself through incorporation into other programs, usually causing damage to the computer.

Web: see *World Wide Web*.

Web site: A file or files accessible through the World Wide Web. A home page is the welcoming or index page (file) at a Web site.

Windows: A graphical interface for personal computers produced by Microsoft.

WorkNet: The South African labour network, set up under conditions of apartheid and continuing to serve popular movements today as SANGONeT.

World Wide Web (WWW): The fastest growing part of the Internet, an interlinked set of hypermedia files, including text, pictures, sound and video.

Selected and Annotated Bibliography

Magazines and Newspapers

Detroit Journal. Online daily strike newspaper, 1995–96.
Labour Telematics News. Published by the Labour Telematics Centre.
PSI Research Network News. Especially useful is the survey of 100 affiliate unions, conducted in 1995.
San Francisco Free Press. Online daily strike newspaper, 1994.
Workers' Education. See especially the regular column 'Online' and issue no. 3, 1993, which was devoted to the subject of computer communications and the labour movement.

Unpublished Papers

Belanger, Marc, untitled. An account on the origins of Solinet, 1995.
Brenner, Joseph E., 'Internationalist Labor Communication by Computer Network: The United States, Mexico and NAFTA'. Paper prepared for a course, The American University, Washington DC, Spring 1994.
Waterman, Peter, 'A New Communications Model for a New Working-Class Internationalism: Still Needed?', 1995.

Conference Reports

Information Technology, Electronic Communications and the Labour Movement. 14–16 April 1992, GMB College, Manchester, UK. Conference Report. The full text of papers presented are available on GeoNet bulletin boards.
Labourtel UK: Information Technology, Electronic Communications and the Labour Movement. 2–4 June 1993, GMB College, Manchester, UK. Conference Report. The full text of papers presented are available on GeoNet bulletin boards.

Articles

Atkins, John, et al., *The Opportunity and Challenge of Telematics*, Labour Telematics Centre, ILO and ICFTU, April 1994.

198   THE LABOUR MOVEMENT AND THE INTERNET

Atkins, John and Dave Spooner, 'Harnessing the potential benefits of computer communications: telematics for workers' organizations', *Labour Education* (ILO) 95-1994/2.

Gallin, Dan, 'Inside the new world order: drawing the battle lines', *New Politics*, Vol, V. No. 1, Summer 1994.

Illingworth, Montieth M., 'Workers of the net, unite!', *Information Week*, 22 August 1994

Lee, Eric, 'Labour and the Internet', *Internet Business Journal*, April 1995.

Lee, Eric, 'Workers unite', *Internet World*, August 1995.

Waterman, Peter, 'Needed: a new communications model for a new working class internationalism', in Peter Waterman (ed.), *For a New Labour Internationalism: A Set of Reprints and Working Papers*, The Hague: International Labour, Education, Research and Information Foundation, pp. 233–55, 1984.

Waterman, Peter, 'International labour communication by computer: the fifth International?', Working Paper Series, No. 129. The Hague: Institute of Social Studies, 1992.

Waterman, Peter, 'From Moscow with electronics: a communication internationalism for an information capitalism', *Democratic Communique*, Vol. 12, No. 2–3, Summer, 1994, pp. 1, 11–16.

Index